N

Cuisines of India

Also by Smita Chandra

Indian Grill:
The Art of Tandoori Cooking at Home

From Bengal to Punjab:
The Cuisines of India

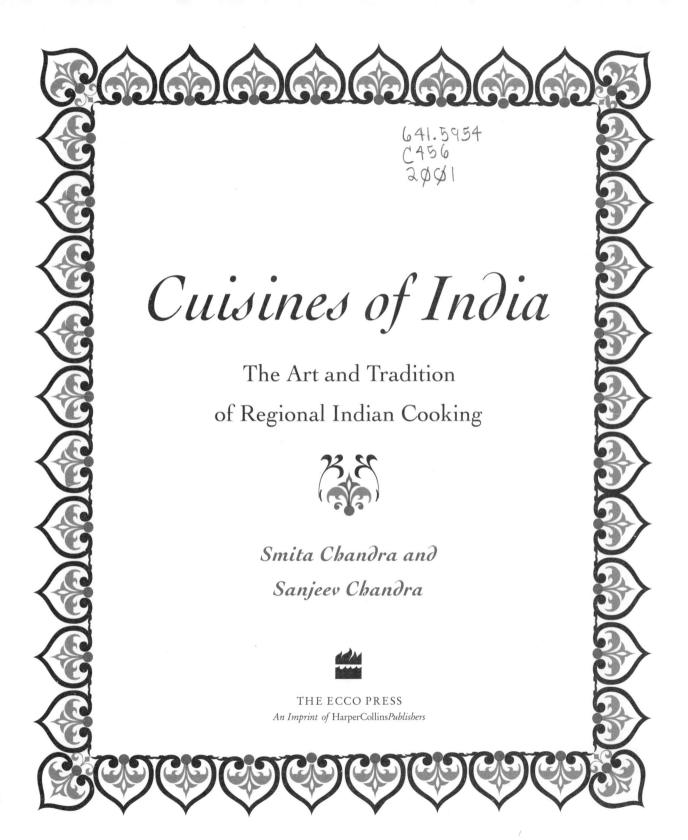

Cuisines of India

The Art and Tradition
of Regional Indian Cooking

Smita Chandra and

Sanjeev Chandra

THE ECCO PRESS

An Imprint of HarperCollins*Publishers*

The following drawings are based on existing paintings:

Food being served to the King of Mandu, from the Nimat Nama (page 112). Saryu Doshi and Karl Khandalavala, eds. *An Age of Splendour: Islamic Art in India.* Bombay: Marg Publications (1983), page 25. *India Office Library Collection, British Library.*

Woman grinding flour (page 200). Mildred Archer. *Company Paintings in the India Office Library.* London: Her Majesty's Stationery Office (1972), page 162. *Additional Oriental Collection 1327, India Office Library Collection, British Library.*

Head table-servant (khansama) carrying a tureen (page 260). Mildred Archer. *Company Paintings in the India Office Library.* London: Her Majesty's Stationery Office (1972), page 162. *Additional Oriental Collection 1307, India Office Library Collection, British Library.*

Grateful acknowledgment is made to Oxford University Press for permission to quote from the following:

The Baburnama: Memoirs of Babur, Prince and Emperor, translated, edited, and annotated by Wheeler M. Thackston. Washington, D.C.: Freer Gallery of Art and Arthur M. Sackler Gallery, Smithsonian Institution. New York: Oxford University Press, 1966.

The Jahangirnama: Memoirs of Jahangir, Emperor of India, translated, edited, and annotated by Wheeler M. Thackston. Washington, D.C.: Freer Gallery of Art and Arthur M. Sackler Gallery, Smithsonian Institution. New York: Oxford University Press, 1999.

HarperCollins books may be purchased for educational, business, or sales promotional use. For information please write: Special Markets Department, HarperCollins Publishers Inc., 10 East 53rd Street, New York, NY 10022.

FIRST EDITION

Printed on acid-free paper

Designed by Cassandra J. Pappas
Drawings by Mamta Malhotra
Maps by Sanjeev Chandra

Library of Congress Cataloging-in-Publication Data
Cuisines of India : the art and tradition of regional Indian cooking / by Smita Chandra and Sanjeev Chandra.
    p. cm.
Includes bibliographical references and index.
ISBN 0-06-093518-9 (hardcover)
  1. Cookery, India.   I. Chandra, Smita.   II. Chandra, Sanjeev.
TX724.5.I4 C85 2001
641.5954—dc21   00–068188

01   02   03   04   05   SP/RRD   10   9   8   7   6   5   4   3   2   1

For Rohan and Varun

Heirs to a great tradition,
which we hope they discover in these pages

Contents

Acknowledgments

Our first thanks go to our children, Rohan, eleven, and Varun, seven, who are always so supportive and enthusiastic about everything we do. Your efforts to keep each other busy so we could work on our book are much appreciated. We also love the way you brag about us to your friends!

Very special thanks go to our parents, who have been very supportive and have contributed recipes and valuable advice.

This book would have been impossible to write without the enthusiastic help of Sanjeev's sister, Mamta Malhotra. She composed the beautiful line drawings, did tireless research for unusual recipe ideas, and has always been there for us.

Many thanks to family members Ashok, Margit, and Mark Tewari; Aloak, Arti, and Sasha Tewari; Ajay, Rachna, and Anubhav Tewari; Nitin, Vishrut, Shantanu, and Avni Malhotra; and Dinesh and Sudhi Misra for their help and encouragement. Atul Trivedi gave us recipes for the section on Rajasthan, which we couldn't have attempted without his help.

Our friends Nina and Peter Trowbridge and their girls Cory and Sophie; Joanne and Don Bain and their children, Christy and Ian; Karen Cormier and

her children, Danielle and Alex; and our children's friends Allan Kent, Greg Dann, and Jeremy Ali deserve our warm thanks for enriching our lives and for praising our culinary experiments. Our warm gratitude goes to Javad and Hélène Mostaghimi for generously supplying us with the best Iranian saffron and for giving us many occasions to taste delicious Persian cooking in their home.

We have enjoyed working with our agent, Madeleine Morel, and editor Beth Thomas over the years. We also appreciate Daniel Halpern, of Ecco Harper-Collins, taking an interest in our book and offering constructive suggestions.

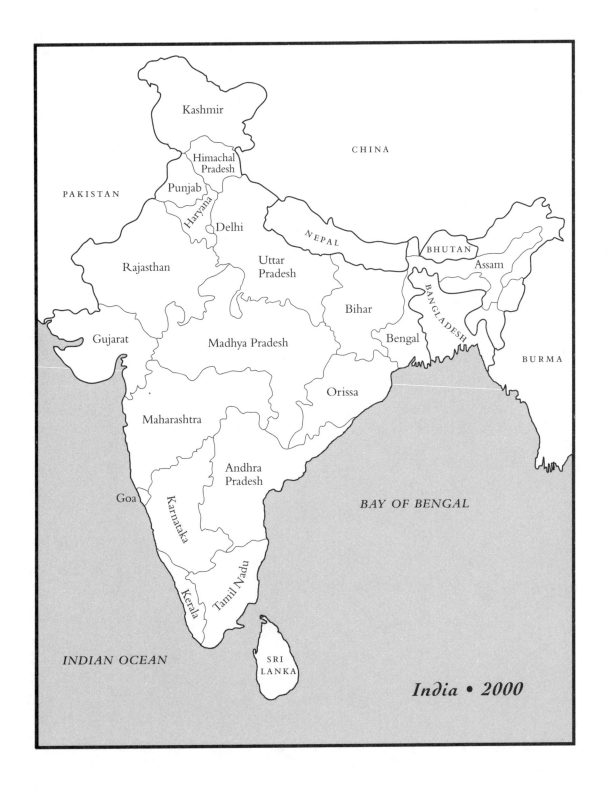

Introduction

"We're going to Delhi!" Those magic words always triggered a storm of anticipation and excitement in my family. Transplanted northern Indians living in the southern state of Kerala, my parents, brothers, and I would set out each year to visit relatives in Delhi. Our delight was not just at the prospect of meeting long-lost cousins: the train journey to Delhi was itself one of the highlights of the vacation. The two-day trip would take us across the borders of six states, each with its own distinct culture, language, and food. Every stop of our train brought exhilarating new sensations. An Indian railway station is a swirling mass of humanity, teeming with travelers rushing to catch trains, porters balancing baggage on their heads, kids getting underfoot, stray cows and dogs wandering about and, loudest of all, hawkers shouting their wares over the general din.

Stepping out of the train in quest of food in the midst of this chaos was always a delicious adventure. Every meal involved delicate negotiations with the vendors, each time in a different language, with a lot of arm waving and gesturing when words failed us. Each city we stopped in had new flavors to offer. At dinnertime we would be passing through Kerala, and our meal would consist of spicy yogurt rice and *masala dosa*s (crisp rice and lentil pancakes, stuffed with spicy potatoes). Next morning we would awaken in Tamil Nadu to the sound of vendors yelling, "*Kapi, kapi,*" and smell the strong coffee even before it reached our coach. Fragrant banana-leaf packages containing *idli*s (steamed rice cakes) and coconut chutney would be passed to us through the window along with the coffee. In Andhra Pradesh, there would be cubes of *aam papad* (sun-dried mango paste) and *bonda*s (potato and chickpea-flour dumplings). Madhya Pradesh brought *dahi bara*s (lentil dumplings in yogurt) and *samosa*s (spicy potato-filled turnovers). In Uttar Pradesh we would dash out to grab a quick meal of *alu puri* (potatoes in a spicy sauce with wheat bread). And when we reached Delhi, our final destination, we would still find time for a quick snack of tea and *pakora*s (potato and onion fritters) while my father went hunting for a porter to carry our baggage out of the station.

Eating my way across India has left me with a deep appreciation for the amazing diversity of its food. When I teach Indian cooking, I like to begin by explaining to my students that "Indian" food is a very broad description of a wide variety of regional cuisines. I tell them how cooks in each part of the country use local ingredients, special spices, and cooking techniques to create unique dishes; and I describe how India's tumultuous history has contributed to this diversity. The food of each region has been shaped by the passage of nomadic tribes, settlers following in the wake of invading armies, trading ships that brought new fruits and vegetables, and the dietary strictures of new religions. India has always embraced these influences and made them part of its own vibrant, constantly evolving cuisine.

In spite of the incredible variety of foods in India, you will find that they all have some common characteristics. Though the *tandoori* chicken of Delhi may bear no obvious resemblance to the *masala dosa* of Bangalore, they are recognizably part of the same cuisine. Both employ the same careful balancing of spices, which is what makes Indian cuisine unique. Each household in India has its own traditional method of spicing that is handed down from one generation to the next. When I got married, I inherited the cooking traditions of my husband's family, which over the years have intermingled with the culinary skills I learned from my mother. When you cook Indian food, you become part of a tradition that stretches back thousands of years.

To help you appreciate the forces that have created the special flavors and aromas of Indian food, I invite you on a journey to India. This journey will take us from the snow-capped mountain peaks of Kashmir to the sun-baked Malabar Coast; from the populous streets of Calcutta to the majestic fortresses of Rajasthan. En route we will sample the dishes that are unique to each region and relive the history that shaped its cuisine. We will explore the fascinating saga of the Aryan tribesmen, the Moghul conquerors, the European explorers, and all the others who came to India in search of wealth and contributed to the rich tapestry of Indian life.

Our journey begins five thousand years ago in the Indus valley, where a remarkably sophisticated civilization flourished around the cities of Harappa and Mohenjodaro. If I were to walk into one of the homes in these cities, the kitchen would seem quite familiar: the circular ovens, the earthen cooking stoves, and stones for grinding grain and spices are like those still used in most village kitchens in India today. And if I were invited to stay for dinner, I would perhaps be served rice, lentils, baked whole-wheat flour chapatis, and chickpeas—pretty much what I eat now.

The cities of the Indus valley flourished for over a thousand years before they came to a catastrophic end. Their demise coincided with the arrival of the Aryans, nomadic tribesmen from Central Asia. The rural farming communities

Pottery, Indus Valley, c. 2000 B.C.

of the Aryans replaced the urban society of Harappa. The wealth of the Aryans centered on their cattle, and their reluctance to slaughter cows evolved into a taboo against eating beef that prevails in India to this day. This age-old instinct is so strong in me that even though I do not count my wealth in cows, I still can't bring myself to enjoy a steak! The growing aversion to meat was reinforced by Buddhism, which originated in India in about 500 B.C. and forbade the slaughter of any animal. This message of nonviolence was absorbed not only by the Buddhists but also by the largely Hindu population, creating a tradition of vegetarianism that prevails even now. As a result, Indian cooks have developed a vegetarian cuisine that is unparalleled in its sheer variety and range of flavors.

The great Hindu empires that flourished across the country slowly retreated before the relentless waves of Muslim invaders who swept down from the mountains of Afghanistan and the plains of Central Asia between A.D. 1000–1500. The Afghans, Arabs, and Turks built an empire in India whose name is still synonymous with pomp and grandeur: the Moghuls. The magnificence of the Moghul court was matched by a rich and luxurious cuisine that centered on meat dishes cooked in lavish cream, nuts, and saffron sauces. Indian cooks were quick to assimilate these new cooking techniques and add to them their own knowledge of spicing and flavoring, creating a delicate and elegant cuisine known as Moghlai.

As the Moghul Empire went into decline in the eighteenth century, the European traders who had come in quest of spices were already poised to colonize the country. By 1850 the British had defeated the Dutch, the French, and the Portuguese in their struggle for domination and established an empire that stretched across the entire subcontinent. Trading ships from the Americas, Africa, and China brought with them new fruits, vegetables, and spices such as potatoes, tomatoes, and chilies, which Indians quickly incorporated into their cooking.

India became independent from British rule in 1947. For the first time, large numbers of Indians began to travel abroad, with many settling in Britain and opening restaurants. Englishmen returning home from India, who had acquired a taste for the local food, were a ready clientele for these restaurants. On a recent visit to London I found more tandoori restaurants than fish and chip shops. My tourist guide called curry the national food of Britain!

In recent years Indian restaurants have appeared in every major city of the world and influenced local cuisines. Fashionable restaurants now have Indian-inspired dishes on their menus, and creative chefs are finding new ways to use Indian spices and ingredients. At a Cajun seafood restaurant in Toronto, I recently saw grilled Atlantic salmon with curried mango salsa on my menu. I ordered it with some trepidation, but when it arrived I was impressed with how beautifully the Indian ingredients had been blended with the Cajun. I shouldn't really have been surprised: after all, Indians have always blithely incorporated ingredients and cooking techniques from every culture they have ever encountered.

The exchange of ideas with other cultures has worked both ways. Indians returning home after living abroad have brought back new ideas and ingredients, which have been embraced by Indian chefs to produce a remarkably innovative fusion of cuisines. Think of this book as a guided tour. Some of the monuments we visit will be dishes that may be already familiar to you. I will also take you down less familiar paths which may hold some delectable surprises. In these pages you will glimpse Indian life through the ages, viewed through the kitchen doors. This book presents recipes from every region of India and describes how such a diverse cuisine was created. As you prepare the *Shahi Kofte ki Biryani,* imagine the royal cooks at the Moghul court four centuries ago, scurrying back and forth in the palace kitchens perfecting each platter for the emperor's banquet. And when you sit down to enjoy your meal, it will truly be fit for a king!

This book is divided into six chapters, each representing the cuisine of a different region. Each chapter is preceded by an introduction that briefly describes the history of the region and explains how it shaped the local food. The recipes are not those from ancient times but represent the food eaten in India today. Most recipes are accompanied by serving suggestions. There are dishes suitable for both simple family dinners and elegant dinner parties. After you've grasped the basic principles of cooking and spicing specific to each region, you can be creative in preparing dishes to suit your own tastes.

Some of the recipes in this book have been cherished for generations in India; others are new, created by me. In preparing these dishes I have worked within the framework of each region's cooking style, sometimes incorporating new ingredients for a fresh twist on old favorites. I hope that you, too, will be inspired to continue this age-old process of creation that has made Indian cuisine so rich and diverse.

Namaskaar!

Helpful Things to Know Before Cooking

This section briefly describes the spices you will need to prepare these recipes. If you have trouble finding any of these ingredients in your area, many are available by mail order from Kalustyan's, 123 Lexington Avenue, New York, NY 10016, tel. (212) 685-3451, fax (212) 683-8458, website www.kalustyans.com. While you may already have most of the cooking implements, I will talk about which ones are best and what to use as substitutes. I will also discuss some special techniques used in cooking Indian food.

Asafetida

This dried resin usually elicits strong reactions from those who eat it: some think its aroma enhances the food, and others find it distasteful. It certainly has a strong pungent aroma which mellows after frying in hot oil. I like the flavor of asafetida and tend to use it a lot. However, since everyone may not feel this way, I have made its use optional in the recipes here. In India it is always used in dried bean and lentil dishes. Although the lump form of asafetida is more aromatic, I recommend the powder for ease of use.

Basmati Rice

I recommend using Basmati rice for all the rice dishes. It comes from the Dehradun region of India and is considered one of the best varieties of rice. It is long-grained and has a nutty aroma and pleasant taste. It holds its shape well during cooking without becoming mushy. If you are cooking a rice dish from this book and find that the rice is not quite done at the end of cooking time, simply transfer everything to a microwave-safe dish, seal tightly with plastic wrap, and microwave on high for 6–8 minutes. Let it sit unopened for 5 minutes before serving. Basmati rice is available at all grocery stores.

Black Pepper

I have used a combination of ground black pepper and cayenne pepper. The taste and aroma of the two blend well together and add to the overall appearance of the dish. I sometimes also use whole black pepper in rice dishes or curries, first lightly frying them in hot oil. I usually don't need to advise my family to pick out the pepper in their food when they are eating! Even if you do bite into one, you will notice that it has lost most of its sharpness in cooking. In some recipes, I have toasted the whole black pepper before powdering to elicit a special roasted aroma. If you feel that the quantity of black pepper used in any of the recipes is too much, you can cut it down to suit your taste.

Black Salt

This is not commonly available in grocery stores—you have to buy it from an Indian store—so I have made its use optional. It is commonly used in Indian dishes such as raitas (yogurt relish), salads, and chutneys. It is pinkish-gray in color and can be bought in powder or lump form. The powder is definitely easier to use.

Cardamom

Two kinds of cardamom are used in Indian cooking: the small green ones and the larger black ones. Green cardamom can easily be found in all grocery stores, either as whole pods or just the seeds. Whole cardamoms keep their aroma and flavor better than seeds or powder. I suggest buying whole pods and storing them in airtight containers.

Black cardamom is usually available only in Indian stores. If you can't find it, you may substitute green cardamom. In all the recipes here, when I refer to cardamom, I mean green cardamom; when black cardamom is required, I specifically say so. Both kinds of cardamom have a lovely aroma that is intensified when fried in hot oil or toasted. I use whole green cardamom, skin and all, to make fresh garam masala and other spice mixtures. I like to fry some whole cardamom pods in hot oil before cooking rice or curries in it as they infuse the dish with their fragrance. I also powder cardamom seeds and sprinkle them over desserts.

Carom Seeds

These tiny seeds bear a strong resemblance to thyme in flavor. They are usually fried in hot oil, in small quantities, before adding the other ingredients. You can buy them in Indian grocery stores: ask for them by their Indian name, *ajwain*. If carom seeds are hard to obtain, you may substitute cumin seeds.

Cashew Nuts, Almonds, and Pistachio Nuts

I have used these raw in a lot of recipes in this book. They are unsalted, unroasted nuts sold in any supermarket. In some places I sauté the nuts lightly along with the onions to draw out a delicious fried aroma. Sometimes in the same recipe I also use the nuts in powder form, sautéing them along with tomatoes or yogurt. This adds body to the sauce and richness to the taste. You might find raw cashew bits, which are cheaper than whole ones, at the grocery store. You may substitute the broken bits for the whole ones.

Cayenne Pepper

Cayenne pepper, or chili powder, is an indispensable part of Indian cuisine. Although most Indians like their food quite hot, I have kept the quantity of cayenne pepper to a minimum. You can increase it or leave it out altogether according to your taste.

Chicken

Some of the recipes in this book call for skinned bone-in chicken, others for boneless chicken thighs. The pieces are usually skinned before being put in the sauce; the skin of the chicken is almost never used. Bone-in pieces are good when the chicken has to be stewed for a long time, as the bones add flavor. Boneless chicken thighs are wonderful to serve when you have guests, because the chicken can be eaten with a fork and knife. You can substitute boneless chicken thighs for bone-in pieces in any recipe you want. Chicken breast is not generally used in curries because it toughens with long cooking. If you wish to use chicken breast instead of legs, first cook the sauce for about 20 minutes, then add the chicken breasts and continue cooking for 15 minutes longer, or until the chicken is tender.

Chickpea Flour

This is pale yellow flour made from ground chickpeas. It is used in Indian food as a thickener, binder, and base for batters, and is an important source of protein. It is available at Indian grocery stores by the name of gram flour or by its Indian name, *besan*.

Chilies, Green and Red

Hot green chilies are used frequently in Indian cooking for their wonderful aroma. They are small in size and hotter than jalapeño peppers. You can substitute any kind of fresh green chili for the Indian variety that I have used here. You can also deseed the chilies before putting them in the food, as this will temper their heat.

Red chilies are usually used dried. They are either broken in half or used whole by frying them lightly in oil or clarified butter and then adding them to the food. Dried red chilies are available at Indian grocery stores. After handling any kind of chilies, wash your hands thoroughly.

Coriander, Fresh

Fresh coriander, or green coriander, is also known as cilantro or Chinese parsley. Indians like to use it liberally as a garnish, in marinades, and in sauces or chutneys. When using it for sauces and chutneys, mince or chop the flavorful stems along with the fresh coriander leaves. Store unused coriander in the refrigerator, wrapped lightly with paper towels in a plastic bag. Rotting leaves should be trimmed away.

Cinnamon

Cinnamon is used in two ways in Indian cooking: whole cinnamon sticks are fried lightly in oil before the food is added, and powdered cinnamon is used to make garam masala (an aromatic spice mixture). Store cinnamon sticks in airtight containers.

Cloves

Cloves are easily available in all grocery stores and should be bought whole. Indian cooks fry cloves lightly in hot oil, then cook rice, meat, or vegetables in it. Cloves are also used in making garam masala.

Coriander Seeds, Ground and Whole

Ground coriander seeds are an essential part of Indian cooking and are used in almost every dish. Whole coriander seeds are toasted or fried lightly in oil before being ground into spice mixtures. Both varieties are available in Indian as well as other grocery stores.

Cumin Seeds, Whole, Ground, and Roasted

Cumin seeds are used in a lot of Indian dishes, especially raitas and chutneys. Whole cumin seeds are lightly fried in oil before the food is added. Ground cumin seeds are added to the dish later, along with other spices. To roast cumin seeds, toast whole cumin seeds for a few minutes in a nonstick or cast-iron frying pan over low heat, then powder them.

Coconut, Fresh and Desiccated, and Coconut Milk

Fresh coconut is an indispensable item in southern Indian cooking. The meat is grated, and the milk is extracted for sauces. When buying a coconut, choose one without any mold on the surface. Shake it and listen for the slosh of milk inside, which is an indicator of freshness. This is Sanjeev's method of breaking open a coconut: using a drill (preferably electric), make holes in the three depressions, or "eyes," on top of the coconut. Upturn the coconut over a glass and collect all the liquid. At this point, you should take a little sip of the liquid; if it is sweet and fresh-tasting, proceed with the next step. If it tastes rancid, save yourself the trouble of breaking open the coconut.

Bang on the coconut, using a hammer, until cracks appear all over its surface. Break it in half and into further little pieces if you wish. Using a sharp knife, pry out the soft meat inside, discarding the outer shell. Wash the pieces well and drain. Some people like to remove the brown skin covering the white meat of the coconut with a peeler or a knife. I don't bother to do this, as it doesn't make much difference to the dish in the end. Cut the coconut meat into smaller pieces and put it in the jar of a blender, along with about ½ cup of water. Blend until all the coconut has been reduced to a grainy paste. This is what is referred to as grated coconut. Take out what you need and freeze the rest in Ziploc bags or in an ice cube tray. This way you can use one or two coconut cubes as needed and let the rest remain frozen. One good-size cube should yield about 2 tablespoons of grated coconut.

Some recipes in this book call for desiccated coconut, which is available in all grocery stores. Make sure you get the unsweetened variety. I don't rehydrate it when using it but just follow the recipe instructions.

I often use coconut milk in my recipes. It is best to use canned unsweetened coconut milk as it tastes good and saves effort. Making fresh coconut milk at home is far too laborious. Remember to freeze unused portions of coconut milk, as it won't last long in the refrigerator.

Cottage Cheese, Cubed and Crumbled

The kind of cottage cheese used in Indian cooking is not the same one sold in plastic tubs in supermarkets. This is hard-pressed cottage cheese with all the liquid drained from it, which makes it easy to cube and sauté. Although it has a hard texture, almost like mozzarella cheese, it softens and absorbs the sauce as it cooks, becoming moist and spongy. This kind of cottage cheese can be found in all Indian stores and in some regular grocery stores in big cities. Look in the refrigerated section for hard-pressed cottage cheese (its Indian name is *paneer*).

I have used crumbled cottage cheese in many recipes in this book. This is now available in all grocery stores; look for it in the refrigerated section, in airtight plastic packets labeled "pressed cottage cheese." It is softer than the hard-pressed variety, though not as liquid as the cottage cheese sold in tubs, and its consistency is wonderful to work with. Use it as stuffing for bread or chicken, in marinades, or as deep-fried koftas. If you need a substitute, grate a hard-pressed block of cottage cheese.

Curry Leaves, Fresh and Dried

Fresh curry leaves are an essential part of most southern Indian cooking. They are used in other recipes in this book too. They have a lovely fragrance, which is intensified by frying in oil. The food is then cooked in this oil and takes on some of the aroma from the curry leaves. I am happy to note that fresh curry leaves are now easily available at Indian grocery stores. Look for them in the refrigerated section, or ask for them by their Indian name—*karipatta*. Refrigerate them in a plastic bag or freeze them in a Ziploc bag. Dried leaves are also available at Indian grocers, but they are not worth using, as they have little aroma or flavor. You can order fresh curry leaves by mail from Indian grocery stores.

Fennel Seeds, Whole and Powdered

Fennel seeds have a delicious licorice-like flavor and a sweet aroma. They are larger than anise seeds, though you can substitute one for the other. When used whole, they are fried lightly in oil first, to draw out their flavor, before the food is added. They are also used in powdered form in many of these recipes. You can powder fennel seeds in a spice grinder, but don't store large quantities, as they lose their aroma quickly. Fennel seeds are an important ingredient in making *panchphoran,* a spice mixture from Bengal. They are also indispensable in chutneys and pickles.

Fenugreek Seeds and Fresh and Dried Leaves

Fenugreek seeds are usually lightly fried in oil to draw out their aroma and flavor before the food is cooked in the oil. They are usually used in small quantities, as they tend to taste bitter, but cooking them after frying mellows them, and they imbue the food with a wonderful aroma. They are an important part of Bengali and southern Indian cooking.

Fresh fenugreek leaves are easily available at Indian grocery stores and in some farmers' markets. Ask for them by their Indian name, *methi*. They are very aromatic and taste mildly bitter, but are wonderful cooked with lamb, chicken, or even potatoes. I like to add a lot of tamarind or lemon juice to the food to balance the flavor of the leaves. I recommend using just the leaves, since the stalks can get too bitter.

I have a passion for dried fenugreek leaves and use them in many recipes. They add a delicious aroma without the bitterness, and are easily obtained at Indian grocers or some of the larger supermarkets. Ask for them by their Indian name, *kasoori methi*, named after Quasur, Pakistan, which produces the world's finest fenugreek.

Fish

I really like salmon and rainbow trout, the two varieties I have used most often in this book, but you can substitute any of your favorites. Make sure that they are thick-cut and firm-fleshed so that they hold their shape when cooking. In most of my recipes, I first marinate the fish for a short while, then grill it lightly in the oven; this loosens the skin, making skinning, deboning, and cutting easier. Marinating also removes any fishy odor and makes the dish more flavorful.

Garam Masala

This aromatic spice mixture is an essential ingredient in almost all northern Indian and Moghlai dishes. It is a combination of cinnamon, cloves, cardamom, bay leaves, nutmeg, cumin seeds, and black pepper. Some people like to add a bit of coriander and fenugreek seeds as well. The ingredients vary from family to family—each has a special blend. Although ready-made garam masala is available in Indian grocery stores, I recommend that you make your own, as the store-bought ones tend to contain fillers and don't taste as good. My recipe for garam masala can be made in small batches in a spice grinder:

1½ tablespoons whole cardamom	2 bay leaves, broken up
4 cinnamon sticks, broken into 1-inch pieces	½ teaspoon fennel seeds
1 teaspoon whole black pepper	1 teaspoon kasoori methi (dried fenugreek leaves) (optional)
1 teaspoon cumin seeds	
1 tablespoon whole cloves	Pinch of saffron (optional)

Put all the spices in a clean spice or coffee grinder and powder finely. You may have to do this in two batches. Transfer to an airtight container and store in a cool dry place. Shelf life is indefinite.

Ghee (Clarified Butter)

Ghee is butter that has been cooked for so long that it no longer contains any milk solids. It has a lovely nutty taste and pleasing aroma. Ready-made ghee can be bought at Indian grocery stores and does not require refrigeration. I have used ghee in some of the recipes in this book, but if you like, you may substitute butter. To make ghee at home, melt 1 pound unsalted butter in a heavy-bottomed saucepan over low heat. When all the solids have settled to the bottom, after about a half hour, carefully pour the liquid butter into a container, leaving the solids behind.

Ginger, Fresh and Dried

Ginger is available in all grocery stores. Store it in the refrigerator in a plastic bag. It has a brown skin that some people like to peel before using; I don't bother, but make sure to wash the ginger well.

Dried, powdered ginger is also used in some of these recipes. It is available in Indian stores as well as other grocery stores. You can substitute fresh ginger for the dried if you wish.

Ground Meat, Chicken, or Lamb

I use ground meat to make grilled kababs and koftas (meatballs). Wrap the meat in paper towels for a little while to absorb the excess juices, which will make the meat less likely to fall apart on the grill. Chilling the meat before shaping it is also recommended, as that will help the kabab hold its shape better. If you find that the mixture is too soft to mold onto skewers or shape into meatballs, add a couple of tablespoons of chickpea flour or all-purpose flour and mince in the food processor. Bread is the best binder, and you can add another slice to the meat mixture if you feel it needs it.

When shaping the meat onto skewers, wet your hands lightly and take a ball of the mixture. Wrap it around the skewers and mold it with your fingers and palm. This is easier than it sounds, so don't be daunted. You can also shape the meat mixture into patties and grill them. Although I have shallow-fried the koftas in most of my recipes, you can try broiling them in the oven or barbecuing them on the grill.

Lamb

I have used lamb in a lot of these recipes. You can substitute beef, veal, or pork if you like. Good-quality fresh lamb can be obtained in any supermarket, and you can ask the butcher to cut bone-in lamb into smaller pieces. Stewing lamb is available already cut up, or you can request cut leg of lamb or lamb shanks with bone in. I sometimes buy lamb chops and cut them up myself. If the recipe calls for boneless lamb, I either use cut-up lamb chops or ask the butcher to debone a leg of lamb. The bone can be used to make broth, and extra pieces of lamb can be frozen for later use.

Mangoes, Green

Green cooking mangoes are hard, unripe fruit that can be found in Indian grocery stores. They have a tart flavor and are used to make chutneys, sauces, and marinades. When buying one, make sure that it is unblemished and firm. The peel and pit of the mango are usually discarded, and the sour flesh from the fruit is minced to a paste or cut into pieces.

Mint, Fresh

Fresh mint is used extensively for making chutneys and flavoring sauces. There are many varieties of mint in grocery stores these days, and the one I have used throughout this book is peppermint, which is most commonly used in India. If you have a lot of mint, you can dry it in the microwave and crumble into the recipe as needed. Fresh mint should be stored in plastic bags and refrigerated. Dried mint needs to be in an airtight container in a cool, dry place.

Mung Beans, Split and Hulled

Yellow mung beans are available at all grocery stores. You can also search for them in Indian stores by their Indian name, *moong dal*.

Mustard Seeds, Black

Although commonly known as "black," these mustard seeds are actually dark brown in color and quite small in size. They are used in two ways in this book: fried lightly in oil before adding the food, and powdered for use in spice mixtures. The first technique draws out a pleasant nutty flavor from the seeds, while the second technique, used mainly in dishes from Bengal, elicits a sharp, pungent flavor. Black mustard seeds can bought in Indian grocery stores; ask for them by their Indian name, *rai*.

Onions

Throughout this book I have used cup measurements for onions, because their sizes vary. In general, you should get about 1¼ cups, finely chopped, from a medium onion and about 1½ cups from a larger one.

Onion Seeds (Nigella)

These are popularly known as onion seeds, though their correct name is nigella. They are black with an oniony flavor. They are usually used whole in Indian dishes like pickles, chutneys, and sauces, where they are first fried lightly in oil. Buy them in Indian grocery stores, where they are known by their Indian name, *kalonji*.

Pomegranate Seeds, Dried

Dried pomegranate seeds are sometimes used whole to add a tart flavor to stuffed breads, or can be powdered and added to sauces for chicken, lamb, or vegetables. Both dried and powdered seeds can be obtained at Indian grocery stores: Look for dried seeds by their Indian name, *anardaana*. If you wish to use a substitute, try tamarind.

Poppy Seeds, White

White poppy seeds are used as a paste or powder to thicken sauces and add a slightly nutty taste. They are available at Indian grocery stores and are called *khus khus* in Hindi.

Saffron

I love saffron and tend to use it in many recipes. It has a lovely color and turns the food a light orange. It also has a delicate aroma that blends well with rice. Saffron is used in rice preparations, desserts, and in some Moghlai dishes. It is an expensive spice, so I use only tiny pinches of it. If you buy a lot, store it in your freezer, which keeps it fresh, crisp, and easier to crumble. Although some people dilute saffron in warm milk before adding it to food, I like to just crumble it lightly with my fingers and sprinkle it over the dish as it cooks. I usually buy saffron in threads.

Spices

Spices are the heart and soul of Indian cooking. Used in the right combination, they enhance the taste of the dish by bringing out the flavor of its main ingredient. Store all spices in airtight containers away from heat. If possible, invest in a spice grinder and powder some of the special spice mixtures yourself. Work with small quantities, as spices lose their freshness if kept too long.

Tamarind

Tart to taste and chocolate brown in color, tamarind is sold in seedless slabs in Indian stores. When you need some, break off a piece and either soak it for a few hours in hot water, mashing it with a fork once in a while, or put it in water and microwave it. Pass it through a sieve and collect the extract in a bowl, then discard the fibrous residue.

Tomatoes, Fresh, Frozen, Canned, Sun or Oven Dried

When using fresh tomatoes, I usually don't peel them but chop or puree them directly as needed. I like to work with plum tomatoes, as they are meatier and sauté well. Toward late summer, when sun-ripened tomatoes are plentiful, I buy a lot and freeze them to use later: Before freezing drop them in boiling water for a few minutes, then drain and cool. Peel the skins and either dice them or leave them whole.

Canned tomatoes can also be used in place of fresh or frozen ones. If using whole or diced tomatoes—I prefer not to use pureed or ground—lift them out of their liquid before measuring and prepare according to the recipe. Their liquid can be used in place of water later in the recipe or for soups in other recipes. Fresh tomatoes should be chopped finely before measuring. They don't need to be peeled unless the recipe specifies it. Plum tomatoes, either fresh or canned, work best. When adding tomatoes to the skillet, make sure to do it on medium heat. Sauté for 5–8 minutes, mashing the tomatoes with the back of your stirring spoon to blend them into the sauce. When all the moisture has evaporated and the oil shows around the edges of the mixture, the tomatoes are done.

Sun- or oven-dried tomatoes are a real treat to have in the kitchen and can be used in marinades, grilled meats, sauces, and breads. Oven-dried tomatoes can be made at home and frozen for later use. Buy a lot of plum tomatoes when they're in season; you can't have too many of them. Preheat oven to 250°F. Wash and halve the plum tomatoes and place them, cut side up, on a lightly greased baking sheet. Bake for at least 8 hours. Toward the end of cooking, check occasionally and remove the ones that are done. They should be shrunken in size and almost leathery in texture. Cool and freeze in Ziploc bags; you don't have to thaw them, just use according to the recipe.

Yellow Split Peas

Indian yellow split peas, called *chana dal,* tend to be slightly smaller than the Western variety. They are not very different in taste, though, and one can be substituted for the other. You can buy chana dal at Indian grocery stores.

Yogurt, Plain and Thickened

Plain yogurt is used as a thickening agent in Indian cooking. Full-fat yogurt sautés well and adds body to the sauce; low-fat yogurt tends to be too watery and the sauce will take longer to thicken. Adding yogurt to a sauce is a tricky job, as the yogurt can curdle at high temperatures and separate from the sauce. It is best to do this with the skillet set at medium heat. Beat yogurt well with a spoon and add it to the sauce in small batches, stirring the sauce constantly. When the yogurt has been incorporated into the sauce, continue sautéing for another 5 minutes, or until all the moisture has evaporated and the raw smell has dissipated. When the yogurt is well sautéed, the oil will appear around the edges of the yogurt mixture.

Thickening yogurt is a technique used in a lot of these recipes. Thickened yogurt has a rich creamy texture and is less likely than regular yogurt to curdle when added to sauces; since it has little moisture, it sautés faster. When used in marinades it clings to the meat, and when combined with spices and other ingredients—such as sun-dried tomatoes or herbs—it makes a delicious low-fat dip.

To thicken yogurt, you may be able to find special cone-shaped plastic, fine mesh strainers available in specialty kitchen stores. They are known as yogurt strainers and sometimes come with a plastic bowl that the strainer fits over. Lacking that, you can improvise by inserting a coffee filter in a fine mesh sieve and setting the whole thing over a bowl to catch the drippings. Put the yogurt in the strainer and let it drain for as long as the recipe requires. Four hours usually gets good results, though keeping it in the refrigerator and letting it drain overnight is even better. Drain and discard the whey at the bottom of the bowl, scrape out the yogurt from the strainer or coffee filter, and use according to the recipe.

Wok or Skillet

Indian cooking is best done in a deep, heavy-bottomed, nonstick wok or skillet with a tight-fitting lid. If you have two of these skillets, so much the better.

Coffee Grinder

These are inexpensive, can be bought in any department store, and are handy to grind nuts and spices.

A Last Word of Advice

Indian cooking is not difficult to master and does not have to be laborious. If your kitchen is well stocked, you can easily prepare delicious Indian food; but don't abandon the recipe even if you don't have all the ingredients. In many cases, substitutions are possible, and you can leave out some ingredients altogether and still get good results. Read through the recipe first and then assemble your supplies close to the stove, as you will need them in quick succession. Taste for seasonings after cooking and adjust salt and lemon juice as required.

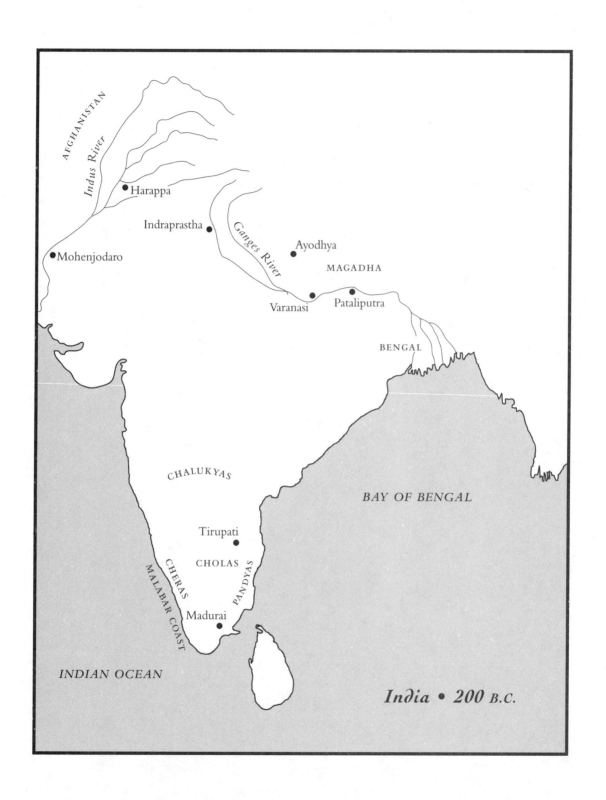

AFGHANISTAN

Indus River

● Harappa

Indraprastha ●

● Mohenjodaro

Ganges River

Ayodhya ●

MAGADHA

● Varanasi ● Pataliputra

BENGAL

CHALUKYAS

BAY OF BENGAL

Tirupati ●

CHOLAS

CHERAS   PANDYAS

MALABAR COAST

Madurai ●

INDIAN OCEAN

India • 200 B.C.

Cuisines of India

Ancient India:
Birth of a Vegetarian Cuisine

When I was born, my grandmother traced the sacred syllable *Om* on my tongue with a finger dipped in honey as a Hindu ceremony of purification. (Or so I have been told. Having tried to do the same for my sons, I can vouch for the fact that it is not easy to get a newborn to stick his tongue out long enough to write anything legible on it!) This ceremony illustrates the Hindu belief that purity of mind and body can only be maintained by a pure diet, which for the majority is strictly vegetarian.

Vegetarianism was not always a central part of Hinduism. The ancestors of today's Hindus, nomadic tribesmen who migrated to India from Central Asia in the second millennium B.C., had no aversion to eating meat. They were farmers and herdsmen who called themselves Arya, meaning "noble." We know them from the rich literature they left behind, including the Vedas, which consist of hymns of praise to the Aryan gods, and the great epics, the Ramayana and Mahabharatha (the longest poem ever composed). Children in India are raised on stories of the great heroes from these epics, and Hindus consider them sacred scriptures. When an enterprising movie producer made a television series of the Mahabharatha, he had enough material for a year's worth of weekly episodes that riveted the country when they aired. Apart from tales of heroism, these stories also contain detailed descriptions of everyday life that give us a fairly clear picture of Aryan times.

Aryan life centered on farming and raising cattle: cows were a source of endless bounty and beef was considered a luxury. Gradually, a growing veneration of cows and their economic value led to a complete taboo against eating beef. Imposing this ban could not have been easy. In one of the ancient texts, the sage Yagnavalkya, on being told that eating beef is a sin, retorts, "That may well be, but I shall eat of it nevertheless if the flesh be tender."

As the Aryans settled down, agriculture became increasingly important, with barley and rice the staple grains. A variety of vegetables were also grown, such as cucumber, lotus stems and roots, gourds, and water chestnuts. Radishes and ginger were eaten, but onions, garlic, and leeks were avoided then, as now, by orthodox Hindus. Turmeric, fenugreek, ginger, pepper, and cardamom were used to spice the food. Many of the preparations would seem quite familiar to Indians today: flour pancakes fried and dipped in honey *(malpuas)*; rice cooked in milk and sugar *(kheer)*; lentils *(dal)*; papads, and sweetened, thickened yogurt *(srikhand)*. Other Aryan cooking techniques, such as cooking pork and mutton in fruit juices and roasting dried meats, have disappeared. I am sometimes tempted to try and revive them—there may be an idea for another cookbook!

Gradually, as the Aryans abandoned their nomadic lifestyle, towns began to take shape over the farming villages. The foundations of Indraprastha (modern-day Delhi), Varanasi (Banaras), and Patliputra (Patna) were laid at this time. Tribal leadership gave way to a new political order, and by 600 B.C. small kingdoms began to emerge. The struggle for supremacy among these kingdoms lasted for a century, with the kingdom of Magadh (now Bihar) emerging victorious. After being ruled by a series of short-lived dynasties, the throne of Magadh was seized in 321 B.C. by Chandragupta Maurya, who founded the first great Indian empire, controlling the area now occupied by the states of Uttar Pradesh, Madhya Pradesh, and Bihar.

A fascinating window into Mauryan times is given by the Arthashastra, a treatise on the art of government written by Kautilya, the chief minister of Chandragupta. In it he describes the duties of the superintendent of slaughterhouses in ensuring the quality of meat in shops. He provides a detailed list of ingredients required for cooking meat sold in markets, including the exact

Sculpture of intoxicated woman, Uttar Pradesh, second century A.D.

proportions of oil, yogurt, salt, and spices. No doubt shopkeepers adhered to the list faithfully, because the Arthashastra also catalogs eighteen forms of torture for those who violated laws. The stability brought about by Mauryan rule produced an era of prosperity, which is still remembered as the dawn of a golden age in Indian history. Social life was sophisticated, and every village boasted at least one tavern. These taverns were large and graced with courtyards, rooms with luxurious seating, and counters where patrons could buy flowers and perfumes. Alcoholic and fermented beverages were sold all through the day and far into the night, with customers offered salt to enhance their thirst.

While Chandragupta Maurya was establishing his empire in eastern India, a new force appeared from the northwest. Alexander of Macedonia, in his quest to conquer the world, had defeated the Persian Empire and reached the Punjab in 327 B.C. With his army exhausted, he retreated after establishing a number of Greek settlements in India. Alexander died in Persia a few years later and his empire soon disintegrated, with Chandragupta Maurya sweeping these settlements into his own empire. Alexander's brief incursion gave the Western world its first direct contact with India. Soldiers in his army brought back tales of the wonders they had witnessed, which were to attract fortune seekers for many centuries. Some of these accounts, though strange to European ears, were quite true: reeds that produced honey without bees (sugarcane) and plants standing in water that yielded grain (rice). Other reports were less than accurate: Megasthenes, the Greek ambassador to the Mauryan court, sent back reports of ants larger than foxes who dug for gold and piled it in glittering heaps. Nearchus, Alexander's admiral, spoke of "places where brass rains from the sky in brazen drops." If nothing else, these stories confirm the age-old Indian custom of telling tall tales to gullible tourists.

The expansion of the Mauryan Empire was continued by the heirs of Chandragupta and reached its height with his grandson, Ashoka. He extended his domain across almost the entire Indian subcontinent, from Afghanistan to Bengal, but the brutality of war appalled him. Searching for peace, he turned to a new religion that was preaching a message of nonviolence—Buddhism. Ashoka had a series of edicts inscribed in stone, exhorting the people in his empire to cultivate simplicity, show gentleness and compassion to all living beings, and embrace vegetarianism. One of his edicts states "No living being may be slaughtered. . . . Formerly slaughter in the king's kitchen was great: now it has almost been stopped."

Buddhism, at the time of Ashoka's conversion, was still a relatively new religion. Founded in the fifth century B.C. by Gautama Buddha, it proclaimed the sacredness of all life and advocated nonviolence. Once Ashoka gave it official sanction, Buddhism spread rapidly, as did the doctrine of vegetarianism. Buddhist missionaries also traveled to China, Tibet, Sri Lanka, and all over Southeast Asia; these countries proved receptive to the new faith, but they declined the vegetarian diet.

After Ashoka's death, his empire fragmented into smaller kingdoms, and the next 600 years of Indian history are a confused tale of the rise and fall of minor monarchs as they struggled for supremacy. It was not until A.D. 300 that another great dynasty rose to unite the entire land under one rule—the Guptas. Starting from their ancestral lands in Magadh, where Ashoka had once reigned, the Guptas rapidly expanded their domain, and by the time of the third king, Vikramaditya, it stretched across the entire country.

The Gupta age is best remembered for its flourishing cultural and intellectual life. The Kamasutra was written in this period as a guide to the young man about town, advising him to excel in poetry, painting, and cooking, and instructing him in the delicate art of love. Medical science made great strides, with the physician Charak cautioning against the dangers of eating too many fried foods, a warning that many doctors have echoed since. Charak also recommended as an aphrodisiac an omelet made with crocodile eggs and rice flour. History does not record the effectiveness of this prescription.

Vegetarianism was firmly established by this time, a fact that was often remarked upon by foreign visitors. The Chinese monk Fa Xian, who visited India in A.D. 399, commented, "throughout the country, no one kills any living thing, nor drinks wine, nor eats onion or garlic. In this country, they do not keep pigs or fowls, there are no dealings in cattle, no butcher shops or distilleries in the market place." Over a century later, another monk, Xuan Zang, stated, "Onions and garlic are little known and few people eat them; if anyone uses them for food, they are expelled beyond the walls of town." To this day, most cooks in the region of Uttar Pradesh do not use onions and garlic in their food, considering them impure.

Three thousand years of vegetarianism have fired up the creativity of Indian cooks, producing a vegetarian cuisine that is unmatched anywhere in the world for flavor and variety. Because vegetables were the main course, chefs brought all their ingenuity into devising countless unique ways to cook every vegetable. Having tried for years to make two small boys eat their vegetables, I appreciate the advantages of serving the same vegetable in ways that taste totally different.

The recipes in this chapter are drawn from the Hindu heartland of Uttar Pradesh, Madhya Pradesh, and Bihar, which were once the center of Ashoka's empire, where Buddha first preached. The food of these regions is simple, lightly spiced, and totally vegetarian. Traditionally, onions and garlic were used sparingly, if at all, but these days many people will use sautéed onions and garlic to add flavor. Food is cooked in a *masala* (sautéed spice mixture) made by putting a pinch of asafetida in hot oil, followed by ground spices such as turmeric, cayenne pepper, ground coriander, and cumin. Yogurt or tomatoes are used for thickening sauces, and they may be sautéed for a while in the spice mixture before a main ingredient is added.

A typical meal eaten at home would consist of two vegetable dishes, one "wet" (cooked in a sauce) and one "dry." Dal (lentils) or dried bean preparations, such as chickpeas or kidney beans, are an important part of the diet and may be substituted for one of the vegetables. There is usually a salad or a raita (yogurt relish with chopped or grated vegetables) and rice or Indian bread.

The food described in this section includes both simple, everyday dishes and more elaborate meals reserved for special occasions. The cuisine is a product of an ancient tradition, but I have not attempted to recreate two-thousand-year-old recipes. This is food as it is cooked and eaten in India nowadays, though I like to think that if Emperor Ashoka had tasted it, he certainly would have enjoyed it. As I hope you will too.

Banks of Ganges River at Varanasi, 1825

Chewra Matar • Beaten rice cooked with peas, tomatoes, and spices

Patty Pan Squash Korma • Patty pan squash cooked in a sauce of sautéed onions, tomatoes, coconut, and yogurt

Chatniwale Alu Gobhi • Oven-roasted potatoes and cauliflower tossed with an herb and mango dressing

Alu ki Sabzi • Potatoes cooked with tomatoes, thickened yogurt, and spices

Saag Khumb • Spinach and mushrooms cooked with sautéed onions, tomatoes, and yogurt

Matar Paneer Khumb Masala • Cottage cheese, peas, and mushrooms cooked in a sautéed onion, tomato, and yogurt sauce

Paneer Khumb aur Mirch ki Sabzi • Cottage cheese, mushrooms, and sweet peppers stir-fried with spices and tomatoes

Khumb Chole Kasoori • Chickpeas and mushrooms cooked in a sauce of onions, tomatoes, and dried fenugreek leaves

Saag Matar • Spinach cooked with green peas, onions, tomatoes, and spices

Gobhi Matar ki Sabzi • Grated cauliflower and peas stir-fried with onions and spices

Masala Baby Corn Curry • Baby corn cooked in a spicy sauce of sautéed onions and tomatoes

Moong ki Dal Palakwali • Yellow mung beans cooked with fresh spinach

Palak ka Raita • Spinach served in spiced yogurt with sautéed onions

Kele ka Raita • Sliced bananas in sweetened cardamom-flavored yogurt

Kele wali Saunth • Sweet and sour tamarind mint chutney with sliced bananas

Tamatar ka Salat • Tomato rounds with roasted cumin, fresh coriander leaves, and lemon juice

Sirkewali Pyaz • Onion rings marinated in vinegar

Subz Paneer Pulao • Rice stir-fried with cottage cheese and sautéed vegetables

Tamatari Kasoori Pulao • Rice stir-fried with spicy tomato puree, scented with dried fenugreek leaves

Bhutte ki Biryani • Rice layered and baked with a spicy corn curry

Makka aur Khumb ka Pulao • Rice cooked with sautéed onions, portobello mushrooms, and baby corn

Kesari Chawal ki Badami Kheer • A rice dessert with milk, sugar, saffron, and almonds

Chewra Matar

Beaten rice cooked with peas, tomatoes, and spices

Considered the holiest of all cities by Hindus, Varanasi (Banaras) has stood on the banks of the river Ganges for over 3,000 years. A dip in the waters of the Ganges is said to wash away all sins, and judging from the throng of pilgrims crowding the riverbank, a lot of people are eager to do so.

My favorite memory of Varanasi is from a visit to my sister-in-law Mamta's home, when we went on a moonlit boat ride. The waters were shimmering with thousands of small flickering clay lamps that people had floated on to the river for good luck. Leaving these serene surroundings for the bustling, brightly lit streets of the town, we were tempted in by appetizing smells from the rows of food stalls that lined the narrow alleyways. I just had to stop and sample one of my favorite street foods from Varanasi—Chewra Matar. This is traditionally made in winter, when fresh peas are in season. It is prepared early in the day and kept warm on a griddle over a portable stove. When you place your order, the cook will stir a pat of fresh butter into your portion.

When you buy beaten rice at an Indian store, be sure to ask for it by its Indian name, poha. There are two varieties, but the thicker kind is best for this recipe. I like to serve Chewra Matar at brunch on a lazy Sunday morning, accompanied by a freshly brewed pot of coffee.

- Briefly wash the beaten rice in a fine mesh sieve. Drain well and transfer to a large mixing bowl. Add the milk and heavy cream and toss gently. Let sit for 20 minutes or until the milk gets absorbed; stir occasionally. Cover the peas with water in a microwave-safe container, seal with plastic wrap, and microwave on high for 5 minutes, then drain and set aside.

1 cup poha (beaten rice)
½ cup milk
2 tablespoons heavy cream
1 cup frozen peas
1 pound red ripe tomatoes
2 tablespoons vegetable oil
½ teaspoon cumin seeds
1 bay leaf
½-inch piece of ginger, grated
2 hot green chilies, finely chopped
Salt to taste
½ teaspoon ground coriander seeds
½ teaspoon ground cumin seeds
½ teaspoon garam masala
½ teaspoon turmeric
¼ teaspoon cayenne pepper
1 medium cooked potato, peeled and
    diced into ½-inch pieces
20 raw cashews
2 tablespoons golden raisins
½ teaspoon sugar
2 tablespoons orange juice
1 cup fresh coriander leaves and
    tender stems, chopped
1 tablespoon melted butter or ghee
Dash of lemon juice (optional)

(You can also cook the peas in a saucepan.) Wash and halve the tomatoes, then puree in a food processor or blender.

- Warm the oil in a nonstick skillet over high heat. Add the cumin seeds and the bay leaf. After a few seconds, add the grated ginger and chopped green chilies. Sauté for 30 seconds, then add the pureed tomatoes. Reduce the heat to medium and cook the tomatoes for 5 minutes, until they have thickened slightly. Add the salt, ground coriander and ground cumin seeds, garam masala, turmeric, and cayenne pepper. Cook for 1 minute, then add the peas, diced potato, cashews, and raisins. Cover and cook for 5 minutes, stirring once in a while.

- Gently stir in the soaked beaten rice, making sure it comes in contact with the sides of the skillet and roasts lightly. Stir-fry for about 10 minutes, then add the sugar and orange juice. Cook for another 5 minutes, then mix in the fresh coriander and butter or ghee. Add ¼ teaspoon more of garam masala and a dash of lemon juice if desired.

- SERVES 3 TO 4

Patty Pan Squash Korma

Patty pan squash cooked in a sauce of sautéed onions, tomatoes, coconut, and yogurt

*1 pound green patty pan squash,
    scraped or peeled and quartered*
1½ cups finely chopped onions
*½ cup diced tomatoes, canned
    or fresh*
½-inch piece of ginger, chopped
2 garlic cloves, chopped
*1 tablespoon grated coconut,
    preferably fresh*

 Kings in ancient India led pampered lives: There were servants whose only duty was to prepare the king's bath, while others laid out his clothes. One person perfumed the clothes, and another selected the right jewelry and flowers to accent them. But no person on the royal staff had a job as exacting as that of the palace's head cook. This poor man was responsible for feeding the entire royal family, as well as an army of retainers, and each day had to create new and exciting dishes to tempt sophisticated palates. His kitchen was in an open courtyard, part of which was covered by a tiled roof. The cook sat cross-legged on the floor, toiling amid the heat and smoke of the kitchen fires. He had to defend against the crows and dogs that were always on the lookout for a quick snack. But the biggest bane of his life was the official food taster, who dropped in for surprise inspections to make sure none of the food was poisoned.

I can sympathize with the cook's predicament when I am rushing to put dinner on the table. On those days, this korma recipe is a godsend: it is easy to put together no matter how often you are interrupted, and is sure to impress the most jaded appetite. This is a good recipe to try out in the summer when a large variety of fresh and tender squash is in season. You can substitute any squash of your choice, baby zucchini, or a medley of vegetables.

3 tablespoons vegetable oil

½ teaspoon cumin seeds

2 tablespoons plain yogurt, not low-fat

Salt to taste

¼ to ½ teaspoon cayenne pepper

½ teaspoon turmeric

½ teaspoon ground coriander seeds

½ teaspoon ground cumin seeds

1 cup water

½ teaspoon garam masala

2 tablespoons chopped fresh coriander leaves

1 tablespoon heavy cream (optional)

- Wash and drain the patty pan squash. In a blender or food processor, blend the onions, tomatoes, ginger, garlic, and coconut till smooth.
- Warm the oil in a nonstick skillet over medium-high heat. Add the cumin seeds, then, after a few seconds, the blended onion paste. Sauté, stirring frequently for 8 to 10 minutes, until the oil appears around the edges. Reduce heat to medium and stir in the yogurt. Cook for 5 minutes, stirring frequently, then add the salt, cayenne, turmeric, and ground coriander and cumin seeds. Cook for 2 minutes, then add the squash and the water. Mix well, cover the skillet, and increase the heat to high. Bring to a boil, reduce heat to low, and cook for 30 minutes or until the squash is very tender. Stir once in a while. Turn off the heat and mix in the garam masala, fresh coriander leaves, and cream if desired. You can make this dish up to 3 days ahead of time.

    • SERVES 3 TO 4 WITH OTHER DISHES

Chatniwale Alu Gobhi

**Oven-roasted potatoes and cauliflower tossed
with an herb and mango dressing**

1½ pounds small white new potatoes,
  unpeeled and halved or quartered

½ pound cauliflower, cut into
  long-stemmed florets,
  1 inch at top

1 medium onion, peeled and chopped
  into 1-inch chunks

1 garlic clove, grated

4 tablespoons vegetable oil

Salt to taste

¼ teaspoon ground black pepper

½ teaspoon ground coriander seeds

½ teaspoon ground cumin seeds

½ teaspoon garam masala

1 small green cooking mango, peeled
  and pitted, pulp retained

1 cup packed fresh mint leaves,
  washed well

1½ cups packed fresh coriander
  leaves and tender stems,
  washed well

1 hot green chili (optional)

½ teaspoon roasted ground
  cumin seeds

¼ teaspoon garam masala

2 tablespoons water

 The sage Manu, who lived in the first century A.D., was acknowledged in his time as the authority on social laws in India. He described how a host should behave after serving guests:

> Invite them to partake of each [dish], proclaiming its qualities; cause them to partake gradually and slowly of each, and repeatedly urge them to eat by offering the food and extolling its qualities. All the food shall be very hot and the guests shall eat in silence. Having addressed them with a question: "Have you dined well?," let him give them water to sip, and bid farewell to them with the words: "Now rest."

I am not sure I agree with Manu on the subject of silence at the dinner table and am reluctant to extol my own cooking. But when I need a dish that all the guests will eat without my repeated urging, this is the recipe I reach for.

I like the taste of roasted cauliflower and have tossed in a few florets with the potatoes, but you can always leave those out and make up the amount with more potatoes. You can even try adding other vegetables, such as sweet green or red peppers or zucchini. The green mango in the dressing is also optional; you can substitute lemon juice. This dish tastes just as good sandwiched in a bun or served with Indian bread and Chicken Curry (chicken cooked with onions, tomatoes, yogurt, and spices, page 231).

- Preheat the oven to 400°F. Combine the potatoes, cauliflower, onion, and garlic in a large mixing bowl, then add the oil, salt, pepper, ground coriander, ground cumin, and garam masala. Toss well to coat, then spread the vegetables in a single layer on a baking sheet or tray. Bake for 45 minutes to an hour, turning the vegetables 2 to 3 times for even roasting. After turning off the oven, keep the tray in for 20 minutes to lightly brown the vegetables. You can roast the vegetables up to 3 days ahead of time and toss them with the dressing just before serving. You can also lightly steam the cauliflower florets before baking, which will soften and roast them faster.

- To make the chutney dressing, in a blender, combine the mango pulp, mint and coriander leaves, and the green chili, if using it; then add the roasted cumin, garam masala, and water and blend to a smooth paste. Add an extra teaspoonful or more of water if needed.
- Transfer the roasted vegetables to a serving bowl and pour on the herb dressing from the blender. Toss gently to coat the vegetables with the dressing and serve.

- SERVES 4 TO 6

Alu ki Sabzi

Potatoes cooked with tomatoes, thickened yogurt, and spices

It was love at first sight for Princess Savitri and Satyavan, but her father opposed their marriage, for the sages foresaw that Satyavan would die within the year. But Savitri could not be persuaded to change her mind, so her father reluctantly consented. Their year of wedded bliss passed quickly, and soon Satyavan's foretold day of death approached. For three days Savitri fasted to purify herself, but at the appointed time Satyavan fell into a deep slumber. Immediately, Yama, the god of death, appeared to carry Satyavan's soul to the underworld. But Savitri would not part from her husband. Moved by her love and devotion,

1 cup plain yogurt,
   not low-fat
4 medium potatoes
¾ teaspoon ground coriander
   seeds
½ teaspoon ground cumin seeds
½ teaspoon turmeric
¼ to ½ teaspoon cayenne pepper
2 tablespoons vegetable oil
½-inch piece of ginger, grated
½ teaspoon cumin seeds

Tiny pinch of crushed asafetida
(optional)

Salt to taste

½ teaspoon garam masala

2 cups water

½ cup chopped fresh coriander leaves

Yama granted her three wishes, on the condition that she not ask for the life of her husband. Savitri's first two wishes were for the welfare of her father and father-in-law, and they were quickly granted. Her third wish was for herself—that she would have a hundred sons. Unthinkingly, Yama granted this boon too, only to realize that he had been outwitted, for without her husband, Savitri could not have children. Together, the pair lived long and had a hundred sons, though I am not entirely sure this is a happy ending: With two sons of my own, I consider a hundred too much of a good thing!

In memory of Savitri's devotion, married Indian women fast once a year. The fast is traditionally broken by a meal of Alu ki Sabzi with puris (deep-fried bread). The yogurt is not usually thickened, but I like to do so, because it is less likely to curdle while frying. If you wish to add the yogurt without thickening it, fry it for a few minutes longer so that all its moisture evaporates, stirring it continuously to prevent curdling.

- Line a fine mesh sieve with a coffee filter or 2 layers of cheese cloth and place it over a bowl. Add the yogurt and let it drain for 4 hours on the countertop or overnight in the refrigerator.
- Boil the potatoes until tender, then cool, peel, and dice into 1-inch cubes. In a small bowl, mix the ground coriander and cumin seeds, turmeric, and cayenne pepper. Keep the bowl handy near the stove.
- Warm the oil in a nonstick skillet over medium heat. Add the grated ginger and fry it for 30 seconds, then stir in the cumin seeds and asafetida if desired. As soon as the cumin begins to crackle, pour in the spice mixture from the small bowl. Give it a quick stir, then add the thickened yogurt. Stir constantly for 5 minutes, until all the moisture has evaporated and specks of oil appear around the edges. Add salt and ¼ teaspoon of the garam masala, then the water and diced potatoes. Cover the skillet and increase the heat to high.

Bring the contents to a boil, then reduce heat to medium-low and cook for 20 minutes, stirring occasionally. Turn off the heat and fold in the remaining garam masala and chopped fresh coriander. You can make this dish up to 3 days ahead of time.

- SERVES 3 TO 4 WITH OTHER DISHES

Saag Khumb

Spinach and mushrooms cooked with sautéed onions, tomatoes, and yogurt

 Specific rituals governed mealtimes in an Indian family. Beforehand, the children washed their parents' feet as a gesture of respect. The man of the house ate first, served by his wife. He ate alone while sitting on the ground, always facing either east or north. A banana leaf was laid before him and the different foods placed on it, each in its assigned spot. He would sprinkle a few drops of water on the leaf to purify it and set aside a portion of food for crows, which were believed to carry messages to the spirit world. He used only his right hand for eating, never touching the food with his left hand. His wife ate when he was finished, following the same rituals and served by her children, who ate last.

Mealtimes at my house deviate considerably from this ancient ritual, but one thing that has not changed over time is the popularity of this dish in my family. I used to enjoy Saag Khumb as a child when my father (who loved to cook anything with mushrooms) brought it to the table with a huge dollop of butter in the center and a swirl of cream around it. My children, just like my brothers and I before them, always contrive to scoop out all the cream and mushrooms onto their plates.

If you aren't fond of mushrooms, you can substitute diced,

½ pound fresh spinach, washed, with woody stems trimmed

¼ cup water

1 cup finely chopped onions

2 garlic cloves, chopped

½-inch piece of ginger, chopped

1 hot green chili (optional)

2 tablespoons vegetable oil

½ teaspoon cumin seeds

30 small, whole white mushrooms, washed and dried with paper towels

1 cup diced tomatoes, canned or fresh

Salt to taste

½ teaspoon turmeric

¼ to ½ teaspoon cayenne pepper

½ teaspoon ground coriander seeds

½ teaspoon ground cumin seeds

½ teaspoon garam masala

1 cup water

1 tablespoon chilled butter

1 tablespoon heavy cream

peeled potatoes or lightly stir-fried cubed cottage cheese (paneer)—the dish will taste just as good. Serve it with Gobhi Matar ki Sabzi (grated cauliflower and peas stir-fried with onions and spices, page 23) and Indian bread.

- In a large microwave-safe bowl, combine the spinach with the water. Cover tightly with plastic wrap and microwave on high for 6 minutes. (You can also cook the spinach in a saucepan.) Uncover the bowl and let the spinach cool.
- In a food processor, finely mince the onions, garlic, ginger, and chili. Warm oil in a nonstick skillet over medium-high heat. Add the cumin seeds, and, after a few seconds, the minced onion mixture. Sauté the onions for about 8 minutes, until they are lightly browned. Add the mushrooms and sauté for 3 minutes.
- While the onions are sautéing, puree the tomatoes in the food processor. Add them to the mushrooms in the skillet and cook for 5 to 8 minutes, stirring gently now and then, until all their moisture has evaporated and the oil shows up around the edges of the sautéed mixture. Add the salt and all the spices and cook for 1 minute.
- While the tomatoes are cooking, lift the spinach out of its accumulated liquid, reserving the liquid. In the food processor, puree the spinach and ¼ cup of its cooking liquid until smooth. Add this spinach puree to the tomatoes in the skillet, along with 1 cup of water. Cover and bring the contents of the skillet to a boil over high heat. Immediately reduce the heat to medium-low and cook for 30 minutes, stirring occasionally. Turn off the heat, add the butter to the skillet, then let the spinach cool for a few minutes before mixing in the cream. You can make this dish up to 3 days ahead of time.
- SERVES 3 TO 4 WITH OTHER DISHES

Matar Paneer Khumb Masala

Cottage cheese, peas, and mushrooms cooked in a sautéed onion, tomato, and yogurt sauce

"Spices such as cloves and cardamom should be wrapped in betel leaves with betel nuts and chewed after meals to increase saliva and aid digestion." This prescription from the *Charak Samhita*, a text by ancient India's greatest medical authority, Charak, is still followed by many Indians. Spices were valued not just for their flavor, but also for their medicinal properties. Charak recommended ginger to cure gout, sweet basil to bring down fever, pepper boiled in oil for ear ailments, and turmeric paste for a clear complexion. Arabs and Persians adopted Indian medical theories, and in turn passed them on to Europeans. Physicians in the West reserved the use of spices, which were very expensive, for the wealthy, while prescribing cheaper herbs to the poor. Copho, a doctor in twelfth-century Salerno, explained with disarming frankness: "For empty words we give herbs from the hills in exchange, but for precious money we give spices."

Indian cooking is still strongly influenced by ancient beliefs. For example, ginger and asafetida are always added to lentil and dried bean preparations to help with digestion. This recipe from Uttar Pradesh uses such an array of spices that it's bound to be good for you—and it tastes wonderful!

Matar paneer is not traditionally made with mushrooms; I like to add them because their flavor blends well with the cottage cheese. You can also try the dish without mushrooms. Team it with Chatniwale Alu Gobhi (oven-roasted potatoes and cauliflower tossed with an herb and mango dressing, page 12) and any kind of Indian bread.

3 tablespoons vegetable oil

8 ounces paneer (cottage cheese), diced into ½-inch cubes

½ teaspoon cumin seeds

2 garlic cloves, grated

½-inch piece of ginger, grated

1 cup finely chopped onions

1 cup diced tomatoes, canned or fresh

2 tablespoons plain yogurt, not low-fat

Salt to taste

½ teaspoon turmeric

¼ to ½ teaspoon cayenne pepper

1 teaspoon ground coriander seeds

½ teaspoon ground cumin seeds

½ teaspoon kasoori methi (dried fenugreek leaves) (optional)

½ teaspoon garam masala

10 medium white mushrooms, washed, dried, and halved

¾ cup frozen peas

2 cups water

2 tablespoons chopped fresh coriander leaves

1 tablespoon heavy cream (optional)

1 tablespoon lemon juice

- Warm the oil in a nonstick skillet set over medium-high heat. Add the cottage cheese cubes and fry until lightly browned all over, about 5 minutes; avoid stirring too much, as they will break up. Remove, drain on paper towels, and set aside. In the same oil, add the cumin seeds. After a second, add the grated garlic and ginger. Sauté for about 30 seconds, then add the onions. Sauté, stirring for about 5 minutes, until the onions are lightly browned. Reduce heat to medium and add the tomatoes. Cook for about 8 minutes, mashing them with the back of your spoon to blend them into the sauce. When all the moisture has evaporated and the oil appears around the edges of the sautéed mixture, add the yogurt. Stir constantly for 5 minutes, until the oil appears again. Stir in all the salt and all the spices and cook for 1 minute.

- Add the mushrooms to the skillet and stir-fry for 2 minutes. Add the frozen peas, water, and cottage cheese. Mix gently and cover. Bring to a boil over high heat, then reduce to medium-low and cook for 30 minutes, stirring occasionally. Cool for 5 minutes, then mix in the fresh coriander leaves, cream if desired, and lemon juice. This dish can be made up to 3 days in advance.

- SERVES 3 TO 4 WITH OTHER DISHES

Paneer Khumb aur Mirch ki Sabzi

Cottage cheese, mushrooms, and sweet peppers stir-fried
with spices and tomatoes

3 tablespoons vegetable oil
½ teaspoon cumin seeds
1 medium onion, peeled and cut
  into 1-inch cubes
8 ounces paneer
  (cottage cheese),
  diced into 1-inch cubes

 As a cookbook writer, I feel a certain kinship with M. Gavius Apicius, who lived in first-century A.D. Rome, and was the author of the world's first cookbook. Apicius believed, as I do, that a cook should spare no expense in creating the perfect sauce. His recipe for fish called for pepper and cardamom from India; mace, nutmeg, and cloves from Indonesia; cinnamon from Sri Lanka; coriander and cassia from China; sugar from Persia; asafetida from Parthia, and onions from Wales. The cost of these ingredients must have been staggering; we are told that Apicius spent a hundred million sesterces on food alone. Left with only ten million sesterces (enough to buy three quarters of a ton of gold!), he decided this amount was inadequate to maintain him in the style to which he was accustomed and killed himself.

In spite of the sad tale of Apicius, I continue to use spices with a free hand in my cooking. Fortunately for us, the spices in this dish are available in grocery stores at a very reasonable price.

This dish is quickly stir-fried and is best made just before serving so that the vegetables retain their crispness. You can obtain a pretty mix of colors by adding purple or yellow sweet peppers along with the red and green ones. Serve it with Masala Baby Corn Curry (baby corn cooked in a spicy sauce of sautéed onions and tomatoes, page 24).

1 each small sweet green and red pepper, stems and seeds removed, cut into 1-inch cubes
10 medium white mushrooms, washed and quartered
2 medium tomatoes, cut into thick chunks
Salt to taste
½ teaspoon garam masala
½ teaspoon ground roasted cumin seeds
¼ teaspoon ground black pepper
¼ to ½ teaspoon cayenne pepper
Lemon juice to taste
Chopped fresh coriander leaves

- Warm the oil in a nonstick skillet over medium-high heat and add the cumin seeds. After a second, add the onions. Sauté them for about 5 minutes, then add the cottage cheese. Stir-fry for 2 to 3 minutes, then add the peppers. Stir-fry them for 5 minutes, then add the mushrooms. Cook until the mushrooms start releasing their liquid, 3 to 4 minutes. Add the tomatoes, salt, garam masala, ground roasted cumin seeds, ground black pepper, and cayenne pepper. Stir-fry for a minute, then switch off the heat, but let the pan sit on the stove. Mix in the lemon juice gently. Cover and let the pan sit on the hot stove for a few minutes for the flavors to mingle. Serve garnished with chopped fresh coriander leaves.

● SERVES 4 TO 6

Khumb Chole Kasoori

Chickpeas and mushrooms cooked in a sauce of onions, tomatoes, and dried fenugreek leaves

1 cup finely chopped onions

2 garlic cloves, chopped

½-inch piece of ginger, chopped

1 hot green chili (optional)

1 cup diced tomatoes, canned or fresh

2 tablespoons vegetable oil

½ teaspoon cumin seeds

½ pound small whole white mushrooms, washed well

Salt to taste

½ teaspoon turmeric

¼ to ½ teaspoon cayenne pepper

1 teaspoon ground coriander seeds

½ teaspoon ground cumin seeds

½ teaspoon garam masala

1 tablespoon kasoori methi (dried fenugreek leaves)

3 cups cooked chickpeas

2 cups water

1 tablespoon lemon juice

2 tablespoons chopped fresh coriander leaves

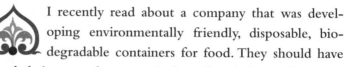 I recently read about a company that was developing environmentally friendly, disposable, biodegradable containers for food. They should have saved their research money. Indians found the perfect solution thousands of years ago: dried leaves stitched together to form cups and plates. Even today food is served on leaf plates when people don't want to bother with washing up. As far back as the tenth century, an Arab visitor noted that Indians ate on

> tables made of interlaced leaves of the coconut palm; with these same leaves they make kinds of plates and dishes. At mealtime the food is served on these interlaced leaves and, when the meal is finished, the tables and leaf plates are thrown into the water with whatever may remain of the food. They disdain to have the same thing served up the next day.

In this dish from Uttar Pradesh, the chickpeas and mushrooms are cooked with tomatoes and infused with the aroma of dried fenugreek leaves. It should be cooked until the sauce is sufficiently thickened to be placed in a dried leaf bowl without leaking. You can also cook the chickpeas without the mushrooms or substitute diced cottage cheese (paneer) for them. I like to serve this dish with plain cooked rice and Gobhi Matar ki Sabzi (grated cauliflower and peas stir-fried with onions and spices, page 23).

- In a food processor, finely mince the onions, garlic, ginger, and chili. Transfer to a small bowl and puree the tomatoes in the food processor.

- Warm the oil in a nonstick skillet over medium-high heat. Add the cumin seeds. After a few seconds, add the minced onion mixture. Sauté for 5 to 8 minutes, until the onions are lightly browned. Reduce the heat to medium and add the pureed tomatoes. Cook for 5 to 8 minutes, until the moisture has evaporated and the oil appears around the edges. Add the mushrooms and sauté for 3 to 4 minutes, just until they begin to release their liquid. Add the salt and all the spices and cook for 1 minute. Add the chickpeas. If you are using canned chickpeas, drain and wash them before adding. If they're home-cooked, reserve their cooking liquid. Mix in the chickpeas, then add the water or cooking liquid, which should measure to 2 cups (supplement the liquid with water if necessary). Cover and bring to a boil. Reduce heat to medium-low and cook the chickpeas for 30 minutes, stirring occasionally. Mix in the lemon juice and fresh coriander leaves. This dish can be made up to 4 days in advance.

- SERVES 3 TO 4 WITH OTHER DISHES

Saag Matar

Spinach cooked with green peas, onions, tomatoes, and spices

 Jainism is an Indian religion. It originated in the sixth century B.C. with the teachings of Mahavira, a contemporary of Gautama Buddha, the founder of Buddhism, and the two religions have much in common. Jainism carries the doctrine of nonviolence to such an extreme that even killing an insect by accident is considered a sin. Jain monks sweep the ground before them as they walk to remove any creatures in their path and wear a cloth over their nose and mouth to avoid inhaling any insects. Jains are forbidden to farm since it requires killing pests. It is not enough to be a vegetarian: any food that could potentially harbor a living creature is prohibited. This includes root vegetables, tubers,

½ pound fresh spinach, washed, with woody stems trimmed

¾ cup water

3 tablespoons vegetable oil

½ teaspoon cumin seeds

1 cup finely chopped onion

2 cloves of garlic, finely chopped

1 cup diced plum tomatoes, canned or fresh

Salt to taste

½ teaspoon ground coriander seeds

½ teaspoon ground cumin seeds

½ teaspoon turmeric

¼ to ½ teaspoon cayenne pepper

½ teaspoon garam masala

1 cup frozen green peas

rancid or fermented food, and pickles. Tomatoes are taboo because they are blood-colored. All liquids have to be strained before drinking. Given the stringent rules, it is not surprising that the religion never became widely popular, but several million Jains still faithfully follow its strictures.

Leafy green vegetables, lentils, and rice are the mainstay of Jain cuisine. Jains would consider the spinach and peas in this dish acceptable but would probably cook it without the onions, tomatoes, and garlic.

My sister-in-law, Mamta, gave me this recipe; it is unusual to cook spinach and peas together, but what a good combination they are! I usually serve it with chapatis or naan and Masala Baby Corn Curry (baby corn cooked in a spicy sauce of sautéed onions and tomatoes, page 24).

- In a microwave-safe container, combine the spinach leaves and ¼ cup water. Cover tightly with plastic wrap and microwave on high for 6 minutes. (You can also cook the spinach in a saucepan.) Lift the spinach from its cooking liquid, then mash it well with a fork on a chopping board. Transfer to a bowl and set aside.

- Warm the oil in a nonstick skillet over medium-high heat. Add the cumin seeds. As soon as they sputter, add the chopped onions and garlic. Sauté, stirring occasionally, for about 5 minutes, until the onions are lightly browned. Reduce heat to medium and add the tomatoes. Cook for another 5 minutes, until the tomatoes are softened and blended into the sauce. Add the salt and all the spices and cook for 1 minute. Mix in the mashed spinach. Finally add the peas and the remaining water, cover, and bring to a boil. Immediately reduce heat to medium-low, cover the skillet, and cook for 20 minutes, stirring occasionally.

- If the sauce is still watery, remove the lid, raise the heat, and boil off some of the excess liquid. You can make this dish up to 3 days ahead of time.

- SERVES 3 TO 4 WITH OTHER DISHES

Gobhi Matar ki Sabzi

Grated cauliflower and peas stir-fried with onions and spices

"If people eat animals in this world, the animals will eat them in the other world," says a Sanskrit verse. According to the Hindu belief in reincarnation, when a living creature dies, its soul is reborn in another body, either at a higher or lower level of existence depending on how it lived its life. By this token, the chicken on your plate could well be a former acquaintance whose behavior was a little regrettable. I have used cauliflower in this dish, which I think we can eat quite safely.

Most cauliflower preparations call for small florets to be cooked with peas. In this unusual recipe, grated cauliflower is stir-fried with peas and spices until it is quite dry. Grating the cauliflower not only reduces cooking time but also helps brown it thoroughly during sautéing, enhancing the flavor of the dish. Serve it with Moong ki Dal Palakwali (yellow mung beans cooked with fresh spinach, page 25) and rice.

1 small cauliflower
3 tablespoons vegetable oil
½ teaspoon cumin seeds
1½ cups finely chopped onions
2 garlic cloves,
  finely chopped
Salt to taste
1 teaspoon ground coriander seeds
½ teaspoon ground cumin seeds
½ teaspoon garam masala
¼ to ½ teaspoon cayenne pepper
½ teaspoon turmeric
1 cup frozen peas
1 tablespoon lemon juice

- Cut the cauliflower into florets and grate them coarsely in a food processor or with a hand grater. Set aside.
- Warm the oil in a nonstick skillet over medium-high heat and add the cumin seeds. After a few seconds, add the chopped onions and garlic. Sauté for about 8 minutes, until they are lightly browned. Stir in the grated cauliflower, salt, and all the spices, then add the peas. Reduce heat to medium-low, cover, and cook until the cauliflower is tender, about 20 minutes. Stir occasionally. Turn up the heat, uncover, and boil off any accumulated liquid, stirring gently for a few minutes. The cauliflower should be cooked dry when done. Add the lemon juice and serve hot. This dish can be made up to 3 days ahead of time.

  - SERVES 3 TO 4 WITH OTHER DISHES

Masala Baby Corn Curry

Baby corn cooked in a spicy sauce of sautéed onions and tomatoes

1 cup chopped onions

2 garlic cloves, chopped

½-inch piece of ginger, chopped

2 tablespoons vegetable oil

½ teaspoon cumin seeds

½ cup diced tomatoes, canned or fresh

Salt to taste

¼ teaspoon ground black pepper

¼ to ½ teaspoon cayenne pepper

½ teaspoon turmeric

½ teaspoon ground coriander seeds

½ teaspoon ground cumin seeds

½ teaspoon garam masala

½ teaspoon kasoori methi
   (dried fenugreek leaves)

1 cup water

One 12-ounce can whole baby corn,
   drained and rinsed

2 tablespoons heavy cream

2 tablespoons chopped fresh
   coriander leaves

 Vegetarianism is a state of mind. Some Indian vegetarians have no qualms about eating fish, which they call "fruit of the sea." Christians in medieval Europe, forbidden meat but allowed fish on days of fasting, were also extremely creative in defining fish. John Russell, who wrote *Of the Kervying of Fische* in the fifteenth century, thought that a beaver's tail so resembled a fish that it was permissible to eat during Lent. Frogs were in too. Even the barnacle goose was classed as a fish, since it was rumored to hatch from seashells. Leo of Rozmital, a Bohemian visiting England in 1465, was perplexed by dinner at the house of the Duke of Clarence on a fast day:

> Among other dishes they gave us to eat what should have been a fish, but it was roasted and looked like a duck. It has its wings, feathers, neck and feet. It lays eggs and tastes like a wild duck. We had to eat it as fish but in my mouth it turned to meat, although they say it is indeed a fish because it grows at first out of a worm in the sea, and when it is grown, it assumes the form of a duck and lays eggs, but its eggs do not hatch out or produce anything. It seeks its nourishment in the sea and not on land. Therefore it is said to be a fish.

This recipe uses baby corn, which is a vegetable. I think.

Baby corn is a fairly recent addition to Indian vegetable markets and is used in a number of recipes. It is usually available fresh, but husking a lot of baby corn is daunting, so I prefer to use canned corn, which tastes just as good. If you make this dish a day ahead of time, the corn will absorb the flavors of the sauce and will taste wonderful. Any Indian bread or rice would go well with it, with perhaps Paneer Khumb aur Mirch ki Sabzi (cottage cheese, mushrooms, and sweet peppers stir-fried with spices and tomatoes, page 18) on the side.

- In a food processor, mince the onions, garlic, and ginger.
- Warm the oil in a nonstick skillet over medium-high heat. Add the cumin seeds, then after a few seconds, the minced onions. Sauté, stirring for about 8 minutes, until lightly browned. Reduce heat to medium and add the tomatoes. Cook for 5 minutes, mashing them into the sauce with the back of your spoon. Add the salt and all the spices and cook for 1 minute. Add the water and the baby corn and mix well. Cover and bring to a boil. Immediately reduce the heat to medium-low and cook for 30 minutes.
- Taste for seasonings and let the curry cool for 5 to 10 minutes. Mix in the cream and fresh coriander leaves and serve. This curry can be made up to 3 days ahead of time.

- SERVES 3 TO 4 WITH OTHER DISHES

Moong ki Dal Palakwali

Yellow mung beans cooked with fresh spinach

From earth sprang herbs, from herbs food, from food seed, from seed man. Man thus consists of the essence of food. . . . From food are all creatures produced, by food do they grow. . . . The self consists of food, of breath, of mind, of understanding, of bliss.

—*The Upanishads (circa 1000 B.C.)*

The first food a child tasted was once believed to determine his future personality. At the age of six months, he was given his first taste of solid food in a ceremony known as *annaprashan*. The parents carefully chose the ingredients of their child's first

1 cup yellow moong dal
  (yellow mung beans), washed
4¾ cups water
Salt to taste
½ teaspoon turmeric

½ pound fresh spinach, washed,
   with woody stalks trimmed
2 tablespoons ghee (clarified butter)
   or unsalted butter
½ teaspoon cumin seeds
1 cup finely chopped onions
1 garlic clove, finely chopped
½ cup diced tomatoes, fresh or canned
½ teaspoon cayenne pepper
½ teaspoon garam masala
Lemon juice
Chopped fresh coriander leaves

meal: rice mixed with ghee (clarified butter) to ensure future glory; fish to make him gentle; partridge meat to instill saintliness; and goat meat to give him strength. The father first tasted the food himself and then fed the baby with his fingers.

The annaprashan ceremony is still important in Hindu families, but meat is no longer included. Nowadays a baby's first taste of real food is of dal (lentils) mixed with rice and ghee. My younger son, Varun, downed his first spoonful of dal and rice with gusto at the age of five months and has been very fond of it since. This dal is almost a meal by itself and needs only rice to complete it.

- In a large heavy-bottomed saucepan, combine the dal, 4 cups of water, salt, and turmeric. Bring to a boil, reduce the heat to medium-low, and partially cover the pan. Stir occasionally, skimming off the yellow scum that rises to the top. Cover the pan completely after removing the scum and cook for 30 minutes.

- Meanwhile, in a large microwave-safe bowl, combine the spinach and ¼ cup of water. Seal tightly with plastic wrap and microwave on high for 6 minutes. (You can also cook the spinach in a saucepan.) Lift the spinach out of its cooking liquid and mash it well with a fork on a chopping board. Add to the dal when it has cooked for 30 minutes and turn off the heat.

- Warm butter in a nonstick skillet over medium heat. Add the cumin seeds and, after a few seconds, the onions and garlic. Sauté, stirring occasionally, for about 5 minutes. Reduce heat to medium and add the tomatoes. Cook for 5 minutes, blending them into the sauce with the back of your spoon. Add the cayenne and garam masala. Now add the dal and mix well. Add ½ cup water, cover the skillet, and bring the dal to a boil over medium-high heat. Immediately reduce heat to medium-low and cook for 10 minutes. Serve with a dash of lemon juice and a garnish of chopped fresh coriander leaves.

- SERVES 4 TO 6

Palak ka Raita

Spinach served in spiced yogurt with sautéed onions

The village children were always the first to race home with the news that a marriage procession was in sight. The groom, who walked in splendor with his friends and family, was received by the bride's relatives and led to her house, where he was greeted and offered refreshments. Villagers leaned from their balconies to shower petals on the guests. The wedding ceremony was held in a specially constructed pavilion in which a sacred fire burned. The bride and groom sat separated by a curtain until the priest pronounced them husband and wife. Then the curtain was drawn aside, the corners of their garments were knotted, and together they walked around the sacred fire. The husband recited the wonderful words that bound them together: "I am he, you are she, you are she, I am he; I am the sky, you are the earth; I am the song, you are the verse. Come, we shall marry and give children to the world! Loving, agreeable, joyful in heart, may we live for a hundred autumns!"

This description of a wedding in ancient times would be quite familiar to anyone who has attended a modern Hindu marriage ceremony. The merrymaking lasts for several days and occasions lots of feasting. My own wedding was such a whirl of festivities that most of the memories have blurred together, but I do remember that the Palak ka Raita tasted good!

This recipe was given to me by my friend Anita Srinivasan. Its secret lies in the sautéed onions, garlic, and green chili that she folds into the raita, along with lots of fresh coriander leaves. I recommend using fresh spinach. You can also substitute ¼ inch fresh ginger for the dried kind that I have used here. Just grate and sauté it along with the onions.

½ pound trimmed spinach leaves, washed

1 cup water

1 cup plain yogurt, not low-fat

Salt to taste

¼ teaspoon powdered black salt (optional)

¼ teaspoon dried powdered ginger

¼ teaspoon ground roasted cumin seeds

1 tablespoon chopped fresh coriander leaves

1 tablespoon vegetable oil

¼ teaspoon cumin seeds

1 small onion, finely chopped

1 small garlic clove, finely chopped

1 hot green chili, deseeded if desired, finely chopped

- In a microwave-safe bowl, combine the spinach and ¼ cup water, cover with plastic wrap, and cook on high for 6 minutes. (You can also cook the spinach in a saucepan.) Lift the spinach out of the accumulated liquid and mash it well with a fork on a chopping board. Transfer to a bowl.
- Combine the yogurt and ¾ cup water in a serving bowl and beat well with a spoon to break up all the lumps. Add the salt, black salt if using, ginger, roasted cumin seeds, and fresh coriander. Mix well, then stir in the spinach.
- Heat the oil in a small skillet over medium-high heat. Add the cumin seeds, then, after a few seconds, the chopped onion, garlic, and green chili. Sauté for 4 to 5 minutes, until the onions are lightly brown. Cool for a few minutes, then pour into the yogurt mixture, leaving behind as much oil as possible. Take care to scoop out all the cumin seeds clinging to the pan. Mix gently into the raita and let it sit for an hour at room temperature or in the refrigerator overnight or up to 2 days. This raita can be prepared up to 2 days ahead of time.

- SERVES 3 TO 4 WITH OTHER DISHES

Kele ka Raita

Sliced bananas in sweetened cardamom-flavored yogurt

1 cup plain yogurt, not low-fat
½ cup water
3 to 4 tablespoons sugar
Tiny pinch of saffron
    (optional)
2 whole cardamom
2 ripe bananas,
    sliced into thin rounds

 Alexander's soldiers, returning to Greece from India in 327 B.C., spoke of "stones the color of frankincense, sweeter than figs or honey." They had discovered rock sugar—India's greatest gift to sweet-toothed people around the world. The word "sugar" is of Indian origin, derived from the Sanskrit word *sharkara*. The Persians introduced the Western world to sugar brought from India, but it remained a very rare commodity in medieval Europe. By the sixteenth century, the Spanish were growing sugarcane in South America and the Caribbean, and sugar became widely available in Europe. The English were especially fond of sugar, adding copious amounts to tea, coffee, and chocolate; the Venetian ambassador was aghast to see them stirring sugar into their wine!

Indians are equally fond of sugar and find any excuse to use it in their cooking. This is a raita (yogurt relish) from Uttar Pradesh that is fragrant with crushed cardamom seeds and sweetened with sugar and sliced bananas. Though sweet, it is not a dessert and is served along with the meal. Its sweet and sour flavors are wonderfully soothing after a spicy curry. You can also add diced pineapple or other fruit in place of, or along with, the bananas.

- In a serving bowl, beat the yogurt with a spoon for a few seconds to break up all the lumps. Add the water, sugar, and saffron. Mix well. Remove the seeds from the cardamom and crush them in a mortar and pestle or between 2 sheets of wax paper. Add to the yogurt, along with the sliced bananas, and stir gently to mix. Let the raita chill at least 30 minutes for the flavors to mingle.

- SERVES 3 TO 4

Kele wali Saunth

Sweet and sour tamarind mint chutney with sliced bananas

 Aryans celebrated special occasions with a drink known as *madhuparka,* made from honey, sugar, yogurt, herbs, and clarified butter. This drink was used to welcome guests, honor pregnant women, and moisten the lips of a newborn child. The word *madhu* means "honey" in Sanskrit and is related to the English word "mead," suggesting that the use of honey dates back to prehistoric times,

4-ounce piece of seedless
*   tamarind, about*
*   the size of a small*
*   orange*
1 cup water
1 cup sugar
Salt to taste

½ teaspoon roasted ground
   cumin seeds
½ teaspoon powdered black salt
   (optional)
¼ teaspoon cayenne pepper

FOR THE HERB CHUTNEY
1 cup fresh mint leaves,
   washed and drained
¼ cup water
½-inch piece of ginger, chopped
1 hot green chili, stemmed
¼ teaspoon cumin seeds
½ teaspoon roasted ground
   cumin seeds
2 ripe bananas, sliced thinly
   or chopped fine

before the Aryans migrated to India. Though Europeans continued to use honey as their principal sweetening agent well into the sixteenth century, Indians had learned by the fifth century B.C. to make sugar from sugarcane, which replaced honey in their cooking.

The cuisine of Uttar Pradesh uses sweeteners in many preparations. Condiments combine sweet, sour, spicy, and hot flavors in intriguing ways. Tomato or green mango chutneys contain raisins, sugar, and vinegar and are often spiced with cumin, asafetida, fennel seeds, onion seeds, and mustard seeds. A taste of this delightful mix leaves your palate tingling.

Saunth is a condiment made with tamarind extract, sugar, spices, and dried fruits and is generally used as either a dip or a topping. This recipe, given to me by my mother, uses sugar to balance the tartness of the tamarind and adds a blend of minced herbs and chopped bananas. If you wish, you can make this chutney without the minced fresh herbs; it will keep longer in the refrigerator. Add the bananas just before serving.

- In a microwave-safe bowl, combine the tamarind and water and microwave uncovered on high for 2½ minutes. Mash well with a fork and allow to cool for 20 minutes. Set a fine mesh sieve over a bowl and pour the tamarind and its soaking liquid through. Squeeze out all the pulp with your hands, discarding the fibrous residue left behind.
- In a saucepan, cook the tamarind extract and sugar over medium heat for a few minutes, until all the sugar has dissolved and the mixture starts coming to a boil. Mix in the salt, roasted cumin seeds, powdered black salt if using, and cayenne pepper, then cool completely.
- In a blender, blend the fresh mint, water, ginger, chili, cumin seeds, and roasted cumin seeds to as smooth a paste as possible. Mix into the cooled tamarind chutney, then gently stir in the bananas. Serve chilled or at room temperature.

• SERVES 6

Tamatar ka Salat

Tomato rounds with roasted cumin, fresh coriander leaves, and lemon juice

Ayurveda, the ancient Indian system of medicine, has played an important role in the structure of an Indian meal. Ayurvedic theory states that the taste of any food has a direct impact on the human body. Flavors are classified into six categories—sweet, sour, salty, bitter, pungent, and astringent—and in a balanced meal, all six are present. Each flavor has specific connotations in Hindu folklore. Sweetness is associated with happiness, and every joyful occasion is celebrated with platters of sweets. Sourness also has pleasant associations because expectant mothers crave sour foods. Pungency is believed to excite the passions—celibate monks are advised to avoid garlic and onions. Bitter foods are considered inauspicious, and though they're eaten regularly, won't be served in a festive meal.

Ayurveda places importance on the texture of food, insisting that a well-balanced meal include a combination of soft, chewy, and crisp dishes. The crunchiness in a meal is usually provided by a fresh vegetable salad. Indian salads are simple platters of sliced vegetables mixed with salt and lemon juice.

This tomato salad is lightly spiced with ground roasted cumin seeds, which have a very distinctive flavor. It's easy, can be served with any Indian meal, and is especially nice in the summer, when the tomatoes are sun-ripened.

1 large ripe beefsteak tomato, washed and sliced into thin rounds

1 tablespoon lemon juice

Salt to taste

¼ teaspoon ground black pepper

¼ teaspoon ground roasted cumin seeds

1 tablespoon chopped fresh coriander leaves

- Arrange the tomato slices in a single layer on a serving platter and set aside. Mix the lemon juice with all the remaining ingredients except the fresh coriander leaves. Spoon this mixture evenly over the tomato slices. Sprinkle the chopped fresh coriander leaves on top. Cover tightly with plastic wrap and refrigerate for 1 hour.

- SERVES 2 TO 3

Sirkewali Pyaz

Onion rings marinated in vinegar

1 large red onion, peeled and sliced
into rounds
2 tablespoons cider or malt vinegar
Salt to taste
¼ teaspoon ground black pepper
¼ teaspoon garam masala
¼ teaspoon sugar

 The high level of personal hygiene practiced by Indians deeply impressed the Chinese traveler Xuan Zang, who came to India in A.D. 629 and spent sixteen years there.

> They are very particular in their personal cleanliness, and allow no remissness in this particular. All wash themselves before eating; they never use that which has been left over; they do not pass the dishes. . . . After eating they cleanse their teeth with a willow, and wash their hands and mouth. Until these ablutions are finished they do not touch one another.

Medieval European writers of etiquette books could only hope their readers would achieve this level of refinement. Fra Bonvicino da Riva sternly admonished diners in A.D. 1290: "Let thy hands be clean. Thou must not put either thy fingers into thine ears, or thy hands to thy head. The man who is eating must not be cleaning by scraping with his fingers at any foul part."

The onions in this salad are separated, making them easier to pick up with your fingers—so let them be clean!

Grilled kababs go well with this dish. You can either arrange the kababs on top of the onions or toss the two together.

- Separate the onion rounds and arrange on a serving platter. In a small bowl, mix the vinegar with the salt, pepper, garam masala, and sugar. Spoon this mixture evenly over the onions. Cover tightly with plastic wrap and refrigerate for at least an hour.

- SERVES 2 TO 3

Subz Paneer Pulao

Rice stir-fried with cottage cheese and sautéed vegetables

 The great epic poem *Mahabharata* gives thrilling descriptions of battles fought by Aryan kings in northern India more than three thousand years ago. It also describes the feasts enjoyed by warriors from both sides who sat and ate together when the day's fighting was done:

Clean cooks, under the supervision of diligent stewards, served large pieces of meat roasted on spits; meat cooked as curries and sauces made of tamarind and pomegranate; young buffalo calves roasted on spits with ghee dropping on them; the same fried in ghee, seasoned with acids, rock salt and fragrant leaves; large haunches of venison boiled in different ways with spices and mangoes, and sprinkled over with condiments; shoulders and rounds of animals dressed in ghee, sprinkled over with sea salt and powdered black pepper, and garnished with radishes, pomegranates, lemons, fragrant herbs, asafetida and ginger.

The ancient armies were obviously not recruiting any vegetarians! The platters of meat served at these banquets were usually accompanied by rice. The term pulao, referring to a dish of meat or vegetables cooked with rice, can be traced as far back as the second century A.D.

This pulao does not contain any meat but would go well with any meat dish. It would also make a delicious meal with only a simple raita as an accompaniment. For quicker results, you can substitute frozen mixed vegetables. Day-old refrigerated rice works better in this recipe, as it won't get mushy while stir-frying.

3 tablespoons vegetable oil
½ teaspoon cumin seeds
1 whole cardamom
1 whole clove
½-inch cinnamon stick
1 bay leaf
1 cup thinly sliced onions
20 raw cashews (optional)
2 tablespoons golden raisins (optional)
½ sweet green pepper, seeded and diced into ¼-inch bits
½ small zucchini, diced into ¼-inch bits
½ stalk of celery, finely diced
3 spears of asparagus, finely diced
½ cup shredded cabbage
½ medium carrot, grated
½ cup paneer (cottage cheese), diced into ½-inch pieces
Salt to taste
½ teaspoon ground black pepper
½ teaspoon garam masala
4 cups cooked Basmati rice, cooled

- Warm the oil in a nonstick skillet over medium-high heat. Add the cumin seeds, cardamom, clove, cinnamon stick, and bay leaf. After a few seconds, add the sliced onions and sauté, stirring occasionally for about 4 minutes, or until translucent. Reduce heat to medium and add the cashews and raisins, if using, and sauté for 1 minute. Add the green pepper and cook for 3 minutes. Mix in the remaining vegetables individually, sautéing each for 3 minutes before adding the next. Add the cottage cheese and stir for 2 minutes. Add the salt, pepper, and garam masala and cook for 1 minute. Gently stir in the rice and cook for 3 minutes, then turn off the heat, cover, and let the flavors blend together for 5 minutes before serving.

- SERVES 4 WITH OTHER DISHES

Tamatari Kasoori Pulao

Rice stir-fried with spicy tomato puree, scented with dried fenugreek leaves

2 tablespoons vegetable oil
½ teaspoon cumin seeds
1 whole cardamom
1 whole clove
½-inch cinnamon stick
1 bay leaf
1½ cups finely chopped onions
1 garlic clove, finely chopped
1 cup paneer (cottage cheese),
  diced into ½-inch pieces
15 raw cashews
1 cup canned diced tomatoes,
  pureed in food processor

 The life of a wealthy young man-about-town in fourth-century India was one of luxury and indolence. The *Kamasutra,* a guide to good living written during that period, gives us a glimpse of how he spent his time. The young dandy's day started with a stroll down to the riverbank, where he relaxed on a couch while being massaged with scented oils. He then exercised, bathed, and returned home. He concluded his ablutions by perfuming his body, marking his forehead and arms with sacred symbols, outlining his eyes with black kohl, and coloring his lips with red dye. Before leaving home, he ate a breath-freshening pill consisting of saffron, musk, cardamom, cloves, and camphor, ground with mango juice. With a garland of flowers around his neck and a parasol in his hand, he was ready to face the world. The morning was spent gambling with friends, followed by a midday meal. Exhausted by his exertions, he retired for a refreshing nap. In the evenings, he received guests, listened to music, attended cockfights, and drank wine. He ended the day with his beloved, languorously reclining with her on the moonlit terrace, sipping mango and lemon juice, coconut milk, or wine, and nibbling on delicacies.

This fragrant pulao will provide the perfect ending to your day, even if it hasn't been quite as leisurely as this one. It is simple to prepare and a perfect way to use up leftover cooked rice. If you don't have any cottage cheese, you can easily make this pulao without it. Serve it with Palak ka Raita (spinach served in spiced yogurt with sautéed onions, page 27).

Salt to taste
½ teaspoon turmeric
½ teaspoon ground coriander seeds
½ teaspoon ground cumin seeds
½ teaspoon ground black pepper
¼ to ½ teaspoon cayenne pepper
½ teaspoon garam masala
1 tablespoon kasoori methi
　(dried fenugreek leaves)
1 cup cooked green peas, drained
4 cups cooked Basmati rice, cooled

- Warm the oil in a nonstick skillet over medium-high heat. Add the cumin seeds, cardamom, clove, cinnamon stick, and bay leaf. After a few seconds, add the chopped onions and garlic. Sauté, stirring occasionally for about 5 minutes, until the onions are lightly golden. Add the cottage cheese and cashews and sauté for another 3 minutes, until the cottage cheese picks up brown specks. Reduce the heat to medium and add the tomatoes. Cook, stirring gently, for about 5 minutes. Add the salt and all the spices and cook for another 3 to 4 minutes until all the moisture has evaporated from the tomatoes and the oil appears at the sides of the skillet. Then gently stir in the peas and rice and cook for 4 to 5 minutes, stirring occasionally.

- SERVES 4 WITH OTHER DISHES

Bhutte ki Biryani

Rice layered and baked with a spicy corn curry

FOR THE CORN CURRY

3 ears of peaches-and-cream corn,
   shucked and washed

2 tablespoons vegetable oil

½ teaspoon cumin seeds

2 garlic cloves, grated

½-inch piece of ginger, grated

1½ cups finely chopped onion

1 cup diced tomato, canned or fresh

3 tablespoons plain yogurt,
   not low-fat

½ teaspoon turmeric

Salt to taste

½ teaspoon paprika

½ teaspoon ground cumin seeds

½ teaspoon ground coriander seeds

1 tablespoon fennel seeds,
   powdered in spice grinder

1 teaspoon kasoori methi
   (dried fenugreek leaves)

½ teaspoon garam masala

¼ teaspoon ground black pepper

1 cup canned unsweetened
   coconut milk

1 cup water

¼ cup fresh coriander leaves, chopped

FOR THE RICE

2 cups Basmati rice, washed and
   drained

¾ cup water

 Hospitality in India is not just a matter of being polite—it also has religious significance. Guests had to be greeted at the front door in a manner appropriate to their age and social status. The host was expected to touch the feet of a respected elder, such as a teacher or parent; formal acquaintances were to be greeted with the host's palms joined together in front of his chest; friends could be embraced. The guest was seated and offered water and a cup of madhuparka (a drink made with honey, yogurt, and herbs), which he was expected to drink in three mouthfuls. In very early times, the visit of a king or a priest was marked with the ritual sacrifice of a cow; later this became purely symbolic. The host would hand a knife to the guest, who returned it saying: "Do not kill the innocent cow; she is the very goddess of Earth. My sins have been slain. Let her go, let her drink water and graze." Though I have never seen anyone do the bit with the knife, feeding guests remains a very important part of social life in India.

Corn is not often used in Indian cooking. Usually, fresh corn is roasted over a slow charcoal fire and rubbed with salt and spices. In this recipe, I use fresh corn to make a flavorful curry, which is then layered with rice and baked on low heat. I suggest using fresh corn, even though it requires a little more work: The flavor of sun-ripened corn will make this biryani memorable, although you may substitute about 3 cups frozen corn kernels. A simple salad or raita (yogurt relish) would make a good accompaniment.

- Wrap each corncob tightly in plastic wrap and microwave on high for 3 minutes each. You can also put the corn in a saucepan, cover with water, and boil until tender. Cool and remove the kernels with a sharp knife, collecting them in a bowl. Set aside.

- Warm the oil in a nonstick skillet over medium-high heat. Add the cumin seeds and, after a few seconds, the grated garlic and ginger. Sauté for 30 seconds, then add the chopped onions and sauté for about 5 minutes, stirring occasionally. Reduce heat to medium, then add the tomatoes and cook for 5 minutes, blending them in with the back of your spoon. Stir in the yogurt and cook for 3 to 4 minutes, stirring all the while, then add all the spices and salt. Cook for 2 minutes, then mix in the corn kernels, coconut milk, and the water. Cover and bring to a boil, then immediately reduce heat to low and cook for 15 minutes, stirring once in a while. Mix in the fresh coriander, then remove the pan from heat.
- To make the rice, combine in a pan with the water, milk, salt, saffron, and whole spices. Cover and bring to a boil, then immediately reduce heat to very low and cook for 12 minutes. Do not uncover the pan in between.
- For the garnish, warm the oil in a nonstick skillet or frying pan over medium heat. Add the sliced onions, almonds, and cashews. Sauté for about 8 minutes, until the onions are golden. Drain on paper towels.
- To assemble the biryani, preheat the oven to 200°F. In an ovenproof dish, spread a thin layer of rice. Evenly spoon over half the corn curry. Spread the remaining rice over the curry and top with the remaining corn curry. Arrange the fried onions and nuts, as well as the boiled egg if using, over the biryani, cover tightly with foil, and bake for 30 minutes. To serve, fluff gently with a fork or transfer to a platter. (If the rice seems a bit underdone, cover the biryani tightly with plastic wrap and microwave for about 10 minutes.)

- SERVES 4 TO 6

¾ cup milk

½ teaspoon salt

Pinch of saffron (optional)

1 whole cardamom

1 whole clove

¼-inch cinnamon stick

1 bay leaf

FOR THE GARNISH

2 tablespoons vegetable oil

1 medium onion, peeled and thinly
   sliced into half rounds

10 raw almonds

10 raw cashews

1 hard-boiled egg, sliced into 1-inch
   chunks (optional)

Makka aur Khumb ka Pulao

Rice cooked with sautéed onions, portobello mushrooms,
and baby corn

1½ cups Basmati rice, washed

3 cups water

4 medium portobello mushrooms,
  washed and dried

1 medium onion

2 tablespoons vegetable oil

½ teaspoon cumin seeds

1 bay leaf

1 whole cardamom

1 whole clove

½-inch cinnamon stick

One 12-ounce can precut baby corn,
  washed and drained

Salt to taste

¼ teaspoon ground black pepper

 Alexander's empire, which spanned most of the world known to Europeans at that time, fragmented soon after his death in 323 B.C. Seleukos Nikator, one of Alexander's generals, ruled the eastern half. His ambassador to India, Megasthenes, wrote detailed descriptions of the people:

> The Indians all live frugally . . . nevertheless happily enough, being simple in their manners. . . . They never drink wine except at sacrifices. Their beverage is a liquor composed from rice instead of barley, and their food is principally a rice-pottage. . . . These things indicate that they possess good, sober sense; but other things they do which one cannot approve: for instance, that they eat always alone, and that they have no fixed hours when meals are to be taken by all in common, but each one eats when he feels inclined. The contrary custom would be better for their ends of social and civil life.

My sons still prefer to eat when they are so inclined instead of at fixed hours, even though I point out that the contrary custom is better for our social life.

This delicate pulao is definitely not a simple rice pottage, but we've come a long way since Megasthenes' time. I came up with this recipe especially for my son Rohan, who dearly loves rice, mushrooms, and baby corn. Serve it with Khumb Chole Kasoori (chickpeas and mushrooms cooked in a sauce of onions, tomatoes, and dried fenugreek leaves, page 20) and Palak ka Raita (spinach served in spiced yogurt with sautéed onions, page 27) for an impressive meal.

- Combine the rice and water in a large bowl. Cut off the mushrooms' stems and slice thinly, then thinly slice the caps from the top and set aside. Peel the onion and slice it in half. Now slice each half into thin half circles. You should have about 1½ cups of sliced onions when you are done.
- Warm the oil in a large heavy-bottomed saucepan over medium-high heat. Add the cumin seeds, bay leaf, whole cardamom, clove, and cinnamon stick. After a few seconds, when the spices begin to sizzle, add the sliced onions. Sauté, stirring occasionally for about 5 minutes, until the onions are lightly browned. Add the mushrooms and sauté for about 3 minutes, just until they begin to release their juices. Add the corn and sauté for 1 minute. Now add the rice and its soaking water, the salt, and the pepper. Mix gently, cover and bring to a boil, then immediately reduce the heat to low and cook for 25 minutes. Uncover and let the pan sit for another 5 minutes before you fluff the rice gently with a fork and serve.

- SERVES 3 TO 4 WITH OTHER DISHES

Kesari Chawal ki Badami Kheer

A rice dessert with milk, sugar, saffron, and almonds

The epic poem *Ramayana* tells the story of Rama, noble prince of Ayodhya, who was banished from his kingdom for fourteen years owing to the machinations of his wicked stepmother. Even greater misfortune befell him during his exile, when the evil demon king Ravana abducted his wife, Sita. But virtue triumphed when Rama returned victorious to Ayodhya, and the people of Ayodhya illuminated the entire city with clay lamps to welcome back their beloved prince.

1½ cups cooked Basmati rice, unsalted

3 cups whole or 2% milk

One 13-ounce can evaporated milk

¾ cup sugar

2 tablespoons golden raisins

Few strands of saffron (optional)

25 raw almonds

10 whole cardamom

2 tablespoons heavy cream (optional)

The Hindu festival of Diwali celebrates this conquest. People light up their homes, as did the citizens of Ayodhya many centuries ago, don new clothes, and offer sweets to one another. The day ends with prayers and feasting, while the night reverberates with the sound of fireworks. The Diwali dinner always concludes with bowls of kheer—rice cooked with lots of milk, sugar, and nuts.

Traditionally, the rice had to be constantly stirred with milk and sugar until it thickened. Here, I have adapted it to the microwave for convenience and used cooked rice to further shorten cooking time. You can serve it either chilled or slightly warmed.

- In a large microwave-safe bowl, combine the rice and milk and microwave uncovered on high heat for 12 minutes. Remove and stir, scraping down the sides, then microwave uncovered on high for another 12 minutes; remove carefully, stir and scrape again, then cook once more on high heat for 5 minutes. Stir well and add the evaporated milk and sugar. Cook on high for 10 minutes, stir and scrape again, then mix in the raisins and the saffron if using.
- In a mortar and pestle or a food processor, coarsely chop the almonds almost to the consistency of bread crumbs, then mix into the rice pudding. Peel the cardamom, first smashing them with a rolling pin, then removing their seeds. Powder the seeds coarsely in a mortar and pestle. (If you do not have a mortar and pestle, you can put the cardamom seeds between 2 pieces of wax paper and pound them with a rolling pin.) Mix the seeds into the rice pudding. Add the heavy cream if using and chill for at least 2 hours before serving. You can make kheer up to 4 days ahead of time.
- SERVES 3 TO 4

South India:
A Cornucopia of Spices

"Samay eshtu aghidhe?" It was the second time the cabdriver had asked me that question, in an increasingly urgent voice, but I had no idea what it meant. It was also beginning to dawn on me that I was lost. I was in a cab in Bangalore, a city in southern India to which I had recently moved from Delhi, and was heading for lunch at a friend's house. The cabdriver did not speak English or Hindi, and I spoke no Kannada, the local language. I had tried to give him directions using sign language, but after half an hour of driving through increasingly unfamiliar streets, I realized that I had a serious communication problem on my hands. If it had not been for a friendly bystander who acted as a translator, I never would have gotten lunch that day. It was right then that I resolved to learn Kannada. Even though I never became fluent, I can now at least manage to find my way around the city in a cab. Oh, and the cabdriver's question—he just wanted to know what time it was.

When I moved to America, people often asked me whether adapting to a new country was difficult. While I did have some problems, they were nothing compared to the culture shock I had experienced when moving from the north of India to the south. At least in America I spoke the language! Even though Bangalore is geographically much closer to Delhi than New York, culturally it feels just as distant.

Walk through any southern Indian city, and contrasts with the north become immediately obvious: the people have darker complexions and their clothes are different; their language does not resemble any in the north; even the landscape and lush tropical vegetation are quite unlike those of the northern plains. Southern Indian food, spices, and cooking techniques are equally distinct. Coconuts, coconut milk, and tamarind combined with spices and herbs such as mustard seeds, coriander seeds, fenugreek seeds, and curry leaves give the food a flavor quite unlike that of northern Indian food, which uses cumin seeds and the spice mixture known as garam masala. The southern Indian technique of frying mustard seeds, yellow split peas, asafetida, and curry leaves in hot oil adds a distinctive aroma and taste. In the south whole spices are fried, then ground with onions and coconut, while northern cooks powder the spices and then fry them with onions, tomatoes, or yogurt. Southern Indians never adopted Persian and Turkish cooking techniques popular in the north, such as cooking with yogurt or cream, use of saffron, and grilling marinated meats.

The northern and southern halves of India developed separately for much of their history. Hills and vast forests covered the center of the country in ancient times, making travel difficult. The Aryan tribes that migrated into India remained in the north, which was just as well, since the southern peninsula was already inhabited by another race—the Dravidians. The origin of these people is uncertain: perhaps they had moved to India before the Aryans. Historians have speculated that the Dravidians were descendants of the people who built the great cities that flourished in the Indus valley during the second and third millennia B.C., before being suddenly and mysteriously destroyed.

The people of the south form four main groups, each occupying a separate state in modern India: the Tamils of Tamil Nadu; the Malayalis of Kerala; the Telugus of Andhra Pradesh, and the Kannadigas of Karnataka. Each community speaks its own language and follows distinct customs and food habits. The histories of these people entwined over the centuries as they alternately warred, forged alliances, traded, and intermarried. The southern kingdoms were ruled by dynasties that spanned more than a millennium, first mentioned in records from the first century B.C. and surviving as late as the fourteenth century. They were the Cholas and Pandyas who ruled Tamil Nadu, the Cheras

Meenakshi Temple, Madurai, Tamil Nadu

of Kerala, and the Chalukyas of Andhra. Rival kings constantly vied for supremacy, but none ever succeeded in completely vanquishing the others.

Though the Aryan kingdoms of the north were never able to conquer Dravidian lands, Aryan religion and culture were carried southward by traders and priests. These influences became evident after the fourth century with widespread adoption of Hinduism by commoners and use of the Sanskrit language by priests and royalty. The mingling of Dravidian and Aryan cultures produced a vibrant, sophisticated civilization, which lives on in the majestic temples of southern India that were hewn out of rock by hand and decorated with intricate sculptures. Trade with distant lands brought prosperity and liveliness to cities in southern India. A Tamil poem from the fifth century A.D. captures the excitement of the marketplace in the Pandya capital of Madurai:

Sacks of pepper and the sixteen kinds of grains such as paddy, millet, gram, peas and sesame seeds are heaped in the grain merchant's street; the brokers move to and fro with steelyards and measures in their hands weighing and measuring the pepper and grams purchased by the people. . . . The hotels and restaurants are now, in the cool of the evening, crowded by visitors who feast upon luscious fruit such as the jack, mango and banana, and on sugar candies, tender greens, edible yams, sweetened rice or savory preparations of meat.

This description of Madurai is still apt—it still bustles with pilgrims visiting its famed temples. Even the restaurant menus are much the same!

Rice was, and still is, the staple grain of the south. If this makes you think of boiled white rice, be prepared for a delicious surprise. The amazing variety of southern Indian rice preparations and their rush of flavors will sweep you off your feet. In a southern home you will eat rice at every meal and for snacks in between, but no two dishes will taste alike. A typical day would start with a breakfast of *idli*s (steamed fermented rice cakes), *dosa*s (paper-thin pancakes made of fermented rice and lentil batter), or *aval* (spicy beaten rice with peas). Lunch might be cooling yogurt rice spiced with mustard seeds and curry leaves or tart and spicy tamarind rice. Dinner may consist of a delicate *biryani* cooked with vegetables or meat and coconut milk followed by a dessert of *payasam* (rice cooked with tender coconut, milk, and sugar). If this isn't enough food, you can snack on *bajji*s (vegetable fritters dipped in a rice flour batter), *chakli* (crispy rice flour and lentil pretzels), or *upama* (spicy cream of rice with vegetables and tomatoes).

Today most inhabitants of southern India are vegetarian. This is one of the results of Aryan influence on the south, because ancient Dravidians had no reservations about eating meat. A poem from the third century A.D. describes the different foods eaten by a minstrel in his travels across the south:

The hunters served him, on the broad leaf of a teak tree, with coarse rice of a red color and the flesh of the iguana. The shepherds gave him sorghum and beans and millet boiled in milk. In the agricultural tracts, the laborers invited him to a meal of white rice and the roasted flesh of the fowl. On the seacoast, the fishermen fed him with rice and fried fish in dishes made of palmyra leaves. The brahmin gave him fine rice with mango pickle and the tender fruit of the pomegranate cooked with butter and fragrant curry leaves. The farmers feasted him with sweetmeats, the fruit of the jack and the banana, and the cooling waters of the coconut.

Southern India produces some of the world's best spices—pepper, cardamom, cloves, cinnamon, mustard seeds, and bay leaves—and you taste all their flavors in the cuisine. The importance of spices extends far beyond their use in cooking, because much of the economy and history of the south has been shaped by its spice industry. From the first century onward, Roman ships were regular visitors to southern ports. Indians called Romans "Yavanas," and Tamil poems depict "Yavanas of fine physique and strange speech whose well-built ships rode the waves of foaming rivers." Roman merchants brought huge pottery jars of wine, a favorite drink of southern Indian kings who drank it "cool, green and fragrant . . . served in golden goblets held by bright-bangled girls."

The ships carried home sugar, pearls, ivory, and muslin, but their most valuable cargo was spice. Romans were the most prodigious consumers of spices the world has ever seen. Legions marched into battle perfumed with cinnamon, cardamom, and sweet marjoram; athletes anointed their bodies with spice-scented oils; royalty slept on pillows filled with saffron. Roman cooks flavored dishes with pepper, cardamom, cinnamon, mace, nutmeg, and cloves and doctors prescribed anise, basil, fennel leaves, coriander, and garlic as aphrodisiacs. Indians demanded gold as payment for their spices, draining so much bullion from Rome that the writer Pliny complained, "No year passes in which India does not impoverish us of fifty million sesterces, and does not furnish us with merchandise, which is sold amongst us for a hundred times that amount."

Control of the spice trade passed into Arab hands as the Roman Empire declined, but Europe's demand for spices did not diminish. When Alaric, king of the Goths, besieged Rome in the fifth century, he demanded and received three thousand pounds of pepper as part of the ransom; Rome had civilized the barbarians only too effectively! By the seventh century, Arab ships carried spices from the Malabar Coast and sold them in Europe for exorbitant prices. Many Arab traders settled permanently in southern India and married local women.

Southern India had close cultural contacts with other Asian kingdoms, including Cambodia, Burma, Malaysia, and Indonesia. These countries adopted Indian religions, architectural styles, and the Tamil script. The largest Hindu temple in the world was built at Angkor Wat in Cambodia. The Chinese were also big consumers of Indian spices. Any person addressing the Chinese emperor was required to perfume his breath with a clove.

New religions came to India aboard ships from the West. It is said that one of the apostles, Saint Thomas, traveled to Malabar in A.D. 52 and converted many whose descendants still form a large Christian community in Kerala. Jewish merchants came to live in India, and there are records of a Chera king granting land to Joseph Rabban in the tenth century to build a settlement. Zoroastrians fleeing the Arab armies that were invading Persia in the eighth century were given sanctuary in the Chalukya kingdom, where they were called "Parsis" after their homeland.

The tolerance of the southern Indian kingdoms, which permitted all these different cultures and religions to coexist, was threatened by upheavals after the fourteenth century. The foreigners that came after this time were intent on conquest, not trade. Turkish and Afghan invaders had been tightening their hold over northern Indian kingdoms since A.D. 1000 and by A.D. 1300 had set their sights on the south. Muslim armies were constantly probing for any weakness in the defenses of southern borders and snapped up some of the out-lying provinces. While the southern kingdoms were resisting this onslaught over land, an even greater danger was approaching from the sea.

European explorers had long been searching for a direct sea route to India in order to bypass the Arab monopoly of the spice trade. The first to succeed was Vasco da Gama, who landed in Calicut in 1498. The Portuguese lost no time in capturing Goa and establishing a stronghold there. Other European traders soon followed, and within the next century, the British, French, Dutch, and Danes had outposts along the Indian coast. The Europeans struggled with one another, and with the local rulers, until by the mid-nineteenth century the British controlled all of India. The south's isolation was ended forever.

As travel between the north and south increased, southern Indian food became increasingly popular in the north. Idlis and dosas have long been favorite snack foods in every part of India and are becoming better known in other countries too. There is, however, a whole world of southern Indian cook-ing, rarely found in restaurants, which you will encounter in this chapter. The recipes here are drawn from the cuisines of the four major southern Indian states: Kerala, Tamil Nadu, Andhra Pradesh, and Karnataka. Although their food is similar, there are some regional variations: the coastal areas of Kerala and Tamil Nadu have developed a wonderful seafood cuisine; Karnataka cooking empha-sizes vegetable and lentil preparations; Andhra Pradesh food is reputed to be the hottest and spiciest in India. Taste these dishes and see for yourself why southern food is so different from that in any other part of India. I miss it so much that I often want to move back to Bangalore. You might be tempted too!

Fruit Punch • Mixed fruit juices

Chana Dal Vadai • Deep-fried dumplings made with yellow split peas and fresh dill

Cabbage Thoran • Shredded cabbage stir-fried with coconut and spices

Vendakai Thengai Mundri Poriyal • Okra cooked with cashews and coconut

Vegetable Kurma • Mixed vegetables cooked with onions, coconut, spices, and nuts

Kozhi Kurma • Chicken cooked with coconut milk and almonds

Vendakai Kozhi • Chicken cooked with onions, spices, and tamarind, folded with spicy okra

Aatu Kari • Lamb curry with coconut milk and tomatoes

Thakkali Scallops • Pan-seared scallops cooked in a sweet and spicy tomato-tamarind sauce

Erra Kari • Shrimp cooked with onions, tomatoes, coconut, and tamarind

Konju Thiyal • Shrimp and zucchini cooked with onions, coconut, and tamarind

Meen Molee • Fish cooked in an onion, tomato, tamarind, and coconut-milk sauce

Chapa Pulusu • Sour fish curry with toasted coconut and spices

Tarkari Thayir Sadam • Yogurt rice with mixed vegetables

Molagu Koli Thakkali Biryani • Pepper chicken layered and baked with tomato rice

Erra Sadam • Spicy fried rice with shrimp and eggs

Fruit Punch

Mixed fruit juices

Thursday, 8th March, 1688. Mrs. Francis, wife of the late Lieutenant Francis killed at Hoogly by the Moors, being sent hither from Bengal very poor, she made it her petition that she might keep a Punch house for her maintenance. But she being a notorious bad woman, it is agreed that she be not permitted to keep a public house, lest it be the occasion of many debaucheries and disorders; she having lived very scandalously formerly here.

—*Entry in the Consultation Book, Fort St. George, Madras*

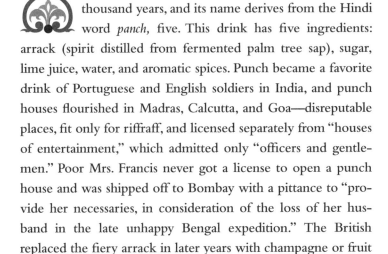 Punch has been drunk in India for at least two thousand years, and its name derives from the Hindi word *panch,* five. This drink has five ingredients: arrack (spirit distilled from fermented palm tree sap), sugar, lime juice, water, and aromatic spices. Punch became a favorite drink of Portuguese and English soldiers in India, and punch houses flourished in Madras, Calcutta, and Goa—disreputable places, fit only for riffraff, and licensed separately from "houses of entertainment," which admitted only "officers and gentlemen." Poor Mrs. Francis never got a license to open a punch house and was shipped off to Bombay with a pittance to "provide her necessaries, in consideration of the loss of her husband in the late unhappy Bengal expedition." The British replaced the fiery arrack in later years with champagne or fruit juices, but the original recipe is still followed in southern India; it uses only fruit juices and ginger ale.

12 ounces frozen pineapple juice concentrate, thawed

12 ounces frozen orange juice concentrate, thawed

12 ounces frozen peach juice concentrate, thawed

½ quart mango juice

1 teaspoon powdered black salt (optional)

1 teaspoon dried ground ginger (optional)

2 quarts ice water, ginger ale, or alcoholic beverage

- Mix all the juices together in a large pitcher. Add black salt and dried ginger if using. Mix well and refrigerate. To serve, fill half a glass with punch concentrate, then top with ice water, ginger ale, or alcohol of your choice.

• SERVES 8 TO 10

Chana Dal Vadai

**Deep-fried dumplings made with yellow split peas
and fresh dill**

*1 cup chana dal (yellow split peas),
    washed*

1 garlic clove

¼-inch piece of ginger

1 hot green chili, stemmed

¼ cup water

½ cup finely chopped onions

*2 to 3 tablespoons finely chopped
    fresh dill*

*10 to 15 fresh curry leaves, finely
    chopped (optional)*

Salt to taste

¼ to ½ teaspoon ground black pepper

Vegetable oil for deep frying

 When kings sat down to eat, their feast inspired the court poet to new heights of imagery. The simple act of eating a *kadubu* (savory steamed cake) was described by a fifteenth-century Kannada poet:

The Kings are relishing the kadubu made of black gram: it looks like a full moon; like a mass of mist set together; as if heavenly nectar had solidified into circles; or as if a drop of moonlight had hardened.

These delectable dumplings scented with fresh dill inspire lyricism too. Vadai are circular, flat lentil dumplings. They are great as appetizers or as a snack, accompanied by some chutney. They can also be served immersed in lightly spiced yogurt, in curries, or in rasam—a spicy lentil and tomato broth. Traditionally these dumplings are deep-fried, but you can also shallow-fry them in a little bit of oil. Make them just before serving so you can eat them still crisp. If you have any leftovers, try cooking them lightly in any sauce from this chapter. You can also substitute fresh coriander for the dill.

- Soak the dal in enough water to cover for at least 2 hours. Drain and set aside. In a food processor, mince the garlic, ginger, and chili. Add the drained dal and mince again, adding ¼ cup of water to achieve a fairly smooth paste. Take care not to add too much water—it will make the dumplings difficult to shape.
- Transfer the mixture to a large mixing bowl. Add the onions, dill, curry leaves, salt, and pepper. Mix well. Warm

oil for deep-frying in a wok or deep fryer set over medium-high heat. With your fingers, make rounded walnut-size balls of the dal mixture and drop them gently into the hot oil, spooning some over the dumplings to seal them. When the underside has browned lightly, gently turn them to cook on the other side. Cook for a few minutes until lightly golden all over. Drain on paper towels and serve hot.

● SERVES 3 TO 4 AS AN APPETIZER

Cabbage Thoran

Shredded cabbage stir-fried with coconut and spices

Ancient legends tell of a time when the great king Mahabali ruled so well and wisely in Kerala that the gods were consumed with jealousy. Vishnu, greatest of all deities, descended from heaven and went to Mahabali's court disguised as a dwarf. Appearing before the king, he begged for a boon: as much land as he could cover in three paces. Amused by how little he wanted, Mahabali granted his wish. Vishnu transformed himself into a being so colossal that in three paces he strode across the entire earth. Mahabali was forced to honor his promise and retreat to the underworld, but before leaving he made one request: that he be allowed to visit his beloved people, the Malayalis, once a year. The day of his return is celebrated joyously in Kerala with the festival of Onam, and is marked by feasts, dances, boat races, and gift giving.

The highlight of the celebrations is the traditional festival meal, the *Onam Sadhya*, which can include over thirty dishes. Cabbage Thoran is a favorite at this feast. The cabbage is usually finely shredded by hand and is mixed with grated fresh coconut and spices before cooking. It is then stir-fried until

4 tablespoons grated or shredded
    fresh coconut

1 hot green chili, stemmed

1 garlic clove

4 cups finely chopped or shredded
    cabbage

Salt to taste

½ teaspoon turmeric

¼ to ½ teaspoon cayenne pepper

¼ to ½ teaspoon ground black pepper

½ teaspoon ground coriander seeds

10 curry leaves, preferably fresh,
    chopped

2 tablespoons vegetable oil

½ teaspoon black mustard seeds

½ teaspoon yellow split peas
    (optional)

10 curry leaves, preferably
    fresh

1 cup finely chopped onions

tender-crisp and served with rice or puris (deep-fried Indian bread).

- In a food processor or blender, mince the grated coconut, chili, and garlic. In a large mixing bowl, combine the cabbage, minced coconut, garlic, and chili, the salt, turmeric, cayenne pepper, ground black pepper, ground coriander seeds, and curry leaves. Mix well.
- Warm the oil in a nonstick skillet over medium-high heat and add the mustard seeds and yellow split peas. After a few seconds, when they sizzle, add the curry leaves and chopped onions. Sauté for about 5 minutes, until lightly browned. Add the cabbage mixture and stir-fry for 7 to 8 minutes. Reduce heat to medium and stir-fry again for 6 to 7 minutes, until the cabbage is just tender but not overcooked. Serve right away.

- SERVES 3 TO 4 WITH OTHER DISHES

Vendakai Thengai Mundri Poriyal

Okra cooked with cashews and coconut

Very small piece of seedless
   tamarind, 1 ounce

¼ cup water

2 tablespoons vegetable oil

½ teaspoon black mustard seeds

15 curry leaves, preferably fresh

2 garlic cloves,
   finely chopped

1 cup thinly sliced onions

20 raw cashews

1¼ pounds fresh okra, washed, ends
   trimmed, cut into ¼-inch pieces

 If the way to a man's heart is through his stomach, then surely the same approach should work with a god. Feeding the gods is an important part of Hindu worship, and at the Tirupati temples, the largest in southern India, the gods are fed up to six times daily. Each day, for over a thousand years, temple cooks have prepared a sumptuous feast for the deities. Tradition dictates that only a very limited range of vegetarian ingredients—such as rice, lentils, and a few vegetables—can be used, but working within these constraints, the cooks have built an amazing repertoire. Inscriptions from the fifteenth century describe five different kinds of rice preparations, eleven varieties of savory cakes, and a range of lentil dishes, milk desserts, and drinks. Many of the temples are famous for a particular dish, and pilgrims travel far to savor these delicacies.

All food served at the temples is paid for by donors who select the dishes and the time they are to be offered. A priest holds up a sample of the food to the mouths of the stone idols in the temple, who are presumed to have accepted the offering. Priests and pilgrims eat the rest of the food. Thousands of people consume these divine leftovers every day, which they consider to be blessed by the gods.

In Tamil a poriyal is any stir-fried vegetable dish without sauce. Okra is a favorite vegetable in the south, and this recipe from Tamil Nadu is a delicious way to prepare it. I sauté whole cashews along with the onions and okra, then add powdered cashews and coconut to the dish. The okra is then enveloped in a tart, spicy, nutty sauce of tamarind, onions, and cashews.

Salt to taste
½ teaspoon turmeric
½ teaspoon cayenne pepper
½ teaspoon ground coriander seeds
1 tablespoon desiccated unsweetened coconut
¼ teaspoon garam masala
2 tablespoons chopped fresh coriander leaves

- In a small microwave-safe bowl, microwave the tamarind and water on high for 1 minute. Mash with a fork and microwave on high again for 30 seconds. Set aside to cool. (You can also soak the tamarind in the water for 2 hours instead of softening it in the microwave.)

- Warm the oil in a nonstick skillet over medium-high heat. Add the mustard seeds and, after a few seconds, the curry leaves and chopped garlic. Sauté for 30 seconds, then add the onions and 10 of the raw cashews. Sauté for 5 minutes, until the onions are lightly browned.

- Reduce the heat to medium-low and mix in the okra, salt, turmeric, cayenne pepper, and ground coriander seeds. Cover and cook for 15 minutes.

- Meanwhile, set a fine mesh sieve over a bowl and pour the tamarind and its soaking liquid into it. Squeeze the pulp through with your fingers, discarding the fibrous residue. You should have about 2 tablespoons of tamarind extract.

- Put the remaining 10 cashews and coconut in the jar of a spice grinder and powder finely. Add this powder and the tamarind extract to the okra. Mix gently, cover, and cook for another 15 minutes, stirring occasionally. If the okra is not completely dry, turn up the heat slightly and cook uncovered for a few minutes longer, stirring gently now and then. Mix in the garam masala and fresh coriander leaves. This dish can be made up to 3 days ahead of time.

- SERVES 3 TO 4 WITH OTHER DISHES

Vegetable Kurma

Mixed vegetables cooked with onions, coconut, spices, and nuts

¼ cup raw cashew bits

1 tablespoon fennel seeds

1 teaspoon white poppy seeds

2 tablespoons unsweetened
    desiccated coconut

Salt to taste

½ teaspoon turmeric

¼ to ½ teaspoon cayenne pepper

½ teaspoon ground coriander seeds

½ teaspoon ground cumin seeds

2 tablespoons vegetable oil

½ teaspoon black mustard seeds

2 whole cardamom

2 whole cloves

½-inch cinnamon stick

1 bay leaf

15 curry leaves, preferably fresh

2 garlic cloves, grated

½-inch piece of ginger, grated

1 hot green chili, sliced (optional)

 The English gardens outside the walls of Madras abounded with fruits and vegetables. John Fryer, a ship's doctor who visited Madras in 1673, reported that there were "Gourds of all sorts for Stews and Pottage, Herbs for Sallad, and some few Flowers as Jassamin, for beauty and delight; . . . Cocoes, *Guiavas,* a kind of Pear; . . . *Mangos* the delight of *India;* a Plum, Pomegranets, *Bonanoes* which are a sort of Plantain." The gardeners seemed to have less luck in growing grass and flowers, if we are to believe William Hickey, a Calcutta businessman who was given a tour of a "boasted garden" when he visited Madras:

After going over what I conceived to be a wild and uncultivated piece of ground, with scarcely a blade of grass or the least sign of vegetation, he suddenly stopped and asked me what I thought of a Madras garden, to which, in perfect simplicity, I answered, "I would tell him my opinion when I had seen one." This answer he replied to with, "When you see one, Sir, why you are now in the middle of mine." The devil I am, thought I.

From what I have seen, flower gardens in Madras have improved considerably since Hickey's time. What has not changed is the profusion of vegetables and vegetable kurma is an example of how local cooks make good use of them.

This popular recipe from Madras allows cooks to use different combinations of vegetables. I have put all my favorite vegetables in this kurma, but you can make it with any of your choice, or even use frozen mixed vegetables. It goes well with Erra Sadam (spicy fried rice with shrimp and eggs, page 75). Before you start cooking, chop all the vegetables and have them nearby.

- In a clean coffee or spice grinder, powder the cashews, fennel seeds, poppy seeds, and coconut, then transfer to a small bowl. Mix in the salt, turmeric, cayenne pepper, ground coriander seeds, and ground cumin seeds. Set aside.
- Warm oil in a nonstick skillet over medium-high heat. Add the black mustard seeds, cardamom, cloves, cinnamon, and bay leaf. After a few seconds, stir in the curry leaves, garlic, ginger, and green chili and sauté for about 30 seconds. Mix in the onions and sauté for about 5 minutes, stirring now and then, until lightly browned.
- Reduce the heat to medium and add the tomatoes. Cook for about 8 minutes, blending them in with the back of your spoon. When all the moisture has evaporated and the oil shows around the sides, add the yogurt. Stir continuously for about 5 minutes, until the oil separates again. Add the reserved spice and nut powder and cook for 1 minute, then mix in the water. Stir in all the vegetables and cover. Bring to a boil, then immediately reduce heat to medium-low and cook for 45 minutes to an hour, until all the vegetables are tender. Check for seasonings, mix in the fresh coriander, and serve. This dish can be made up to 3 days ahead of time.
  - • SERVES 4 TO 6

1½ cups finely chopped onions
1 cup diced tomatoes, canned or fresh
½ cup plain yogurt, not low-fat
1 cup water
1 cup finely diced green beans
1 cup finely diced carrots
1 cup tiny cauliflower florets
½ cup finely diced zucchini
4 raw baby potatoes,
*   peeled and halved*
10 white mushrooms,
*   washed and halved*
1 small sweet green pepper
¼ cup chopped fresh coriander
*   leaves*

Kozhi Kurma

Chicken cooked with coconut milk and almonds

Walnut-size piece of seedless
  tamarind (2 ounces)

1½ cups water

½-inch piece of ginger, chopped

2 garlic cloves, chopped

1 hot green chili, chopped

20 curry leaves, preferably fresh

½ teaspoon ground black pepper

2 tablespoons lemon juice

2 pounds skinned chicken thighs,
  bone-in, washed

2 tablespoons vegetable oil

½ teaspoon black mustard seeds

¼ teaspoon fenugreek seeds

2 whole cloves

2 whole cardamom

½-inch cinnamon stick

1 bay leaf

1 cup thinly sliced onions

30 raw almonds: 10 whole,
  20 powdered fine in a
  spice grinder

Salt to taste

½ teaspoon turmeric

½ teaspoon ground coriander seeds

¼ to ½ teaspoon cayenne pepper

1 cup canned unsweetened
  coconut milk

2 tablespoons chopped fresh
  coriander leaves

 The Roman writer Livy knew exactly when things started going downhill in Rome: 187 B.C., when Rome's army returned from a campaign in Asia with some strange foreign ideas:

> For the beginnings of foreign luxury were introduced into the City by the army from Asia. At that time the cook, to the ancient Romans the most worthless of slaves, both in their judgement of values and in the use they made of him, began to have value, and what had been merely a necessary service came to be regarded as an art.

In spite of Livy's disapproval, Romans wholeheartedly embraced good cooking and a taste for spices. Their cooks must have been grateful! Roman ships sailed all the way to southern India for spices, coconut oil, and ghee (clarified butter) to use in dishes and religious ceremonies. Even Livy might have reconsidered his disdain for Asian luxuries had his cook served him Kozhi Kurma.

A kurma (pronounced korma in the north) is a meat or vegetable dish braised in a rich creamy sauce, versions of which are found all over India. In northern India, kormas are cooked in a sauce of sautéed onions, nuts, and cream. Southern Indian recipes substitute coconut milk for cream to provide richness. Kurmas are very sumptuous and wonderful to serve at dinner parties accompanied with a rice pulao and perhaps Vendakai Thengai Mundri Poriyal (okra cooked with cashews and coconut, page 52).

- In a small microwave-safe bowl, microwave the tamarind and ½ cup of the water uncovered for 2 minutes on high.

Mash well with a fork and cool for 10 minutes. (If you prefer you can soak the tamarind in the water for 2 hours instead.) Set a fine mesh sieve over a bowl and pour the tamarind and its liquid through, squeezing out all the pulp and discarding the fibrous residue. Set aside this extract.

- In a food processor, mince the ginger, garlic, green chili, and 10 curry leaves. Scrape down the sides and add the ground black pepper and lemon juice. Process again till well blended. Transfer to a large mixing bowl and toss in the chicken. Mix well with the marinade and set aside for 15 minutes at room temperature or 2 to 3 hours in the refrigerator.

- Warm the oil in a nonstick skillet over medium-high heat. Add the mustard seeds, fenugreek seeds, cloves, cardamom, cinnamon, and bay leaf. After about 30 seconds, add 10 curry leaves and, after another 30 seconds, the sliced onions. Sauté for about 5 minutes, until lightly browned. Add the whole almonds and sauté for 1 minute.

- Lift the chicken pieces out of their marinade, reserving the marinade, and sauté uncovered for 5 minutes, to seal the juices; turn occasionally. Add the salt, turmeric, ground coriander seeds, and cayenne pepper, then stir in the reserved marinade, coconut milk, tamarind extract, and the remaining water. Mix well, cover and bring to a boil. Immediately reduce heat to medium-low and cook for about 30 minutes or until the chicken is tender. Mix in the powdered almonds and fresh coriander leaves and serve. This dish can be made up to 3 days ahead of time.

- SERVES 4 WITH OTHER DISHES

Vendakai Kozhi

**Chicken cooked with onions, spices, and tamarind,
folded with spicy okra**

Hail and Prosperity! The following gift was graciously made by him who has assumed the title of King of Kings! . . . To Joseph Rabban Prince of Anjuvannam and to his descendants, . . . so long as the world and moon exist. Anjuvannam shall be his hereditary possession. Hail!

—*Proclamation of King Ravi Varman, tenth century A.D.*

FOR THE CHICKEN

*Walnut-size piece of seedless
  tamarind (2 ounces)*

½ cup water

2 tablespoons vegetable oil

¼ teaspoon black mustard seeds

¼ teaspoon fenugreek seeds

10 to 15 curry leaves, preferably fresh

2 garlic cloves, grated

½-inch piece of ginger, grated

1¼ cups finely chopped onions

Salt to taste

½ teaspoon turmeric

½ teaspoon ground black pepper

¼ to ½ teaspoon cayenne pepper

1 teaspoon ground coriander seeds

*8 boneless, skinless chicken thighs,
  washed*

FOR THE OKRA

2 tablespoons vegetable oil

¼ teaspoon black mustard seeds

10 to 15 curry leaves, preferably fresh

The Jewish settlement at Anjuvannam in Kerala, established on land granted by King Ravi Varman, grew into an independent principality, which the Jews called Shingly, that survived for more than five centuries. The Jews prospered as pepper traders in Kerala, but the tiny domain given to them "so long as the world and moon exist" did not survive. An attack by Arabs in the fifteenth century almost destroyed their city. Even more hostile were the Portuguese, who had recently arrived in India and persecuted the Jews mercilessly. The survivors fled to the Hindu kingdom of Cochin, where they were welcomed by the king and given land next to his own palace. Their descendants still live in the Jewish community that was rebuilt in Cochin in 1567.

Later Jewish immigrants to India came mostly from Iraq and Syria; Indian Jewish cuisine and customs are an interesting mix of Jewish, Kerala, and Arab traditions. The festival of Purim coincides with the Hindu celebration of Holi, and Jewish children adopted the Hindu custom of dousing each other with colored water. A Rosh Hashanah meal includes Arab rice pulaos and an impressive variety of chicken and vegetable curries from Kerala. Okra, commonly eaten by both Indians and Arabs, is a favorite vegetable.

This recipe from Kerala combines chicken and okra in a

spicy tamarind sauce. The chicken is cooked until the sauce is very thick, then the cooked okra is gently folded in and simmered for a few minutes to blend the flavors. It is best eaten with an Indian bread. If you celebrate Rosh Hashanah, try serving this dish next time. If your guests wonder about it, tell them it is an old Jewish tradition.

1¼ cups finely chopped onions
1 garlic clove, finely chopped
1 pound small fresh okra, washed,
  ends trimmed, and halved
Salt to taste
½ teaspoon turmeric
½ teaspoon ground coriander seeds
½ teaspoon ground black pepper

- In a small microwave-safe bowl, microwave the tamarind and water for 2 minutes on high. Mash with a fork and set aside to cool for 10 minutes. (If you prefer, you can soak the tamarind in the water for 2 hours.) Set a fine mesh sieve over a bowl and pour the tamarind and its soaking liquid through, squeezing out all the pulp with your hands and discarding the fibrous residue. Set this extract aside.

- Warm the oil in a nonstick skillet over medium-high heat. Add the mustard seeds, fenugreek seeds, and curry leaves. After a few seconds, add the grated garlic and ginger. Sauté for 30 seconds, then add the onions. Sauté, stirring occasionally for 5 minutes, until the onions are lightly browned. Stir in the salt, turmeric, ground black pepper, cayenne, and ground coriander seeds, then add the chicken, coating the pieces well with onions and spices. Pour the reserved tamarind extract over the chicken, stir to mix, and cover. Cook over medium-low heat for about 30 minutes or until the chicken is tender, stirring once in a while.

- While the chicken is cooking, warm the oil in a nonstick skillet over medium-high heat and add the mustard seeds and curry leaves. After a few seconds, add the chopped onions and garlic and sauté for about 5 minutes, until lightly browned. Stir in the okra, salt, turmeric, ground coriander seeds, and ground black pepper, cover, and cook on medium-low heat for about 20 minutes or until the okra is soft. Stir very gently once in a while.

- When the chicken is done, divide it into smaller pieces. This can be done right in the skillet with your stirring spoon and a fork. The sauce should be very thick and clinging to the chicken at this point; if it is not, uncover, increase heat, and boil off excess liquid. Gently fold the cooked okra into the chicken and cook uncovered at medium heat for 5 minutes. Stir very gently once or twice. This dish can be made up to 3 days in advance.

• SERVES 4

Aatu Kari

Lamb curry with coconut milk and tomatoes

1 teaspoon fennel seeds
½ teaspoon black mustard seeds
½ teaspoon fenugreek seeds
1½ cups chopped onions
3 garlic cloves, chopped
1-inch piece of ginger, chopped
1 cup diced tomatoes, canned or fresh
1 hot green chili, stemmed
15 curry leaves, preferably fresh
1 cup fresh coriander leaves and
  tender stems, washed well
1 cup canned unsweetened
  coconut milk
Salt to taste
½ teaspoon turmeric
¼ to ½ teaspoon cayenne pepper
1 teaspoon ground coriander seeds
½ teaspoon ground cumin seeds
½ teaspoon garam masala
2 pounds bone-in lamb, cubed by
  the butcher, washed and drained
1 tablespoon vegetable oil
1 tablespoon lemon juice

 Arab traders who lived in every southern Indian port city accumulated great wealth from the spices they shipped to Europe and sold at exorbitant prices. They were careful not to reveal where spices were grown and fabricated fantastic stories about their origin. Spices were expensive, they explained to their European customers, because they grew in Paradise. A thirteenth-century English account described exactly how spices were obtained:

> And it is said that these things came from the earthly paradise, just as the wind blows down the dry wood in the forests of our own land; and the dry wood of the trees in paradise that thus falls into the river is sold to us by the merchants.

Even at the time there were skeptics. Bartholomeus Anglicus noted cynically: "These men do feign, to make things dear and of great price." It was not until the Portuguese landed in India, and saw for themselves where spices were grown, that they realized the truth.

Arabs who settled in South India and married local women never lost their fondness for lamb, the mainstay of all Middle Eastern cuisines. Their wives prepared the lamb with coconut milk and spices in the cooking style they knew best, with delightful results. You can serve this dish from Tamil Nadu with plain rice and Vegetable Kurma (mixed vegetables cooked with onions, coconut, spices, and nuts, page 54).

- In a clean spice or coffee grinder, powder the fennel, mustard, and fenugreek seeds. In a food processor or blender, mince the onions, garlic, ginger, tomatoes, green chili, curry leaves, and fresh coriander. Add coconut milk, salt, turmeric, cayenne, ground coriander, ground cumin, and garam masala, as well as the powdered fennel, mustard, and fenugreek seeds, and mince again, scraping down the sides if necessary. Transfer to a large mixing bowl and add the lamb. Toss well to coat with the marinade, cover, and refrigerate overnight if possible, or for at least 4 hours.
- Warm the oil in a nonstick skillet over medium-high heat. Add the lamb and all its marinade. Stir well to mix, cover, and bring to a boil. Reduce heat to medium-low and cook for 1½ hours, until the lamb is tender. The sauce should be very thick after cooking; you will have to stir occasionally to prevent sticking. (You can also pressure-cook the lamb and its marinade for 20 minutes, then boil off the excess liquid over medium heat, with the lid off.) Mix in the lemon juice and serve. This dish can be made up to 3 days ahead of time.

- SERVES 4 WITH OTHER DISHES

Thakkali Scallops

Pan-seared scallops cooked in a sweet and spicy tomato-tamarind sauce

 The ancient Greeks, Romans, and Egyptians were frequent visitors to the southern coast of India, with eleven ports of call listed in Ptolemy's *Geography*. Ships sailed from the Malabar Coast of Kerala to the Arab port of Aden, carrying cargoes of spices, pearls, sandalwood, camphor, and salt. Indian cotton and silk fabrics were

½ pound large scallops
  (10 to 12), washed

FOR THE MARINADE
Salt to taste
¼ teaspoon ground black pepper

1 tablespoon lemon juice

2 tablespoons vegetable oil

FOR THE SAUCE

Walnut-size piece of seedless
*   tamarind (2 ounces)*

1 cup water

1 garlic clove, chopped

¼-inch piece of ginger, chopped

1 hot green chili, stemmed

15 curry leaves, preferably fresh

1 cup diced tomatoes, canned or fresh

2 tablespoons vegetable oil

½ teaspoon black mustard seeds

Salt to taste

¼ teaspoon turmeric

¼ teaspoon ground black pepper

1 tablespoon desiccated
*   unsweetened coconut*

2 teaspoons sugar

prized in the West and some marketing whiz in first-century India gave them wonderfully evocative names such as "Webs of Woven Wind" and "Vapors from Milk." But the most eagerly sought-after product from Kerala was pepper, known locally as "the passion of the Greeks."

Pepper vines grow in wild abandon all over Kerala, twining themselves around trees. Some green berries plucked by hand from these vines are used fresh to make pickles and sauces. Others are spread out in the sun to dry, giving us the familiar black peppercorns. To obtain white pepper, berries are plucked once they are ripe, then hulled.

In this recipe from Kerala, I have used pepper in both the marinade for the scallops and the sauce. The tart and sweet tomato coconut sauce enhances the delicate sweetness of the scallops. Plain cooked rice is all that is needed to enjoy this dish.

- In a mixing bowl, combine the scallops, salt, pepper, and lemon juice. Toss to mix, cover, and let sit for 15 minutes. Lift them out of their marinade and place on paper towels.
- Warm the oil in a small nonstick frying pan over medium-high heat. Cook the scallops in two batches, about 2 minutes per side, and remove to drain on paper towels.
- In a small microwave-safe bowl, microwave the tamarind and ½ cup water on high for 2 minutes. Mash well with a fork and set aside to cool for 10 minutes. (If you prefer, you can soak the tamarind in the water for 2 hours instead.) Set a fine mesh sieve over a bowl and pour the tamarind and its liquid through, squeezing out all the pulp and discarding the fibrous residue. Set this extract aside.
- In a food processor, mince the garlic, ginger, chili, and curry leaves, then transfer to a bowl. In the same food processor jar, pulse the diced tomatoes till they are pureed. Transfer to a bowl.
- Warm the oil in a nonstick skillet over medium heat and add the mustard seeds. As soon as they splutter, add the minced garlic mixture and sauté for 1 minute, then stir in the pureed

tomatoes. Cook for about 5 minutes, until some moisture has evaporated. Mix in the salt, turmeric, ground black pepper, coconut, and sugar and sauté for 1 minute, then add the reserved tamarind extract. Cook for 1 minute, add the remaining water and cover, then bring to a boil. Immediately reduce the heat to medium-low and cook covered for 5 minutes, then add the scallops. Cook for 2 minutes and serve.

- SERVES 2 WITH OTHER DISHES

Erra Kari

Shrimp cooked with onions, tomatoes, coconut, and tamarind

 Mr. Francis Day explained that his reason for establishing the new English settlement at Madras in 1639 was that the East India Company could buy at that place "excellent long Cloath and better cheape by 20 per cent than anywhere else." Local gossips insinuated that Mr. Day selected the site for its proximity to the Portuguese town of St. Thomas, because he "had a Mistris at St. *Thomas* he was so enamoured of, that made him build there, that their Interviews might be the more frequent and uninterrupted." If others suspected Mr. Day's motives, he had only himself to blame; it was reported that:

'Tis no strange thing for Mr. Day to be drunke. Drinkeinge with Moores and Persians at Ballisara hee soe disguised himself in theire presence that they sent him away in a Pallankeene out of which he fell by the way. . . . And another tyme hee made himselfe soe drunke he Rann into the Sea.

In spite of its dubious origins, Madras flourished and became the most important city in southern India. Eliza Fay, who visited Madras in 1780, said, "There is something uncommonly

Walnut-size piece of seedless
    tamarind (2 ounces)
1 cup water
2 tablespoons vegetable oil
¼ teaspoon fenugreek seeds
¼ teaspoon black mustard seeds
15 curry leaves, preferably fresh
2 garlic cloves, grated
½-inch piece of ginger, grated
1 cup finely chopped onions
1 cup diced tomatoes,
    canned or fresh
Salt to taste
½ teaspoon turmeric
¼ teaspoon cayenne pepper
¼ teaspoon ground black pepper
½ teaspoon ground coriander seeds
¼ teaspoon garam masala
1 tablespoon grated coconut,
    fresh or desiccated
    unsweetened

1 pound raw jumbo shrimp, peeled
and deveined

2 tablespoons chopped fresh
coriander leaves

striking and grand in this town, and its whole appearance charms you from novelty, as well as beauty."

The magnificent cuisine of Madras has been shaped by its geographical location. Rice, coconuts, and tamarind grow in profusion inland, and the tranquil waters of the Indian Ocean are home to a rich variety of fish and shellfish. While the majority of Tamilians are vegetarians, people living in coastal communities such as Madras eat a lot of seafood.

This exquisite shrimp curry from Madras is cooked in a delicious coconut and tamarind sauce, and serves nicely with plain cooked rice and a crunchy salad.

- In a small microwave-safe bowl, microwave the tamarind and ½ cup of the water uncovered on high for 2 minutes. Mash well with a fork and set aside to cool for 10 minutes. (If you prefer, you can soak the tamarind in the water for 2 hours instead.) Set a fine mesh sieve over a bowl and pour the tamarind and its liquid through, squeezing out all the pulp and discarding the fibrous residue. Set this extract aside.

- Warm the oil in a nonstick skillet over medium-high heat. Add the fenugreek and mustard seeds. After a few seconds, add the curry leaves, grated garlic, and grated ginger. Sauté for 30 seconds, then add the onions. Sauté, stirring occasionally for about 5 minutes, until lightly browned. Reduce heat to medium and blend in the tomatoes, mashing with the back of your spoon; cook for 5 minutes. Add the salt, all the spices, and coconut and cook for 1 minute, then stir in the tamarind extract and cook for another minute. Add the remaining water, then, after the mixture starts bubbling, the shrimp. Coat well with sauce, then cover and cook on medium-low heat for 10 minutes or until the shrimp are cooked through and pink. Mix in the chopped fresh coriander and serve.

- SERVES 3 TO 4 WITH OTHER DISHES

Konju Thiyal

Shrimp and zucchini cooked with onions, coconut, and tamarind

> Every jilt of the town
> Gets a callicoe gown;
> Our own manufactures are out of fashion.

 Fabrics were, after spices, the most important Indian export passing through the port of Calicut in Kerala, from which calico cloth got its name. "From the greatest gallants to the meanest Cook Maids nothing was thought so fit to adorn their persons as the Fabric from India," complained an English politician. Britain made it illegal in 1700 to import or wear Indian cloth, but this law only provided new opportunities for smugglers, who were already doing brisk business by evading customs duties on coffee, tea, and spices. Much of the contraband from India, including coconuts, spices, and fabrics, originated in Kerala, which, with its long coastline, was a major trade center.

While Kerala farmers produce a bounty of spices and coconuts, coastal villages have a long tradition of fishing. Cooks from this region combine all these ingredients to create a wonderfully spicy seafood cuisine. A few examples: pulicha meen, a whole fish stuffed with spices, wrapped in banana leaves and baked in charcoal; meen avial, fish chunks cooked in a thick coconut-tamarind sauce; meen pada, fish pickled in a mixture of vinegar, tamarind, ginger, garlic, and spices.

Shellfish such as crabs, shrimp, lobsters, clams, and mussels are also abundant in Kerala waters. In this recipe, I have cooked shrimp with zucchini and saved you the trouble of making a vegetable side dish. As far as I know, none of the ingredients are banned in England now. Serve the dish on a calico tablecloth if you want to be really authentic!

FOR THE PASTE

Walnut-size piece of
  seedless tamarind
  (2 ounces)
½ cup water plus 2 tablespoons
1 tablespoon vegetable oil
10 curry leaves, preferably fresh
1 cup finely chopped onions
1 garlic clove, chopped
¼-inch piece of ginger, chopped
1 hot green chili, stemmed
2 tablespoons grated coconut,
  fresh or desiccated
  unsweetened

FOR THE STIR-FRY

2 tablespoons vegetable oil
¼ teaspoon black mustard seeds
¼ teaspoon fenugreek seeds
10 curry leaves, preferably fresh
1¼ cups finely chopped onions
½ teaspoon turmeric
½ teaspoon ground coriander seeds
¼ teaspoon ground cumin seeds
¼ teaspoon ground black pepper
¼ teaspoon cayenne pepper

Salt to taste

*1 medium zucchini, washed and diced
  into ¼-inch pieces*

*½ pound jumbo raw shrimp, peeled
  and deveined*

- In a small microwave-safe bowl, microwave the tamarind and ½ cup of the water on high for 2 minutes. Mash well with a fork and set aside to cool for 10 minutes. (If you prefer, you can soak the tamarind in the water for 2 hours instead.) Put a fine mesh sieve over a bowl and pour the tamarind and its soaking liquid through, squeezing out all the pulp and discarding the fibrous residue. Set aside this extract.

- Warm the oil in a nonstick skillet over medium-high heat. Add the curry leaves and, after a few seconds, the chopped onions, garlic, ginger, chili, and coconut. Sauté, stirring, for about 5 minutes, until lightly browned. Cool slightly and transfer to a blender along with the reserved tamarind extract. Add 2 tablespoons of water and blend to a smooth paste. Scrape out all the paste and transfer to a bowl.

- In the same skillet, warm the oil over medium-high heat. Add the mustard and fenugreek seeds. As soon as they begin to crackle (this will only take a few seconds), add the curry leaves and onions and sauté for 5 minutes, until lightly browned. Add all the spices and salt and stir for a few seconds.

- Reduce heat to medium and stir in the diced zucchini. Cover and cook for 2 minutes. Add the shrimp and cook uncovered for 1 minute, then mix in the coconut tamarind paste. Cover, reduce the heat to medium-low, and cook for 10 minutes, stirring occasionally. The sauce should be very thick, clinging to the shrimp and zucchini, when done; if not, turn up the heat slightly, uncover, and boil off the excess liquid.

  - SERVES 3 TO 4 WITH OTHER DISHES

Meen Molee

Fish cooked in an onion, tomato, tamarind, and coconut-milk sauce

 Meen Molee is a fish stew cooked in all coastal areas of southern India. *Meen* is fish in Tamil, but the source of the word *molee* is obscure. It is a word coined by the British, perhaps derived from "Malay," which gives us a hint as to where the dish came from. Whatever the origin of Meen Molee, it is now cooked in all coastal areas in the south and the recipe has been thoroughly Indianized with spices such as cardamom, cloves, and black pepper.

A lot of fish dishes in the south are cooked in earthenware pots, which infuse the food with its special aroma. Fish curries are never stirred while cooking. The pot is merely tilted around in a gentle swirling motion to prevent the sauce from sticking to the bottom of the pan and the fish from breaking up.

When I cook Meen Molee for dinner, I often team it up with plain cooked rice and Cabbage Thoran (shredded cabbage stir-fried with coconut and spices, page 51) for a very satisfying meal.

- Wash the fillets, dry with paper towels, and lay them skin side down in a single layer in a large flat dish. Mix together all the ingredients for the marinade in a small bowl and pour evenly over the fillets. Cover and refrigerate for 15 minutes.
- Preheat the broiler, with the oven rack on the second rung from the top. Line a large flat ovenproof dish with foil and place a grill or roasting rack over it. Lift the fillets out of their marinade and place them skin side down in a single layer on the grill rack. Grill the fish under the broiler for 5 minutes, just enough to loosen their skin. Cool slightly and

1¼ pounds thick-cut, firm fish fillet such as rainbow trout or salmon

FOR THE MARINADE
2 tablespoons white vinegar
Salt to taste
¼ teaspoon turmeric
¼ teaspoon ground black pepper

FOR THE SAUCE
Walnut-size piece of seedless tamarind (2 ounces)
1½ cups water
2 tablespoons vegetable oil
½ teaspoon black mustard seeds
¼ teaspoon fenugreek seeds
1 bay leaf
1 whole cardamom
1 whole clove
½-inch cinnamon stick
10 to 15 curry leaves, preferably fresh
1 garlic clove, grated
¼-inch piece of ginger, grated
1 cup finely chopped onions
½ cup diced tomatoes, canned or fresh
Salt to taste
½ teaspoon turmeric
½ teaspoon ground black pepper

½ teaspoon ground coriander seeds

1 cup canned unsweetened coconut
   milk

1 hot green chili, sliced thin

2 tablespoons chopped fresh coriander
   leaves

remove the skin, dividing the meat into 2-inch chunks as you do so. Set aside in a bowl.

- To make the sauce, microwave the tamarind and ½ cup water in a small microwave-safe bowl for 2 minutes on high. Mash well with a fork and set aside to cool for 10 minutes. (If you prefer, you can soak the tamarind in the water for 2 hours instead.) Place a fine mesh sieve over a bowl and pour the tamarind and all its soaking liquid through, squeezing out the pulp and discarding the fibrous residue. Set this extract aside.

- Warm the oil in a nonstick skillet over medium-high heat. Add the mustard seeds, fenugreek seeds, bay leaf, cardamom, clove, and cinnamon. After a few seconds, add the curry leaves, grated garlic, and ginger. After 30 seconds, mix in the chopped onions and sauté, stirring occasionally for about 5 minutes, until the onions are lightly browned. Reduce the heat to medium and add the tomatoes. Cook for 5 to 8 minutes, mashing with the back of your spoon to blend. When the moisture has evaporated and the oil appears at the sides, add the salt and all the spices and cook for 1 minute, then add the tamarind extract. Cook for another minute, then add the coconut milk, 1 cup water, and green chili. Mix well, cover, and bring to a boil. Reduce the heat to medium-low, uncover, and gently slide in the fish. Stir to mix and cook covered for 20 minutes, occasionally stirring gently. Mix in the fresh coriander leaves and serve. You can make the sauce up to 3 days ahead and cook the fish in it just before serving.

- SERVES 3 TO 4 WITH OTHER DISHES

Chapa Pulusu

Sour fish curry with toasted coconut and spices

 Hindu custom forbids people to share a drinking cup. To make sure they don't sip from a vessel that someone else has used, Indians pour water into their mouths from a cup held above, without letting it touch their lips. Pietro della Valle, an Italian traveling across southern India in 1623, was delighted by this practice:

> . . . the vessel touches not the lips or mouth of him who drinks; for it is held up on high with the hand over the mouth, and he that lifts it up highest, and holds it furthest from his mouth, shows himself most mannerly . . . they are so dextrous at it, that I remember to have seen one of them take with both hands a vessel as big as a basin and lifting it up above a span higher than his mouth, poure a great torrent of water into his throat and drink it all off. . . . I purposely set myself to learn this manner of drinking, which I call *drinking in the Air,* and at length have learned it. . . . I do it very well; sometimes in conversation we drink healths, *all'Indiana,* after this fashion . . . and he that cannot do it right either wets himself well, or falls a coughing . . . which gives occasion of laughter.

As children, walking home from school in the summer heat, my friends and I would frequently stop for a drink of water at houses we passed on the way. Most of the homes near the school kept an earthen vessel filled with cold water out on the porch, which we were welcome to use. We would dip a cup into this and pour the water into our mouths. The entire school could drink from one cup without anyone ever touching it to their lips!

While some Westerners find Indian food hot and need lots of water to drink with it, even Indians blanch at the mention of

Walnut-size piece of seedless tamarind (2 ounces)
½ cup water
1½ pounds thick-cut, firm fish fillet, such as rainbow trout

FOR THE MARINADE
Salt to taste
½ teaspoon turmeric
½ teaspoon ground black pepper
2 tablespoons lemon juice

FOR THE SAUCE
2 tablespoons desiccated unsweetened coconut
1 teaspoon white poppy seeds
1 teaspoon fennel seeds
¼ teaspoon fenugreek seeds
½ teaspoon cumin seeds
½ teaspoon black mustard seeds
1 whole clove
1 whole cardamom
½-inch cinnamon stick
1 bay leaf, crushed
¼ teaspoon whole black pepper
2 tablespoons vegetable oil
¼ teaspoon black mustard seeds
10 to 15 curry leaves, preferably fresh
2 garlic cloves, grated
½-inch piece of ginger, grated
1¼ cups finely chopped onions

½ cup diced tomatoes, fresh or canned

Salt to taste

¼ teaspoon cayenne pepper

½ teaspoon ground coriander seeds

¼ teaspoon turmeric

1½ cups water

½ cup chopped fresh coriander leaves
    and tender stems

Andhra Pradesh cuisine, which is reputed to be the fieriest in all the country. Fortunately, this dish from Andhra Pradesh, with its heady aroma of toasted spices and coconut, uses tomatoes and tamarind to temper the heat. However, it is still quite spicy, so keep a jug of water on the table—you can even try drinking all'Indiana! Serve Chapa Pulusu with plain cooked rice and Cabbage Thoran (shredded cabbage stir-fried with coconut and spices, page 51) for a complete South Indian meal.

- In a small microwave-safe bowl, microwave the tamarind and water on high for 2 minutes. (If you prefer, you can soak the tamarind in the water for 2 hours instead.) Mash with a fork and set aside to cool for 10 minutes. Set a fine-mesh sieve over a bowl and pour the tamarind and its soaking liquid through, squeezing out all the pulp with your hands and discarding the fibrous residue. Set this extract aside.
- Wash the fish fillets and pat them dry with paper towels. Place them skin side down in a single layer in a large flat dish. Mix together all the ingredients for the marinade and pour over. Cover and refrigerate for at least 15 minutes.
- In a small nonstick frying pan over medium heat, combine the coconut, poppy seeds, fennel seeds, fenugreek seeds, cumin seeds, mustard seeds, clove, cardamom, cinnamon stick, bay leaf, and whole black pepper. Toast for 3 to 4 minutes, stirring occasionally, until the seeds darken and smell roasted. Cool slightly, then transfer to a clean coffee or spice grinder and powder finely. Transfer to a small bowl.
- Preheat broiler, with the oven rack on the second rung from the top. Line a large ovenproof dish with foil and place a grill or roasting rack on it. Lift the fillets out of their marinade and place them skin side down on the rack in a single layer. Broil the fish for 5 minutes, cool slightly, and remove the skin, dividing the meat into 2-inch chunks as you do so. Set aside.
- Warm the oil in a nonstick skillet over medium-high heat. Add the mustard seeds and curry leaves. After a few seconds, add the grated garlic and ginger. Sauté for 30 seconds, then

stir in the onions and continue sautéing, stirring occasionally, for about 5 minutes or until lightly browned. Reduce heat to medium and add the diced tomatoes, blending them in with the back of your spoon. Cook for 5 to 8 minutes until the moisture has evaporated and the oil appears around the edges. Stir in the salt, cayenne, ground coriander seeds, and turmeric, then the toasted spice and coconut powder, and sauté for 1 minute. Add the tamarind extract and water, cover, and bring to a boil. Immediately reduce heat to medium-low and gently slide in the chunks of fish. Cook for 20 minutes, stirring occasionally. Gently mix in the chopped fresh coriander and serve. This curry can be prepared up to 3 days in advance.

• SERVES 3 TO 4 WITH OTHER DISHES

Rider drinking water, Awadh, eighteenth century

Tarkari Thayir Sadam

Yogurt rice with mixed vegetables

2 tablespoons vegetable oil
½ teaspoon black mustard seeds
1 garlic clove, grated
¼-inch piece of ginger, grated
15 curry leaves, preferably fresh
1 hot green chili, sliced thin
1 cup finely chopped onions
½ cup finely diced carrots
½ cup finely diced zucchini
½ cup finely diced sweet green
   and/or red peppers
½ cup shredded cabbage
Salt to taste
3 cups cooked and cooled Basmati rice
1 cup plain yogurt, not low-fat
¼ cup milk
2 tablespoons chopped fresh
   coriander leaves

 "I have not told half of what I saw," said Marco Polo as he lay on his deathbed in 1324, when people asked him to confess that his fantastic stories of the Eastern lands he had visited were lies. Few Europeans at that time believed the Italian traveler's descriptions of the wonders he had witnessed in China and India. But his detailed report of the journey leaves little doubt that he indeed saw these places firsthand. He described the Malabar Coast of Kerala:

> All their things are different from ours—more beautiful, and better. They have no product that is similar to any of ours, nor any beast nor bird. And this is due to the great heat they have. They have no kind of grain except rice alone. They make a wine, or rather drink, from dates, which is very good, and makes you drunk more readily than grape-wine. They have all the necessaries of life in abundance and cheap, except that they have no grain, apart from rice.

Rice is still eaten at every meal. No matter what other dishes are on the menu, a typical meal concludes with simple yogurt rice.

At its most basic, making yogurt rice is just a matter of mixing plain yogurt and salt with cooked rice. For something more elaborate, the rice is fried lightly with curry leaves and sliced green chilies, then tempered with mustard seeds, yellow split peas, and asafetida. I have put sautéed vegetables in the rice, which add a new dimension to its taste. Serve as a snack or light lunch.

- Warm the oil in a nonstick skillet over medium-high heat. Add the mustard seeds, then as soon as they sputter, the grated garlic and ginger, curry leaves, and green chili. Sauté for 30 seconds, then stir in the onions and sauté for 2 minutes. Individually add the carrots, zucchini, sweet peppers, and cabbage, stirring for 2 minutes between each. Mix in the salt, then the rice, and sauté for 2 minutes. Turn off the heat but keep the pan on the stove and gently add the yogurt. Cool to room temperature, then stir in the milk and chopped fresh coriander leaves and serve at room temperature.

• SERVES 3 TO 4 AS A SIDE DISH

Molagu Koli Thakkali Biryani

Pepper chicken layered and baked with tomato rice

Born in America, in Europe bred.
In Africa traveled, in Asia wed;
Where long he lived and thrived, in London dead,
Much good, some ill he did, so hope all's even
And that his soul thro' mercy's gone to heaven.
—*Epitaph on the tomb of Elihu Yale, Wrexham, England*

Born in Boston, Elihu Yale joined the East India Company and traveled to India in 1672, eventually rising to the rank of governor of Fort St. George in Madras. Governor Yale's administrative methods were, to put it mildly, somewhat forceful. When his groom missed work for three days, Mr. Yale ordered him to be arrested and executed. On being informed that being absent without leave was not a capital offense, he immediately amended the charge to piracy and hanged the luckless groom. After serving five years as governor, Elihu Yale was removed from office for neglecting his duties and speculating with company funds. By then he had amassed a huge fortune and returned to England in 1699, carrying five tons of spices, precious stones, and leather goods. His departure

FOR THE CHICKEN

2 tablespoons vegetable oil

¼ teaspoon fenugreek seeds

¼ teaspoon black mustard seeds

10 to 15 curry leaves, preferably fresh

1 hot green chili, sliced thin

2 garlic cloves, grated

½-inch piece of ginger, grated

1 cup finely chopped onions

Salt to taste

½ teaspoon turmeric

½ teaspoon ground coriander seeds

½ teaspoon ground black pepper

6 boneless, skinless chicken thighs,
 washed and drained
1 tablespoon lemon juice
2 tablespoons chopped fresh
 coriander leaves

FOR THE RICE
2 tablespoons vegetable oil
¼ teaspoon black mustard seeds
10 curry leaves, preferably fresh
10 raw cashews (optional)
1 cup thinly sliced onions
2 tablespoons desiccated
 unsweetened coconut
Salt to taste
½ teaspoon turmeric
½ teaspoon ground coriander seeds
¼ to ½ teaspoon cayenne pepper
2 cups canned diced tomatoes, pureed
 in blender or food processor
3 cups cooked Basmati rice, cooled

must have been a great relief to his domestic staff! A Connecticut college contacted him in 1718, requesting financial support. He donated a parcel of goods that sold for £562, enough money to persuade the college to change its name to Yale.

In spite of Mr. Yale's shortcomings as governor, the population of Madras kept burgeoning; farms on the outskirts of the city provided food for its people. Rice was the most important crop grown because it was, and still is, the heart of a Tamil meal.

Tomato rice is a popular dish in Madras. Here I have added pepper chicken to create a complete meal, which needs just a raita (yogurt relish) as an accompaniment.

If you prefer, you can serve the pepper chicken as a curry and skip layering it with the tomato rice. You can also serve the tomato rice without the chicken for a vegetarian dish. This biryani is dedicated to the memory of that old reprobate Elihu Yale, benefactor of American higher education.

- Warm the oil in a nonstick skillet over medium-high heat. Add the fenugreek and mustard seeds. After a few seconds, add the curry leaves, green chili, garlic, and ginger and sauté for about 30 seconds, then add the onions. Sauté for 5 minutes, stirring occasionally. Add the salt, turmeric, ground coriander seeds, and black pepper. Mix in the chicken, coating the pieces with the spicy sautéed onions. Cover, reduce heat to medium-low, and cook for about 25 minutes or until the chicken is tender and the sauce quite thick. Divide each chicken thigh into 3 pieces. You can do this right in the skillet with your stirring spoon and a fork. Mix in the lemon juice and fresh coriander and set aside. You can make this chicken curry up to 3 days in advance.
- To make the rice, warm the oil in a nonstick skillet over medium-high heat. Add the mustard seeds, curry leaves, and cashews. After 30 seconds, add the onions and sauté for about 5 minutes, until lightly browned. Reduce heat to medium and mix in the coconut, salt, turmeric, ground

coriander seeds, and cayenne pepper; sauté for 1 minute, then add the tomatoes. Cook for about 10 minutes, until the moisture has evaporated and the sauce has thickened. Turn off the heat and gently stir in the rice, mixing well.

- To assemble the biryani, preheat the oven to 250°F. Take a large flat ovenproof dish and spread half the rice in it. Ladle half the chicken over the rice and top it with the remaining rice. Spread all the remaining chicken evenly over the rice, cover the dish tightly with foil, and bake for 30 minutes.

- SERVES 3 TO 4 WITH OTHER DISHES

Erra Sadam

Spicy fried rice with shrimp and eggs

Hannah in breeks behav'd so well
That none her softer sex could tell:
Nor was her policy confounded
When near the mark of nature wounded
Which proves, what men will scarce admit
That women are for secrets fit

—*Gentleman's Magazine, July 1750*

 Hannah Snell's husband had abandoned her and run away to sea. Believing him to have sailed for India, she disguised herself as a man and enlisted in a detachment of the Royal Marines that embarked for India in 1748. Hannah was posted to the British force besieging the French fort at Pondicherry in southern India, and fought courageously until she was wounded in the groin. Afraid to let a doctor examine her, she removed the shot herself, helped by a female Indian nurse who loyally kept her secret. After recovering, she sailed home to England, only to dis-

2 tablespoons vegetable oil

½ teaspoon black mustard seeds

1 whole clove

1 whole cardamom

½-inch cinnamon stick

1 bay leaf

1¼ cups finely chopped onions

2 garlic cloves, chopped

1 cup diced tomatoes, canned or fresh

¼ to ½ teaspoon cayenne pepper

Salt to taste

½ teaspoon turmeric

½ teaspoon ground black pepper

1 pound raw shrimp, peeled and deveined, washed and drained

1 tablespoon fennel seeds, powdered

2 eggs, beaten

4 cups cooked Basmati rice, cooled

2 tablespoons chopped fresh coriander leaves

cover that her errant husband had been convicted of murder in Genoa and executed. But Hannah's story ends happily, for on returning to England she published her biography and became quite a celebrity. She prospered as the owner of a pub called the Female Warrior and, though vowing "never to engage with any Man living," married twice more, and we hope lived happily ever after.

Pondicherry survived repeated British assaults and remained a French colony until 1954. Three centuries of French rule has had its effect on the cuisine of the Tamil population of Pondicherry. They use milk, yogurt, and eggs in their cooking, unlike most other southern Indians, who make sauces from coconut milk. The French also introduced Pondicherry to broad beans, which are still popularly known as French beans in India.

My friend Chitra Vidyasagar, whose family has lived in Pondicherry for generations, gave me this exceptional recipe. It is very different from any other southern Indian preparation in its unusual combination of shrimp, eggs, and rice, delicately spiced with powdered fennel seeds. I like to eat it by itself with a raita and crisp fried papadums on the side, but you could also serve it with Vegetable Kurma (mixed vegetables cooked with onions, coconut, spices, and nuts, page 54) for a more elaborate meal.

- Warm the oil in a nonstick skillet over medium-high heat. Add the mustard seeds, clove, cardamom, cinnamon, and bay leaf. After a few seconds, add the onions and garlic and sauté, stirring occasionally, for about 5 minutes or until the onions are lightly browned. Reduce heat to medium and add the tomatoes, blending them in with the back of your spoon, and cook for about 8 minutes. When all the moisture has evaporated and the oil appears around the edges, add the cayenne, salt, turmeric, and ¼ teaspoon of the ground black pepper. Cook for 1 minute. Add the shrimp and cook for 5 minutes, stirring occasionally.

- Mix the powdered fennel, ¼ teaspoon black pepper, and a pinch more salt with the beaten eggs and pour over the shrimp. Wait for 30 seconds, then stir to coat the shrimp. Cook for 1 minute, then add the rice and cook for 2 to 3 minutes, until the eggs have cooked and the shrimp are pink. Mix in the fresh coriander leaves and serve.

• SERVES 4

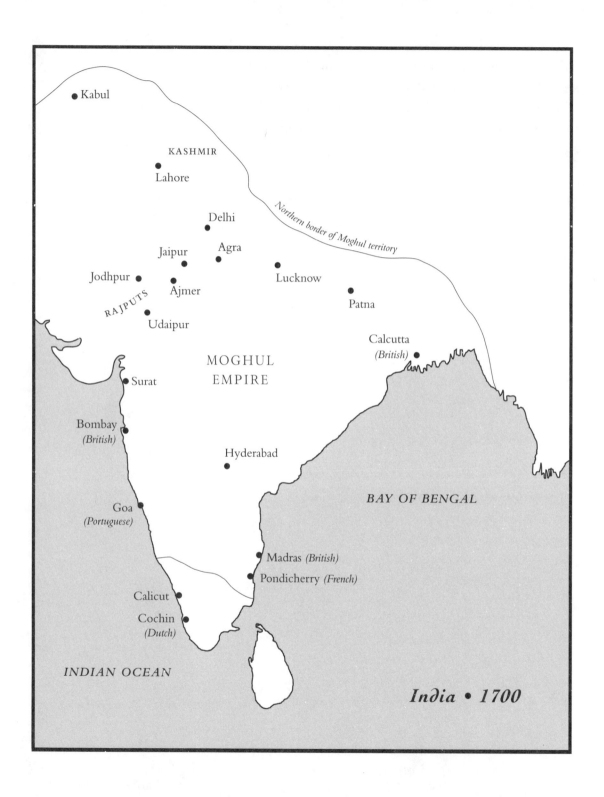

Kabul

KASHMIR

Lahore

Delhi

Jaipur   Agra

Jodhpur

RAJPUTS   Ajmer

Udaipur

MOGHUL
EMPIRE

Surat

Bombay
(British)

Hyderabad

Goa
(Portuguese)

Lucknow

Patna

Calcutta
(British)

BAY OF BENGAL

Madras (British)
Pondicherry (French)

Calicut

Cochin
(Dutch)

INDIAN OCEAN

Northern border of Moghul territory

India • 1700

The Moghuls:
Food Fit for Kings

If there is a paradise on the face of the earth
It is this, it is this, it is this.
—*Inscription in the throne room, Red Fort, Delhi*

The arrogant proclamation on the walls of the majestic Red Fort, where the Moghul emperors once reigned, sounds ironic as you walk through the empty, echoing halls. It is easy to mock the lines now, and they have often been quoted to demonstrate the fleeting nature of power and glory. But the men writing them—the Moghuls whose name has become synonymous with splendor—thought the words a simple statement of fact.

The Moghuls were tribesmen from Central Asia—descendants of the Mongol hordes that swept across Asia and Europe—who came to India and carved out an empire with their swords. They were not the first Muslims to invade India; Afghan and Turkish armies had made repeated incursions since about A.D. 1000. Most of these raiders came only to plunder, but a few stayed to rule the land they seized. By the sixteenth century, several Muslim kingdoms had been established in northern India, but they were weak and divided, constantly feuding with each other and with neighboring Hindu states. It was not until the arrival of the Moghuls that these small kingdoms were welded into a single empire.

Babar, founder of the Moghul dynasty, was born prince of Ferghana, a tiny principality in Central Asia. Dislodged from his throne by dynastic struggles, he was left a king in quest of a kingdom. In 1526 Babar's search brought him to India, where his army defeated the Afghan ruler of Delhi. A few years and several battles later, his rule extended across a large part of northern India.

Babar did not think very highly of his new country, which the Muslims called Hindustan. He disliked its people, food, and climate in equal measure:

> Hindustan is a place of little charm. There is no beauty in its people, no graceful social intercourse, no poetic talent or understanding, no etiquette, nobility, or manliness. The arts and crafts have no harmony or symmetry. There are no good horses, meat, grapes, melons, or other fruit. There is no ice, cold water, good food or bread in the markets.

Babar's soldiers were equally homesick for the cool mountains from which they had come. Khwaja Kalan, a leading Moghul nobleman, hastily retreated to Afghanistan after experiencing his first summer in Delhi, leaving scrawled on the walls of his house, "May my face turn black if I ever desire to see Hindustan again."

Life in India may have held little appeal for the Moghuls, but they were not about to abandon the kingdom they had fought so hard for. Instead, they set out to create a society in accord with their own ideals of good living. Standards of high culture for the Muslim world were set by Persians, from whom the Moghuls derived much inspiration. Persian architects, craftsmen, poets, artists, and musicians brought new ideas that blended with older Hindu traditions, producing a distinctive Moghul culture.

Indian food was profoundly transformed by these Persian influences. The cooking style that evolved at the court of the Moghuls drew upon the cuisine of Isfahan, capital of the Persian Empire. Indian cooks learned to combine apricots, raisins, and almonds with meat dishes. Kababs, pulaos, and biryanis became the mainstay of Moghul banquets; these platters were elaborately garnished with thin sheets of beaten silver or gold. But even as the Indian chefs borrowed from their Persian counterparts, they continued to use traditional spices and ingredients, creating a truly novel cuisine that we now know as "Moghlai."

Dishes served at the Moghul courts diffused into the everyday food of the largely Hindu population, and even today northern Indian food has much in common with Middle Eastern cuisines. Hindus who ate meat soon developed a taste for Persian lamb dishes, though they would still not eat beef. Pork, forbidden by Muslim dietary laws, never became popular in India, so Moghlai food centers on lamb and chicken. Indians also shared the Arab and Persian fondness for sweets. Many of the desserts most beloved in India today were developed in Moghul times: *halwa,* a favorite of the Arabs, made from grated vegetables or semolina cooked with milk and sugar; *barfi* (so called because of its resemblance to snow, which is *baraf* in Persian), made from thickened milk, nuts, and sugar; and *jalebi*s, deep-fried spirals of fermented batter in syrup, whose name derives from the Arabic *zalabia.*

Babar's empire flourished under his descendants, for the Moghul dynasty was fortunate in having six successive emperors of great ability. Babar's son Humayun spent much of his life battling the Afghan chiefs whom his father had defeated, and consolidating his territory. The Moghul Empire reached its zenith during the reign of the third emperor, Akbar, whom most people rank the greatest king in all of Indian history. A military and administrative genius, he was blessed with the tolerance and wisdom needed to rule all the diverse peoples of India. He married Hindu wives and allowed them to practice their religion in his harem. Muslim scholars, Hindu mystics, and Jesuit priests were all equally welcome at his court. Men of all faiths were appointed to high offices in his army and administration. His reign hastened the transformation of the Moghuls from conquerors living in an alien land to Indians at home in their own country.

Akbar left an immense empire to his son Jahangir, with no external enemies powerful enough to seriously threaten it. Jahangir's tranquil reign was one in which art and culture flourished. Shah Jahan, the next emperor, was a great patron of architecture who completely rebuilt his capital city of Delhi. After the death of his beloved wife, Mumtaz Mahal, he constructed the Taj Mahal in Agra as a memorial whose beauty has made it the most famous building in India. Jahangir and Shah Jahan were both famous gourmets who encouraged Moghul cooking into a fine art.

The Moghul tradition of living well and patronizing the arts ended with Aurangzeb, the last of the great Moghul emperors. A very different character from his ancestors, he was known for his puritanical views and austere lifestyle, refusing to eat meat or drink wine. When he banned all music in his realm, the musicians in Delhi protested by conducting a mock funeral procession for their instruments; his only comment was "Bury them deep." With Aurangzeb's death in 1707, the decline of the Moghul Empire set in. His rigid Muslim orthodoxy had alienated the Hindu princes whose support Akbar had so carefully cultivated, and they revolted against Moghul rule. During his lifetime, Aurangzeb had suppressed all insurrection with an iron hand, but the weak, dissipated rulers who succeeded him were unable to hold the empire together, and it soon began to crumble.

The Moghul court at its peak was a glorious sight, carefully designed to awe all those who beheld it. The emperor's day started at sunrise with a public appearance on a palace balcony, where he received petitions from his subjects and reviewed contingents of his army. Meetings with his nobles and foreign dignitaries were held in the palace hall of audience where the emperor sat on the fabulous, gem-encrusted Peacock Throne. As the emperor entered, musicians played, dancing girls pirouetted before him, and attendants sprinkled perfume on the throng of courtiers. François Bernier, a French physician attending the emperor, described the atmosphere of the court:

> Whenever a word escapes the lips of the King, if at all to the purpose, how trifling soever may be its import, it is immediately caught by the surrounding throng; and the chief *Omrahs* [officials], extending their arms towards heaven, as if to receive some benediction, exclaim *Karamat! Karamat!* Wonderful! Wonderful! He has spoken wonders! Indeed there is no Mogol who does not know and does not glory in repeating this proverb in Persian verse:
>> If the monarch say the day is night,
>> Reply:—"The moon and stars shine bright."

At noon the emperor retired to the royal harem to eat and rest. The women's apartments occupied a large portion of the palace, with several thousand residents. Within their walls lived the emperor's many wives and concubines, his other female relatives, and a huge number of attendants. Each of the queens had her own lavishly appointed palace with gardens, fountains, and waterfalls. Competition for the emperor's attentions was often fierce among the women of his harem and created bitter jealousies. Francisco Pelsaert, who saw Jahangir's court while serving as agent for the Dutch East India Company, described life in the imperial harem:

Each night he visits a particular wife and receives a very warm welcome from her and the slaves, who, dressed specially for the occasion, seem to fly, rather than run, about their duties. . . . Some of the slaves chafe the master's hands and feet, some sit and sing, or play music and dance, or provide other recreation, the wife sitting near him all the time. They study night and day how to make exciting perfumes and efficacious preserves . . . containing amber, pearls, gold, opium and other stimulants. . . . The husband sits like a golden cock among the gilded hens until midnight, or until passion, or drink, sends him to bed.

It is hard to know how Pelsaert obtained his information, but it was certainly not from personal observation, for the only men admitted into the harem were the emperor and a few close relatives. The English ambassador, Sir Thomas Roe, described his closest meeting with Jahangir's wives:

At one syde in a window were his two Principall wifes, whose Curiosity made them breake litle holes in a grate of reede that hung before yt to gaze on mee. I saw first their fingers, and after laying their faces close nowe one eye, Now another; sometyme I could discerne the full proportion. . . . When I looked up they retyred, and were so merry that I supposed they laughd at mee.

Food for all the inhabitants of the palace was prepared in a single kitchen, which was open around the clock and ran with military precision. In charge of all food preparation was the *Mir Bakawal,* the Master of the Kitchen, a man held in high esteem. He was given several assistants and could, when necessary, count on the help of the prime minister himself. The palace cooks came from all parts of the world, each specializing in a particular delicacy. It was claimed that given an hour's notice, a hundred dishes could be prepared in the kitchen.

A vegetable garden provided fresh produce. Sheep, goats, and poultry were specially reared for the emperor's table. Fruits were brought from the farthest reaches of the Moghul Empire: cherries, pears, and apricots from Kashmir; melons, almonds, and pistachios from Afghanistan; oranges and mangoes from Bengal.

When a dish was ready, the cook tasted it first, and then the Mir Bakawal, to ensure that it had not been poisoned. The dishes were covered and tied in cloth—red for gold and silver dishes, and white for copper and china. The Master of the Kitchen wrote the contents of the dish on the wrappers and placed his seal on top. A procession of servants headed by a macebearer carried the food to the king and queen. They reclined on carpets placed on the ground and the dishes were spread before them on a white cloth.

Meals included the finest creations of Moghlai cuisine: pulaos and biryanis made from rice, roast spiced meats such as kababs and tikkas, stewed meats such as yakhni (meat cooked in a yogurt sauce) and do pyaza (meat cooked with twice-fried onions). There were also meats cooked with fine wheat flour paste or rice, spices, sugar, saffron, and nuts; rice cooked with lentils, meats, spices, and nuts; saag made with various greens; and halwa made from semolina or wheat flour, sugar, nuts, and saffron. The cooks had a unique technique of removing the bones from a whole chicken through its neck, leaving the fowl intact. They would then bake it in a sauce of onions, tomatoes, spices, and cream on low heat in a wood-fired oven.

Occasionally the royal women would cook some special delicacy for the emperor or a favored guest. Jahanara, sister of Emperor Aurangzeb and a deeply religious woman, wrote of the dishes she had prepared for a visiting sage. Nur Jahan, principal wife of Emperor Jahangir, was famed for her cooking and often created new dishes for her husband.

Though the Moghuls grew accustomed to the heat of the Indian plains, they never gave up longing for their ancestors' cool mountains. Their refuge from the summer heat was the verdant valley of Kashmir, nestling among the towering Himalayan ranges in the north and a two-month journey from Delhi. The Moghul emperor's entourage was a small city on the move: his entire court, harem, and army, all followed by thousands of retainers. In Kashmir, the Moghuls built the formal gardens they loved and filled them with flowers, towering plane trees brought from Persia, cascading streams of water, and sparkling fountains. They planted orchards of fruit that could not be grown anywhere else in India— apples, peaches, apricots, cherries, and strawberries. Life in Kashmir was pure bliss for the Moghuls, an escape from the worries of empire. Tradition has it that as Jahangir lay dying, his grieving attendants begged to know if there was anything that he desired. The emperor's last words were "Kashmir, only Kashmir."

Most people in Kashmir had been Hindus before the advent of Islam, but mountain isolation allowed their customs to evolve quite differently from those of other Indians. They never became vegetarians, as the majority of other Hindus did, and even today Kashmiri Hindus eat meat. When Kashmir was conquered by Muslims, a large number of Kashmiris converted to Islam but otherwise did not change their way of life. The food eaten by Muslims and Hindus in Kashmir has only subtle differences: Hindus refuse to eat onions and garlic, and Muslims do not use asafetida in their cooking. Their cuisine is based on lamb dishes, with chicken rarely eaten and pork never. The dishes are cooked in a lot of yogurt, spiced with fennel seeds and cardamom. Moghul cooking techniques also influenced Kashmiri cuisine, for Kashmiri cooks embraced many Moghlai recipes, while adding familiar ingredients, such as fresh coriander and yogurt. Kashmiri food, like that of the Moghuls, is extremely rich, cooked in clarified butter with abundant use of almonds.

No account of the Moghuls is complete without mention of the Rajputs, who were at one time formidable foes of the Moghuls but, in one of history's strangest twists, became their staunchest supporters. When Babar first arrived in India, the only Hindu armies powerful enough to challenge him were those of the Rajput kingdoms, which lay southwest of Delhi in the Rajasthan desert. Rajput clans lived by a strict code of chivalry, according to which honor could be gained only in battles that they usually fought against one another. The Rajputs remained preoccupied with their own feuds, refusing to unite even when confronted by the Moghuls, and were defeated one by one following years of combat. Faced with the formidable task of keeping the Rajputs subjugated, Akbar realized that they would be much more useful as allies. He offered the Rajput chiefs autonomy in their own kingdoms, high rank in his service, and honored positions at his court. Akbar cemented the alliance by marrying a Rajput princess, a practice his descendants continued: his son Jahangir had a Rajput mother, as did Jahangir's son Shah Jahan. The Rajputs, who became prominent members of the imperial court, brought with them their customs, dress, and food, much of which was adopted by the Moghuls.

Rajput cuisine also shows many Moghul influences, such as the preparation of elaborate rice and meat dishes—unusual for Hindus. They even ate the wild boar they hunted, which Muslims thought unclean and refused to touch. Many traditional Rajput cooking techniques are suited to hunting parties or army camps, where meats were marinated in yogurt and spices, skewered and grilled over open fires. Other favorite foods are made from dried ingredients, which are light and do not spoil, important considerations for warriors on the march. Flour made from dried chickpeas or dried mung beans is used to prepare steamed or sun-dried dumplings, which are lightly sautéed before being added to a yogurt-based spicy sauce. Sun-dried vegetables, easy to prepare under the blazing desert sun, are used all year round.

This chapter describes the cuisine of the Moghuls, the Kashmiris, and the Rajputs, three people whose histories are inextricably entwined. Moghlai cooking developed in Delhi, and even today you find the best samples of it in the homes and restaurants of that city. The recipes in this chapter will show you how to recreate the magnificent cuisine that was once served to emperors. Kashmir is still as beautiful as it was when the Moghuls made it their playground. They left their indelible stamp on Kashmiri cuisine, which you can still taste in the dishes described here. The ancient Rajput kingdoms have all been amalgamated into the state of Rajasthan in modern India, but the cities that gave their names to those kingdoms—such as Jaipur, Jodhpur, Udaipur, and Ajmer—still exist. There you will find traditional Rajput cooking at its best. It has taken centuries to perfect these dishes—cook them and you will discover why they have remained favorites all this time.

Kashmiri Dum Alu • Baby potatoes served in a sautéed onion, tomato, and yogurt sauce

Dhaniya Tamatar Moongodi • Mung bean dumplings served in a tomato-herb sauce

Chane ki Dal Laukiwali • Yellow split peas cooked with zucchini, tomatoes, and spices

Paneer Makhani Masala • Cottage cheese, cashews, and mushrooms in a creamy, buttery tomato sauce

Mughlai Kadhai Paneer • Cottage cheese and sweet peppers cooked in a sauce of tomatoes, nuts, raisins, and cream

Zafrani Paneer Kabab • Chicken marinated and grilled with thickened yogurt, cottage cheese, and cashews, tossed with sautéed onions

Murgh Kabab • Chicken marinated in minced herbs, sun-dried tomatoes, vinegar, eggs, and cream, grilled on skewers

Bhare Kabab • Boneless chicken thighs marinated in yogurt and spices, stuffed with spicy ground chicken kababs

Akhroat Murgh • Chicken breast morsels and portobello mushrooms marinated in powdered walnuts, yogurt, mint, and spices, served in tortillas

Kofte Pistewale • Broiled meatballs made with ground chicken, cottage cheese, and sun-dried tomatoes, baked in a sauce of onions, tomatoes, and pistachios

Shah Jahani Makhani Dum Murghi • Grilled marinated chicken baked in a tomato, nut, and cream sauce

Hara Murga • Chicken cooked with herbs, coconut, and spices

Udaipuri Masala Murgh • Chicken cooked with yogurt, cashews, peas, and spices

Shahi Kofte • Chicken balls cooked in a sauce of tomatoes, onions, and sour cream with pistachios and apricots

Bhindi Jhinga Masala • Shrimp stir-fried with okra and spices

Machali ke Tikke • Fish fillets marinated in yogurt, nuts, and spices, grilled on the barbecue

Khumani Kabab • Ground lamb kababs with sautéed onions, almonds, and spices, stuffed with dried apricots and cottage cheese

Dhaniwal Roghan Josh • Lamb cooked with onions, yogurt, almonds, and fresh coriander

Mookal • Cooked shredded lamb stir-fried with onions, yogurt, and spices

Saag Kofte • Spicy meatballs served in a sautéed spinach and yogurt sauce

Keema Guchchi • Portobello mushrooms stuffed with spicy ground lamb and peas

Gosht Yakhni Biryani • Fennel-scented lamb curry, layered and baked with rice

Shahi Kofte ki Biryani • Rice layered and baked with a spicy meatball curry

Aam ki Kulfi • Ice cream made with thickened, sweetened milk, flavored with mangoes and pistachios

Kashmiri Dum Alu

Baby potatoes served in a sautéed onion, tomato, and yogurt sauce

1¾ pounds small white new potatoes

1¼ cups finely chopped onions

2 garlic cloves, chopped

2 tablespoons vegetable oil

½ teaspoon cumin seeds

1 whole cardamom

1 whole clove

½-inch cinnamon stick

1 bay leaf

½ cup diced plum tomatoes,
    canned or fresh

4 tablespoons plain yogurt,
    not low-fat

Salt to taste

½ teaspoon turmeric

¼ teaspoon paprika

¼ teaspoon ground black pepper

½ teaspoon ground coriander seeds

½ teaspoon dried powdered ginger
    or ½-inch piece of fresh ginger,
    finely chopped

½ teaspoon garam masala

1 teaspoon fennel seeds, powdered

3 cups water

Vegetable oil for deep-frying

2 tablespoons chopped fresh coriander
    leaves (optional)

When John Fryer visited India in 1673, he carefully noted the vegetable crops, which included carrots, turnips, radishes, cabbage, beets, peas, beans, lettuce, parsley, mint, and spinach. He did not mention potatoes, now the mainstay of Indian cooking, for at that time they were very new to the country. Potatoes originated in South America and were brought to India by European traders in the sixteenth century. Sir Thomas Roe, British ambassador to the Moghul court, mentioned being served potatoes at a banquet in 1615, the first recorded instance of their use in India. Even as late as 1780, potatoes were so unusual in India that when the British governor general, Sir Warren Hastings, received a basket of them as a gift, he invited his entire council to dinner. By the nineteenth century, potato cultivation was widespread in India.

Small new potatoes with a taste all their own are used whole in this recipe from Kashmir. They are cooked in a sauce spiced with powdered fennel seeds, a typical Kashmiri seasoning. Cooking them a day in advance will blend the flavors and allow the potatoes to absorb the sauce. Kashmiri Dum Alu goes very well with puris (deep-fried Indian bread) and Saag Kofte (spicy meatballs served in a sautéed spinach and yogurt sauce, page 128).

- Wash the potatoes and put them in a microwave-safe bowl with enough water to cover. Seal with plastic wrap and microwave on high for 10 minutes; the potatoes should be firm to the touch, not mushy. (You can also boil them in a saucepan.) Drain and set aside to cool. Meanwhile, prepare the sauce.

- In a food processor, mince the onion and garlic. Warm the oil in a nonstick skillet over medium-high heat. Add the cumin seeds, cardamom, clove, cinnamon, and bay leaf. After a few seconds, add the minced onions and sauté for about 5 minutes, stirring occasionally, until the onions are lightly browned.
- In the food processor or a blender, whirl the diced tomatoes to a smooth puree. Reduce stovetop heat to medium and stir in the tomatoes. Sauté for another 5 minutes, until the sauce is well blended.
- Mix in the yogurt, salt, then all remaining spices, stirring continuously to prevent the yogurt from curdling. Cook for 5 minutes, then stir in the water. Cover and remove from heat.
- The potatoes should now be cool enough to handle. Peel and dry them lightly with paper towels. Warm vegetable oil for deep-frying in a wok or deep fryer over medium-high heat. Fry the potatoes in batches until lightly browned, then drain on paper towels. (You can also toss the cooked peeled potatoes with 2 tablespoons of oil, spread them on a large baking sheet, and bake them at 400°F for 15 minutes. Turn off the oven and let them brown in the residual heat for 10 minutes before proceeding with the recipe.)
- Using a toothpick or wooden skewer, poke each potato a few times to let the sauce soak in, then slide them into the sauce. Bring to a boil, then cover, reduce heat to low, and cook for 20 minutes, stirring gently once in a while. After cooking, transfer to a serving bowl and garnish with fresh coriander leaves. You can make this dish up to 3 days ahead of time.

- SERVES 3 TO 4 WITH OTHER DISHES

Dhaniya Tamatar Moongodi

Mung bean dumplings served in a tomato-herb sauce

FOR THE DUMPLINGS

½ cup yellow mung beans (moong dal)

4 tablespoons water

2 tablespoons chopped fresh
    coriander leaves

¼ to ½ teaspoon cracked black pepper

Salt to taste

Tiny pinch of baking soda

Vegetable oil for deep frying

FOR THE TOMATO-HERB SAUCE

1 cup packed fresh coriander leaves
    and tender upper stems, washed

2 garlic cloves, chopped

½-inch piece of ginger, chopped

1 hot green chili, stemmed (optional)

1 cup diced tomatoes, canned or fresh

2 tablespoons vegetable oil

Pinch of crushed asafetida

½ teaspoon cumin seeds

1½ teaspoons ground coriander seeds

½ teaspoon turmeric

½ teaspoon ground cumin seeds

Salt to taste

½ teaspoon garam masala

1 teaspoon kasoori methi
    (dried fenugreek leaves)

2 cups water

 Asafetida (known as *hing* in Hindi) is a spice frequently used in Indian cooking, both for its pungent flavor and because it is believed to aid digestion. Many Westerners find the aroma of pure asafetida overpowering. The Reverend John Ovington, an English chaplain in the port of Surat in 1691, thought asafetida quite distasteful:

> The Natives of *Suratt* are much taken with *Assa Fœtida,* which they call Hin, and mix a little of it with the Cakes they eat, which tho' very unpalatable and unsavoury, yet, because they esteem it beyond all things healthful, the *English* are tempted sometimes to taste it. The whole City sometimes smells very strong of the nauseating Vapours which flow from that abundance that is eat in it.

Asafetida still evokes strong reactions from those who eat it for the first time, so this is the only recipe in this book where I have used it. You may leave it out if you wish.

In this recipe, typical of Rajasthani cuisine, the dumplings are made fresh and deep-fried before being combined with the sauce. Another way to prepare the dumplings—well suited to the hot, dry desert climate of Rajasthan—is to spread them in the sun for a few days. The dried dumplings are then lightly fried in oil and cooked in a yogurt-based sauce. This tomato-herb sauce is also great for cooking chicken. Dhaniya Tamatar Moongodi goes well with Indian bread and Mookal (cooked shredded lamb stir-fried with onions, yogurt, and spices, page 126).

- Wash the mung beans and soak in enough water to cover for at least one hour. Drain well, combine in a blender with 4 tablespoons of water, and blend to a smooth paste. Transfer to a bowl and add the chopped fresh coriander, black pepper, salt, and baking soda. Mix well.

- Heat oil for deep-frying in a wok or deep skillet set over high heat. Drop rounded teaspoonfuls (the size of marbles) of the mung-bean batter in the oil and fry gently until lightly browned. Drain on paper towels and set aside.

- To make the sauce, mince the fresh coriander, garlic, ginger, and green chili in a food processor and transfer to a bowl. In the same container, whirl the tomatoes to a puree, then set in a small bowl.

- Warm the oil in a nonstick skillet over medium-high heat. Add the asafetida and cumin seeds and, after a few seconds, the minced herbs. Sauté for 2 minutes, stirring occasionally. Add the ground coriander seeds, turmeric, ground cumin seeds, salt, garam masala, and dried fenugreek leaves and stir for 1 minute, then mix in the pureed tomatoes. Reduce the heat to medium and cook for 8 to 10 minutes, until all the water has evaporated and the oil appears around the edges. Add 2 cups of water, then gently add the fried dumplings, cover, and bring to a boil. Reduce heat to low and cook for 20 minutes. The sauce should not be too thin; the dumplings will absorb some of it and become spongy. You can make this dish up to 3 days ahead of time.

  - SERVES 3 TO 4 WITH OTHER DISHES

Chane ki Dal Laukiwali

Yellow split peas cooked with zucchini, tomatoes, and spices

1 cup chana dal (yellow split peas),
    washed

Salt to taste

½ teaspoon turmeric

2 cups water

2 tablespoons butter, ghee
    (clarified butter),
    or vegetable oil

½ teaspoon cumin seeds

½ teaspoon fennel seeds (optional)

½-inch piece of ginger, grated

2 garlic cloves, grated

1 cup finely chopped onions

1 small zucchini, chopped into
    1-inch cubes

½ cup diced tomatoes

¼ to ½ teaspoon cayenne pepper

½ teaspoon garam masala

1 teaspoon lemon juice

2 tablespoons chopped fresh
    coriander leaves

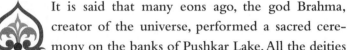

It is said that many eons ago, the god Brahma, creator of the universe, performed a sacred ceremony on the banks of Pushkar Lake. All the deities were assembled for the great occasion, but Brahma's consort, Saraswati, goddess of wisdom, was nowhere to be seen. Brahma waited fretfully, for the ritual could not be performed without his wife, but Saraswati was adorning herself and would not be hurried. When it seemed that the auspicious hour would pass, Brahma saw a young maiden tending her cows nearby. He married her on the spot and completed the ceremony with her assistance. Saraswati, upon arriving, was furious at finding herself displaced and swept off to a shrine on a nearby hill from which she still has not descended; pilgrims must climb the hill to worship her. Before leaving, she decreed, as goddesses can, that from then on Brahma could only be worshiped once a year, and then only at Pushkar.

Since time immemorial, a great camel fair has been held every year at Pushkar Lake, near the city of Ajmer in Rajasthan. People come from great distances to buy, sell, and race camels. At night, in the light of the full moon, people bathe in the lake and worship in the temple of Brahma, the only one in the world. As darkness falls, hundreds of cooking fires are lighted as people prepare their evening meals. Many of them cook dal (lentils), which—because of the scarcity of fresh vegetables in the Rajasthan desert—is an important part of the diet. Often the vegetable supply is stretched by combining it with dal. The dal here is cooked with fresh zucchini and tomatoes in characteristic Rajasthani style and would go well with plain rice or any Indian bread.

- In a heavy-bottomed pot, combine the split peas, salt, turmeric, and water. Bring to a rolling boil, then cover partially and cook on low heat until the split peas are tender, 20 to 25 minutes. Stir occasionally and add more water if needed. (You can also cook them in a pressure cooker for about 10 minutes.)
- Warm the butter or oil in a nonstick skillet over medium heat and add the cumin and fennel seeds, then the grated ginger and garlic, and sauté for 30 seconds. Add the chopped onions and zucchini and sauté until lightly browned, about 8 minutes, then stir in the tomatoes. Cook for about 5 minutes, until soft. Add the spices and cook for 2 minutes. Now add the cooked split peas and mix gently. Cook uncovered for about 10 minutes on low heat. Add the lemon juice and chopped fresh coriander. This dish can be made up to 3 days ahead of time.

- SERVES 3 TO 4 WITH OTHER DISHES

Paneer Makhani Masala

Cottage cheese, cashews, and mushrooms in a creamy, buttery tomato sauce

Emperor Shah Jahan retired at noon every day to the privacy of his harem, where he ate lunch in the company of his wives, played with his children, and listened to musicians, poets, and storytellers. Very few outsiders were permitted into the harem; even when François Bernier, a French doctor at the Moghul court, went to the harem to treat one of the ladies, he was not permitted to see the place:

A *Kachemire* shawl covered my head, hanging like a large scarf down to my feet, and an eunuch led me by the hand as if I had been a blind man. You must be content, therefore, with such a general description as I have received from some of the

2 tablespoons vegetable oil

2 garlic cloves, grated

½-inch piece of ginger, grated

½ pound paneer (cottage cheese),
     cut into 1-inch cubes

½ cup raw cashew pieces

¼ pound (about 25) small white
     mushrooms, washed and dried

2 cups canned diced plum tomatoes

¼ teaspoon sugar

Salt to taste

¼ teaspoon paprika

*1 teaspoon kasoori methi
(dried fenugreek leaves)*
½ teaspoon garam masala
¼ teaspoon ground black pepper
1 cup water
2 tablespoons chilled butter
2 tablespoons heavy cream

eunuchs. They informed me the *Seraglio* contains beautiful apartments, separated, and more or less spacious and splendid, according to the rank and income of the females. Nearly every chamber has its reservoir of running water at the door; on every side are gardens, delightful alleys, shady retreats, streams, fountains, grottoes, deep excavations that offer shelter from the sun by day, lofty divans and terraces, on which to sleep coolly at night.

Niccolò Manucci, an Italian with rather dubious medical credentials, was also taken to the harem in a similar manner to attend one of the royal women. He proved less compliant when his eyes were covered:

I walked as slowly as I could, in spite of the urging of my guides, the eunuchs. The prince, having seen this, ordered them to uncover me, and that in future I was to be allowed to come and go without being covered. He said that the minds of the Christians were not filthy like those of the Mahomedans.

In the seclusion of the harem, the emperor and his close family dined in splendor. The royal cooks vied with one another to prepare elaborate dishes that would catch the emperor's fancy.

Paneer makhani masala is an example of how simple cottage cheese can be turned into a dish fit for a royal banquet. The cottage cheese is cooked with mushrooms and cashews in a rich, creamy tomato sauce. If you wish, you can substitute peanuts or almonds for the cashews, and green peppers for the mushrooms. Serve this dish with Kofte Pistewale (broiled meatballs made with ground chicken, cottage cheese, and sun-dried tomatoes, baked in a sauce of onions, tomatoes, and pistachios, page 108).

• Warm the oil in a nonstick skillet over medium-high heat. Add the grated garlic and ginger and sauté for 30 seconds,

Moghul nobles listening to music, seventeenth century

until lightly browned. Add the cubed cottage cheese (paneer) and the cashew bits and sauté for 3 to 4 minutes, until lightly browned; take care to stir the paneer gently to avoid breaking it. Add the mushrooms and stir-fry for 3 to 4 minutes, just until they begin to release their liquid. Transfer everything to a bowl.

- In the same skillet, cook the tomatoes on medium heat, mashing them with the back of your spoon for about 10 minutes to thicken. Reduce heat to medium-low and mix in the sugar, salt, paprika, dried fenugreek leaves, garam masala, and black pepper. Cook for 1 minute, then add the water. Gently mix in the sautéed paneer, mushrooms, and cashews, scraping out all accumulated liquid from the bowl. Bring to a boil, then immediately reduce heat to low, cover, and cook for 15 minutes. Uncover, stir in the chilled butter, and cook for 1 minute. Remove the skillet from heat and cool for 5 minutes, then gently mix in the heavy cream. Taste for salt and seasonings and serve. If you wish to make this dish ahead of time, add the cream just before serving.

- SERVES 4 WITH OTHER DISHES

Mughlai Kaдhai Paneer

Cottage cheese and sweet peppers cooked in a sauce of tomatoes, nuts, raisins, and cream

3 tablespoons vegetable oil
½ pound paneer (cottage cheese),
  cut into ½-inch pieces
1 small sweet green pepper, seeded
  and thinly sliced into long strips
¼ cup raw cashew bits
2 tablespoons golden raisins
2 garlic cloves, grated

 Bega Begam was feeling a little neglected. Lately she had seen so little of her husband, Emperor Humayun, that she felt compelled to make this poignant complaint:

For several days now you have been paying visits in this garden, and on no one day have you been to our house. Thorns have not been planted in the way to it. We hope you will deign to visit our quarters also, and to have a party and a sociable gathering there, too. How long will you think it right to show all these disfavours to us helpless ones? We too have hearts.

Humayun was indignant: he had been busy visiting his mother and aunts; he was an opium eater and should not be held responsible for his actions; and he wanted a written apology. Bega Begam grumbled that "the excuse looked worse than the fault," but wrote the letter: "What remedy have we? You are Emperor." The pair made up. The women of the harem competed with one another for the emperor's attentions. Being a good cook helped to captivate him. Bega Begam must have planned her party to celebrate their reconciliation with great care. Serving Kadhai Paneer, with its delectable aroma of fried green peppers and sautéed cottage cheese in a rich creamy sauce, would have ensured that her husband did not neglect her again!

½-inch piece of ginger, grated
1 cup canned diced tomatoes, pureed
  in food processor
½ teaspoon ground coriander seeds
½ teaspoon ground cumin seeds
½ teaspoon turmeric
¼ to ½ teaspoon cayenne pepper
½ teaspoon garam masala
1 teaspoon kasoori methi
  (dried fenugreek leaves)
¼ teaspoon ground black pepper
Salt to taste
½ cup water
1 tablespoon heavy cream
Fresh coriander leaves, chopped
  (optional)

- Warm the oil in a nonstick skillet over medium-high heat. Add the cubed cottage cheese, green pepper strips, cashews, and raisins. Stir-fry gently for about 5 minutes, until the cottage cheese is lightly browned. Drain everything on paper towels and set aside.

- In the same skillet, sauté the grated garlic and ginger for 30 seconds, then reduce heat to medium and add the pureed tomatoes. Cook for 8 minutes, stirring occasionally, until the oil appears at the edges. Add all the spices and salt and cook for another 2 minutes. Add the water, mix well, then add the fried cottage cheese, sweet pepper, cashews, and raisins. Mix again, cover, and reduce heat to medium-low. Cook for 15 minutes, until the sauce has thickened and the cottage cheese is soft. Let sit, covered, for 5 minutes, then gently mix in the cream. Serve with a garnish of chopped fresh coriander leaves if desired. If you wish to make this dish ahead of time, add the cream after you reheat it.

  - SERVES 3 TO 4 WITH OTHER DISHES

Emperor Babar feasting, sixteenth century

Zafrani Paneer Kabab

Chicken marinated and grilled with thickened yogurt, cottage cheese, and cashews, tossed with sautéed onions

Only the drinker knows the pleasure of wine.
What enjoyment thereof can the sober have?
>   —*Emperor Babar, 1504*

I have two lips, one devoted to wine and the other apologizing for drunkenness.
>   —*Emperor Jahangir, 1619*

Babar resolved at an early age to renounce wine when he turned forty. With this deadline looming, he wrote in his diary: "With only one year left to my fortieth year I was drinking to excess out of anxiety." It was on the eve of a great battle against the Rajputs in 1527 that he finally smashed all his gold and silver wine goblets and vowed to forsake alcohol forever. Babar's descendants, all of them hard drinkers, had little success in their sporadic efforts to enforce the Islamic ban on liquor. Babar's grandson Akbar forbade the sale of wine throughout his kingdom. He graciously made an exception for Europeans because, he said, "the European people must have been created at the same time as intoxicating drink and if deprived of them, were like fish out of their element, unless they had drink, they would not see plain."

Akbar's son Jahangir continued the ban on intoxicants, at the same time sheepishly noting, "I myself commit the sin of drinking wine and have constantly persisted in doing so from the age of eighteen." The Moghul emperor's subjects appear to have followed his example, because more than fifty years later, Jahangir's grandson Aurangzeb was bemoaning the fact that "there are only two men in India who are not

½ cup plain yogurt, not low-fat

2 garlic cloves, chopped

½-inch piece of ginger, chopped

½ cup crumbled pressed paneer (cottage cheese)

½ teaspoon ground coriander seeds

½ teaspoon ground cumin seeds

½ teaspoon garam masala

½ teaspoon ground roasted cumin seeds

¼ teaspoon ground black pepper

Salt to taste

Tiny pinch of saffron

2 tablespoons fresh coriander leaves

15 raw cashews, powdered fine

1 tablespoon lemon juice

1 pound boneless, skinless chicken breast

2 tablespoons vegetable oil

1 large onion, peeled and sliced into thin half-rounds

drunkards—myself and the Chief Justice." Niccolò Manucci, an Italian who lived for several decades in India and wrote a delightfully gossipy record of his stay at the Moghul court, challenged even this sad accounting of sobriety. "With respect to the Chief Justice," he wrote, "the Emperor was in error, for I myself sent him every day a bottle of spirits which he drank in secret."

Indians do not customarily drink anything but water with their meals. People who drink wine usually do so before the main course, while nibbling on appetizers. When drinks are being served, these kababs make a delightful accompaniment. Serve them with a fresh herb chutney.

- Line a fine mesh sieve with a double layer of cheesecloth or a coffee filter and place over a bowl. Pour in the yogurt, cover, and refrigerate overnight. Scrape the yogurt into a blender or food processor, along with all the remaining ingredients except the chicken, oil, and onion. Blend to a smooth paste and transfer to a mixing bowl.

- Cut the chicken breast into 1-inch pieces and mix into the marinade, tossing to coat. Cover and refrigerate for at least 4 hours.

- When ready to grill, lift the chicken out of the marinade, thread onto skewers, and place on a medium-hot barbecue. Cover and cook for about 15 minutes, turning occasionally for even cooking and basting with any leftover marinade. When cooked through, remove from skewers and set aside.

- Warm the oil in a nonstick skillet over a medium heat and sauté the onions for about 10 minutes, until soft and lightly browned. Toss in the grilled chicken pieces and stir-fry for 1 minute. Transfer to a platter and serve.

  - SERVES 3 TO 4 WITH OTHER DISHES

Murgh Kabab

Chicken marinated in minced herbs, sun-dried tomatoes, vinegar, eggs, and cream, grilled on skewers

Asad Beg, captain of the emperor's bodyguard, saw a strange sight while traveling along the western coast of India in 1604: men blowing smoke out of their mouths! They were smoking tobacco, which had recently been brought to the country by Portuguese traders but had not yet reached the Moghul court. Asad Beg took some back as a present for Emperor Akbar, and described how his gift was received:

> His Majesty was graciously pleased to say he must smoke a little to gratify me, and taking the mouthpiece into his sacred mouth, drew two or three breaths. . . . The first physician said, "In fact, this is an untried medicine, about which the doctor has written nothing. How can we describe to Your Majesty the qualities of such unknown things? It is not fitting that Your Majesty should try it." I said to the first physician, "The Europeans are not so foolish as not to know all about it; there are wise men among them who seldom err or commit mistakes. . . ." When the Emperor heard me dispute and reason with the physician, he was astonished, and being much pleased . . . said, "Did you hear how wisely Asad spoke? Truly, we must not reject a thing that has been adopted by the wise men of other nations merely because we cannot find it in our books; or how shall we progress?"

Despite the royal physician's protests, smoking became extremely popular among Moghul nobles, though the emperor himself never took to it.

Portuguese merchants also brought other, more useful, plants from the Americas. Among the most important were

2 garlic cloves, chopped

½-inch piece of ginger, chopped

1 cup loosely packed fresh coriander leaves and tender stems, washed and drained

1 hot green chili, stemmed (optional)

10 sun- or oven-dried tomato halves

1 egg

1 teaspoon kasoori methi (dried fenugreek leaves)

Salt to taste

1 teaspoon ground coriander seeds

1 teaspoon ground cumin seeds

¼ teaspoon cayenne pepper

¼ teaspoon ground black pepper

Tiny pinch of saffron

½ teaspoon garam masala

2 tablespoons heavy cream

4 tablespoons white vinegar

1 tablespoon vegetable oil

1 pound boneless, skinless chicken breast, washed, dried, and cut into 1-inch pieces

½ cup plain bread crumbs

Lemon juice to taste

tomatoes, which transformed Indian cooking. They are now used in almost every dish: eaten fresh as a simple salad, with salt and roasted cumin seeds; sautéed in sauces; chopped and added to food as it cooks. Sun-dried tomatoes, which I have used in this recipe, are not yet commonly used in India; otherwise, these kababs are made with traditional Moghul ingredients. Purists may frown at my innovation, but we must not reject a thing merely because we cannot find it in our cookbooks, or how shall we progress?

- In a food processor, mince the garlic, ginger, fresh coriander, green chili, and sun-dried tomatoes. Scrape down the sides with a spatula, add all the remaining ingredients except the chicken and bread crumbs, and puree.
- Pour this marinade over the chicken and toss well to coat. Cover and refrigerate for at least 4 hours. When ready to grill, lift the chicken out of the marinade and thread 4 to 5 pieces on each skewer. Place all the skewers side by side on a plate and sprinkle liberally with half the bread crumbs, patting gently with your fingertips to hold them in place. Flip the skewers and repeat on the other side with the remaining bread crumbs.
- In a covered barbecue, grill over medium heat until cooked through and lightly browned all over. Flip once in a while for even cooking. Sprinkle with lemon juice and serve.

- SERVES 3 TO 4 WITH OTHER DISHES

Bhare Kabab

Boneless chicken thighs marinated in yogurt and spices,
stuffed with spicy ground chicken kababs

 Welsh fairies, according to a twelfth-century story of a boy who visited a fairy palace, had rather unusual tastes. The fairies "neither ate flesh nor fish, but lived on a milk diet, made up into messes with saffron." Everyone in Britain wanted saffron; fortunately, it proved the one spice that readily grew in Europe. Soon cooks (and presumably fairies) were using it with abandon.

Saffron had come to India from the Mediterranean countries where it originated almost a thousand years before it reached England. There are records of its growing in Kashmir as early as A.D. 550. Kashmiri cooks have always used saffron in rice pulaos and biryanis, and in sauces for curries and kormas. It is prized both for its delicate flavor and for the rich golden hue it imparts to the food. These kababs from Kashmir use saffron, though probably not in the quantities of medieval days.

Although this recipe may sound complicated, it is quite simple to put together and is sure to dazzle. Leftovers can be sliced thinly and used as filling for wraps or tossed with thickened yogurt spiced with roasted ground cumin seeds, green onions, and tomatoes for a succulent salad. You could also grill the marinated thighs without the stuffing.

- Line a fine mesh sieve with a coffee filter or double layer of cheesecloth and place over a bowl. Pour in the yogurt, cover, and refrigerate overnight. Scrape the thickened yogurt into a bowl and add all remaining marinade ingredients except the chicken thighs. Mix well and rub this marinade into the chicken. Cover and refrigerate for at least 4 hours.
- To prepare the stuffing, mince the ginger, garlic, and onion in a food processor. Add the egg, bread, salt, and all the

FOR THE MARINADE

8 tablespoons plain yogurt,
   not low-fat

Pinch of saffron, crushed

1 tablespoon white vinegar

¼-inch piece of ginger, grated

2 garlic cloves, grated

½ teaspoon ground coriander seeds

½ teaspoon ground cumin seeds

½ teaspoon garam masala

1 teaspoon whole cardamom,
   powdered with skins in spice
   grinder

Salt to taste

¼ teaspoon cayenne pepper

2 tablespoons chopped fresh coriander
   leaves

1½ pounds (8 pieces) boneless,
   skinless chicken thighs, washed
   and dried

FOR THE STUFFING

¼-inch piece of ginger, chopped

1 garlic clove, chopped

1 medium onion, quartered

1 large egg

1 slice of bread, broken up

Salt to taste

¼ teaspoon paprika

1 teaspoon fennel seeds

½ teaspoon ground coriander seeds

½ teaspoon ground cumin seeds

½ teaspoon garam masala

¼ teaspoon ground black pepper

¾ pound lean ground chicken

Lemon juice to taste

spices and whirl again to mix. Add the ground chicken and process until everything is well blended. Transfer to a bowl and refrigerate covered for at least an hour.

- When ready to make the kababs, divide the ground chicken mixture into 8 equal portions. Wetting your hands lightly whenever necessary, mold each portion onto skewers in 4-inch-long sausage shapes, pressing gently with your fingers to hold the meat in place. Grill, covered, on a medium-hot barbecue for about 7 minutes, turning the skewers to cook evenly; the aim is to partially cook the meat before stuffing it in the chicken thighs. Slide the kababs off the skewers and onto a platter.

- Lift a boneless chicken thigh from its marinade onto a flat work surface and stuff a kabab in its center. Now roll up the flaps around the kabab and secure at the center with a couple of toothpicks (the ends of the kabab will stick out from both sides). Stuff all the thighs similarly and spread any remaining marinade on top.

- Grill, covered, on low heat for 25 to 30 minutes, until the meat is tender and lightly browned. Transfer to a serving dish, remove all toothpicks, and sprinkle liberally with lemon juice.

- SERVES 4

Akhroat Murgh

Chicken breast morsels and portobello mushrooms marinated in powdered walnuts, yogurt, mint, and spices, served in tortillas

FOR THE MARINADE

1 cup walnut bits, powdered in a
   spice or coffee grinder

2 garlic cloves, grated

¼-inch piece of ginger,
   grated

"I do not know if there is so much saffron in any other place in the world," wrote Emperor Jahangir, and in "the whole country of Kashmir there is saffron only in this place." He was referring to the village of Pampur, which has India's sole suitable climate for growing crocus bulbs. The stamens of the crocus blossoms are plucked by hand to get strands of saffron. Jahangir, a keen botanist, visited the saffron fields during harvest time to study the flowers, and found the aroma of saffron overpowering: "The breeze in that place scented one's brain." He and all his attendants developed a headache from the odor, though the Kashmiri workers seemed unaffected. The workers could not explain their immunity, for "it was obvious that it had never occurred to them to have a headache."

Jahangir was profoundly interested in the effects of saffron. After reading in a medical text that eating excessive amounts made one laugh so much that it could prove life-threatening, he performed an experiment. A condemned criminal was summoned from prison and ordered to eat a quarter pound of saffron. This having produced no effect, he was given double the amount the next day. "His lips did not crack a smile," noted a disappointed Jahangir, who concluded that there was no danger of dying from laughter after eating saffron.

In this recipe, I have used the popular Kashmiri akhroat raita (walnut yogurt relish) as a base for the marinade and added a few Kashmiri spices, including saffron. I like to reserve a bit of the marinade and use it as a dipping sauce for the kababs. Feel free to increase the amount of saffron if you like—besides tasting good, it might produce unusual hilarity at the table!

½ cup loosely packed fresh mint
    leaves, washed and finely chopped
Few strands of saffron, crushed
1 cup plain yogurt, not low-fat
Salt to taste
1 teaspoon fennel seeds, powdered
1 teaspoon whole cardamom,
    powdered with skins in spice
    grinder
1 tablespoon honey
½ teaspoon garam masala
2 tablespoons olive oil

1 pound boneless, skinless chicken
    breast, washed, dried, and cut into
    1-inch pieces

FOR ASSEMBLING AND SERVING
1 large portobello mushroom, washed,
    with stem removed
6 store-bought Mexican flour tortillas
1 cup shredded lettuce
1 tomato, finely chopped

- Combine all marinade ingredients in a deep mixing bowl and mix well.
- In a small bowl, toss the portobello mushroom with 2 tablespoons of the marinade, coating well. Cover and refrigerate until needed. Reserve and refrigerate another 3 tablespoons of the marinade in a covered bowl. To the remaining marinade, add the chicken and toss well to coat. Cover and refrigerate for at least 4 hours, or overnight if possible, tossing it once in a while.
- When ready to grill, thread the pieces of chicken onto skewers and place on a medium-hot grill. Lift the mushroom cap out of its marinade and grill it alongside the

chicken for 5 to 8 minutes per side, flipping the skewers and the mushroom for even cooking. Baste the skewers occasionally with any leftover marinade.

- When the chicken is tender, slide off the skewers onto a platter. Slice the mushroom thinly into a bowl. Warm the tortillas and serve with the chicken, mushroom, shredded lettuce, chopped tomato, and the reserved marinade. Invite people to roll up their own wraps, using the reserved marinade as a sauce or topping.

- SERVES 2 TO 3

Kofte Pistewale

Broiled meatballs made with ground chicken, cottage cheese, and sun-dried tomatoes, baked in a sauce of sautéed onions, tomatoes, and pistachios

FOR THE KOFTAS (MEATBALLS)

¾ pound lean ground chicken

10 sun- or oven-dried tomato halves, frozen or packed in oil, dried with paper towels

½ cup fresh coriander leaves and tender stems, washed and drained well

⅔ cup grated or crumbled paneer (cottage cheese)

1 egg

2 slices of white bread, broken up

Salt to taste

½ teaspoon ground black pepper

FOR THE SAUCE

¼ cup plus 1 tablespoon raw pistachios

1 tablespoon fennel seeds

 Emperor Jahangir, an avid collector of exotic fauna, was delighted with his latest acquisition. One of his nobles had returned from the Portuguese settlement at Goa with some strange birds never before seen in India. Jahangir described them as "larger in body than a peahen and significantly smaller than a peacock" and ordered the court artist to draw their picture "so that the astonishment one has at hearing of them would increase by seeing them." The birds, as is clear from Jahangir's picture of them, were turkeys brought from America by Portuguese merchants.

In spite of the birds' rarity in India, most Europeans were firmly convinced that it was their country of origin. The French called them *coq d'Inde,* which was shortened to *dinde.* The Italians called them *galle d'India* and the Germans *indianische Henn;* the English, for some mysterious reason, called them turkeys.

The Moghuls may not have eaten turkeys, but they had no shortage of other poultry and game birds. Hawking was a favorite sport, and geese, ducks, pigeons, partridges, quail, herons, and bustard were all hunted and eaten. Koftas (meatballs) could be made from any of these meats, though usually ground chicken or lamb was used. You can even make koftas from ground turkey, but it won't be authentic Moghul food—Jahangir never would have let anyone eat his precious turkeys! You can also serve the koftas as appetizers without the sauce: mold them onto skewers and barbecue.

- Wrap the chicken in 3 layers of paper towels to absorb all the juices. Set aside. In a food processor, mince the sun-dried tomatoes and fresh coriander. Add the cottage cheese, egg, bread, salt, and pepper. Mince again, then add the ground chicken. Process until everything is well blended, then transfer to a large mixing bowl.
- Place your oven rack on the second rung from the top, about 8 inches away from the broiler, and preheat the broiler. Line an ovenproof dish with foil and place a grilling rack on it. Wetting your hands lightly whenever necessary, divide the ground chicken mixture into 25 equal parts and roll each into a smooth ball, about the size of a walnut. Place the meatballs in a single layer on the rack (you may have to broil them in two batches) and broil for 5 minutes. Flip and broil again for 3 to 4 minutes, until lightly browned on all sides. Transfer to a bowl. You can make the meatballs up to 3 days ahead of time; you can also freeze them.
- For the sauce, powder the ¼ cup pistachios and the fennel seeds in a clean coffee or spice grinder. Transfer to a bowl and mix in the salt, turmeric, ground coriander, ground cumin seeds, garam masala, and cayenne pepper. Set aside. In a food processor, mince the onions, garlic, ginger, and green chili (if using).
- Warm the oil in a nonstick skillet over medium-high heat. Add the cumin seeds and, after a few seconds, the minced onions. Sauté, stirring occasionally, for about 5 minutes. Add the tablespoon of whole pistachios and continue sautéing

Salt to taste
½ teaspoon turmeric
½ teaspoon ground coriander seeds
½ teaspoon ground cumin seeds
½ teaspoon garam masala
¼ to ½ teaspoon cayenne pepper
1¼ cups chopped onions
2 garlic cloves, chopped
½-inch piece of ginger, chopped
1 hot green chili, stemmed (optional)
2 tablespoons vegetable oil
½ teaspoon cumin seeds
½ cup diced tomatoes, canned or fresh
3 tablespoons plain yogurt, not low-fat
2 cups water

for another 3 to 4 minutes, until the onions are browned, then reduce the heat to medium.

- While the onions are browning, puree the tomatoes in the food processor and add to the skillet after the onions have browned. Cook on medium heat for about 5 minutes, until the moisture has evaporated and the oil appears around the edges. Add the yogurt, stirring constantly for 3 minutes, then the spice and pistachio powder, and cook for 2 more minutes. Stir in 2 cups of water and the meatballs, cover, and bring to a boil. Reduce heat to medium–low and cook for 30 minutes, stirring occasionally. This dish can be made 3 days in advance.

  - SERVES 3 TO 4 WITH OTHER DISHES

Shah Jahani Makhani Dum Murghi

Grilled marinated chicken baked in a tomato, nut, and cream sauce

FOR THE MARINADE

4 garlic cloves, chopped

1-inch piece of ginger, chopped

1½ cups plain yogurt, not low-fat

2 tablespoons lemon juice

Salt to taste

1 teaspoon ground coriander seeds

1 teaspoon ground cumin seeds

1 teaspoon garam masala

½ teaspoon ground black pepper

1 teaspoon kasoori methi
  (dried fenugreek leaves)

12 boneless, skinless chicken thighs,
  washed and drained

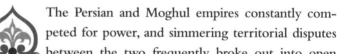 The Persian and Moghul empires constantly competed for power, and simmering territorial disputes between the two frequently broke out into open warfare. Even when the rivals were at peace, Emperor Shah Jahan often vented his animosity on the Persian ambassador at his court, who did not suffer the emperor's insults in silence. At a dinner where Shah Jahan was eating khichadi (rice and lentils), a favorite dish of his, he noticed the Persian ambassador picking all the meat off the bones on his plate. He asked, "Well, My Lord Ambassador, what shall the dogs eat?" "Khichadi" was the prompt reply. François Bernier, a French physician at the Moghul court who reported this exchange, was aghast: "For my part," he wrote, "I think a dignified gravity and respectful demeanor would better become an ambassador."

Khichadi is a simple dish of rice and lentils which has been eaten in the villages of India for thousands of years and is considered a poor man's meal. Emperor Akbar started a custom, which his descendants followed, of not eating meat on certain days of the week. They ate khichadi instead, though their version was cooked in clarified butter with spices and nuts. While the emperors abstained from eating meat, they did not force others to do so; all sorts of delicacies were placed before their guests. This dish is a good example of the food Shah Jahan loved when he was not eating khichadi. Here, the chicken is first marinated, then grilled and baked in an exquisite tomato-nut-cream sauce.

- In a food processor mince the garlic and ginger, then add the yogurt, lemon juice, salt, ground coriander seeds, ground cumin seeds, garam masala, ground black pepper, and fenugreek leaves and process again. Transfer to a large mixing bowl and toss in the chicken, coating well with marinade, then cover and refrigerate for at least 4 hours.
- To cook the chicken, lift the pieces from the marinade and cook on a covered medium-hot grill for 20 to 25 minutes, until the chicken is cooked through and lightly browned. Baste with leftover marinade and turn the pieces occasionally for even grilling. Remove to a platter and set aside. When the chicken is cool enough to handle, cut each piece into 3 parts. You can grill the chicken up to 3 days ahead of time and cook it in the sauce just before serving. (You can also bake the chicken in the oven, on a grill rack set over an ovenproof dish, at 400°F for 30 minutes.)
- To make the sauce, mince the onions, garlic, and ginger in a food processor. Warm the oil in a nonstick skillet over medium-high heat. Add the whole cardamom, clove, bay leaf, and cinnamon stick. After 30 seconds, add the minced onion mixture and sauté, stirring occasionally, for about 5 minutes. Reduce the heat to medium and continue sautéing for another 5 minutes, until the onions are browned.
- Meanwhile, puree the tomatoes in the food processor and keep them handy. Add them to the sautéed onions and cook for 5 minutes, stirring now and then. In a clean coffee or

FOR THE SAUCE

1 cup chopped onions

1 garlic clove, chopped

¼-inch piece of ginger, chopped

2 tablespoons vegetable oil

1 whole cardamom

1 whole clove

1 bay leaf

½-inch cinnamon stick

2½ cups canned diced plum tomatoes

15 raw cashews

15 raw almonds

Salt to taste

¼ teaspoon ground black pepper

¼ teaspoon cayenne pepper

1 teaspoon ground coriander seeds

1 teaspoon ground cumin seeds

¾ teaspoon garam masala

1 teaspoon kasoori methi
  (dried fenugreek leaves)

2 tablespoons butter, chilled

2 cups water

3 tablespoons heavy cream

spice grinder, powder the cashews and almonds finely and add them to the tomatoes along with the salt, black pepper, cayenne pepper, ground coriander seeds, ground cumin seeds, garam masala, and dried fenugreek leaves. Cook for another 5 minutes, until the oil appears around the edges. Now add the butter and cook for 2 minutes. Turn off the heat and add the water and heavy cream. Slide in the pieces of chicken and coat them gently with the sauce.

- Preheat the oven to 250°F. Transfer the contents of the skillet to an ovenproof dish large enough to hold everything comfortably. Cover the dish tightly with foil and bake for 30 minutes. The sauce can be made up to 3 days in advance.

- SERVES 6

Food being served to the King of Mandu, sixteenth century

Hara Murga

Chicken cooked with herbs, coconut, and spices

Niccolò Manucci was ready for a change of career. The Italian gunner had served several years with the Moghul forces, where Europeans were required only to aim the cannon. When Emperor Aurangzeb ordered them to load the guns as well, which involved heavy lifting, Manucci quit. He decided to be a doctor, not viewing his lack of medical knowledge or training as a serious obstacle. He described his first consultation:

> To induce him to believe that I was a great physician, I asked the patient's age and then for a time I assumed a pensive attitude, as if I was seeking for the cause of the illness. Next, as is the fashion with doctors, I said some words making out the attack to be very grave. This was done in order not to lose my reputation and credit if he came to die.

Dr. Manucci prescribed a diet of camel's milk and cheese, and the patient soon recovered.

Manucci was a great favorite of the Rajput prince Jai Singh, commander of the Moghul army, whom he taught the card game Hombre. After losing a lot of money gambling, Jai Singh offered to make Manucci commander of the artillery, and he temporarily abandoned his medical practice to go campaigning with the Moghul army.

Sixty years in the country made Manucci so Indian that he sometimes confused even the natives. He dressed like a Muslim but kept mustaches like the Hindu Rajputs. Some Rajput officers finally inquired whether he was a Hindu or a Muslim. "A Christian," responded Manucci. "Yes, of course," they said, "but would that be a Muslim Christian or a Hindu Christian?"

Walnut-size piece of seedless
   tamarind (2 ounces)
½ cup water
3 tablespoons desiccated
   unsweetened coconut
1 teaspoon white poppy seeds
   (optional)
3 tablespoons vegetable oil
½ teaspoon cumin seeds
1½ cups chopped onions
2 garlic cloves, chopped
½-inch piece of ginger, chopped
1 cup diced tomatoes, fresh or canned
1 cup fresh coriander leaves and
   tender upper stems, washed well
10 to 15 fresh curry leaves (optional)
1 hot green chili, stemmed (optional)
Salt to taste
½ teaspoon turmeric
½ teaspoon ground cumin seeds
½ teaspoon ground coriander seeds
½ teaspoon garam masala
8 skinless chicken thighs, bone-in
   (about 1¼ pounds),
   washed and drained
1 bay leaf
1 whole cardamom
1 whole clove
½-inch cinnamon stick

In this wonderful dish from Rajasthan, the chicken is cooked in a tart and nutty sautéed onion and herb sauce with tomatoes. It is just the sort of thing that Manucci and Jai Singh would have enjoyed after a long evening of Hombre. Serve it with Gobhi Matar ki Sabzi (grated cauliflower and peas stir-fried with onions and spices, page 23) and rice.

- In a small microwave-safe bowl, microwave the tamarind and water uncovered on high for 2 minutes. Mash well with a fork and allow to cool for 10 minutes. (If you prefer, you can soak the tamarind in hot water for 2 hours instead.) Set a fine mesh sieve over a bowl and pour the tamarind and its liquid through, squeezing out all the pulp and discarding the fibrous residue. Set this extract aside.
- Warm a small nonstick frying pan over medium heat, then toast the coconut and poppy seeds for about 3 minutes, stirring occasionally, until lightly golden. Set aside to cool.
- Warm 2 tablespoons oil in a nonstick or heavy-bottomed skillet over medium-high heat and add the cumin seeds. After a second, mix in the chopped onions, garlic, and ginger and sauté for 4 to 5 minutes, until the onions are lightly browned. Cool and transfer to a blender or food processor. Add the tomatoes, fresh coriander, curry leaves, green chili if using, salt, turmeric, ground cumin, ground coriander, and garam masala, then the reserved tamarind extract and the toasted coconut and poppy seeds, and blend to a smooth paste. Transfer to a mixing bowl and toss in the chicken, coating well with the marinade. Cover and refrigerate overnight.
- Warm 1 tablespoon of vegetable oil in a heavy-bottomed skillet. Add the bay leaf, cardamom, clove, and cinnamon. After a few seconds, stir in the chicken and its marinade. Bring to a boil, turn the heat to low, cover, and cook for 25 to 30 minutes, until the chicken is tender, stirring occasionally. If the sauce is too thin after cooking, turn up the heat, uncover, and boil off some of the excess liquid.
  - SERVES 3 TO 4 WITH OTHER DISHES

Udaipuri Masala Murgh

Chicken cooked with yogurt, cashews, peas, and spices

 The towering fortress of Chittor, the last stronghold of Hindu power in north India, lay besieged by the Moghul army in 1568. Facing certain defeat but too proud to surrender, the Rajput warriors defending the fort sallied out one last time to die honorably on the battlefield. Only a handful survived, among them Udai Singh, ruler of Chittor, who retreated and built a new capital—Udaipur. With the fall of Chittor, most of Rajasthan came under the Moghul emperor Akbar's rule, and nearly all the Rajput princes pledged allegiance to him. But the king of Udaipur vowed never to capitulate and resisted the Moghuls to the end of his days. A monument to Rajput heroism, Udaipur is a vision of marble palaces set amid tranquil lakes.

Hunting was a favorite pastime of the Rajputs, and much of their cuisine centers on preparing game. It was the custom in Udaipur to roast an entire boar on a spit called a *soola*. Other game skewered and cooked over an open fire included venison, pheasant, peacock, quail, and duck.

This recipe, based on the Udaipuri style of cooking, is noticeably different from other Rajasthani recipes in its use of peas and hard-boiled eggs and its superb sauce. Serve it with any kind of Indian bread.

- Line a fine mesh sieve with a double layer of cheesecloth or a coffee filter and place over a bowl. Pour in the yogurt and let it drain unrefrigerated for 4 hours. Scrape the thickened yogurt into a small bowl.
- Warm the oil in a nonstick skillet over medium-high heat. Add the cumin seeds and, after a few seconds, the chopped onions, garlic, and ginger. Sauté for about 5 minutes, until the onions are lightly browned. Lift them out of the oil and

---

1 cup plain yogurt, not low-fat

2 tablespoons vegetable oil

½ teaspoon cumin seeds

1¼ cups finely chopped onions

2 garlic cloves, chopped

½-inch piece of ginger, chopped

Salt to taste

¼ teaspoon cayenne pepper

¼ teaspoon ground black pepper

½ teaspoon ground coriander seeds

½ teaspoon ground cumin seeds

Tiny pinch of saffron or
    ¼ teaspoon paprika

½ teaspoon garam masala

15 raw cashews, powdered fine

8 skinless chicken thighs, bone-in
    (about 1¼ pounds),
    washed and drained

1 hot green chili, stemmed

10 small pearl onions or shallots,
    peeled

½ cup frozen peas

3 hard-boiled eggs, peeled and
    halved

2 tablespoons chopped fresh
    coriander leaves

1 tablespoon lemon juice

into a food processor, then add the thickened yogurt and mince well. Add salt, all the spices, and the powdered cashews and whirl again to mix.

- Warm the residual oil in the skillet over medium heat, then sauté the onion-yogurt paste for 5 to 8 minutes, until the oil appears around the edges. Add the chicken and stir-fry for 5 minutes, then cover and bring to a boil. Reduce the heat to low and cook for 20 minutes, then mix in the whole green chili, pearl onions, and peas. Cover and cook again for 20 minutes or until the chicken is tender, stirring occasionally. Now add the eggs to the pan along with the chopped coriander leaves and lemon juice and cook uncovered for 2 minutes. The sauce should be very thick. This dish can be cooked up to 3 days ahead of time.

- SERVES 3 TO 4 WITH OTHER DISHES

Shahi Kofte

Chicken balls cooked in a sauce of tomatoes, onions, and sour cream with pistachios and apricots

FOR THE KOFTAS (MEATBALLS)
1¼ cups chopped onions
1 garlic clove, chopped
¼-inch piece of ginger, chopped
¼ cup fresh coriander leaves and
    tender upper stems, washed
    and drained well
Salt to taste
¼ teaspoon ground black pepper
10 raw almonds, powdered fine
1 egg
2 slices of white bread, broken up

In an age of great explorers, Tom Coryate was a tourist—one who liked to travel economically. He journeyed from England to India ("all which way I traversed afoot, but with divers paire of shooes") with a fairly modest ambition: "to have my picture expressed in my next Booke, sitting upon an elephant." His travels cost little ("victuals beeing so cheape in some Countries where I traveled, that I oftentimes lived competentlie for a pennie sterling a day"), and he was proud to have spent only three pounds on his entire journey. He reckoned that ten shillings of that amount didn't count, having being swindled from him "by certaine lewde Christians of the Armenian Nation." In 1615

Tom Coryate arrived at the Moghul court, where he was granted an audience with the emperor. He took advantage of the opportunity to beseech Jahangir for money, to the great embarrassment of the English ambassador, Sir Thomas Roe, who considered it shameful that "one of our Countrey should present himselfe in that beggerly and poore fashion to the King."

Though Tom Coryate may have eaten cheap victuals elsewhere on his travels, I doubt he found any at the Moghul court: for that cuisine was designed to be as rich as possible, with lavish use of cream, fruits, and nuts. These delectable koftas, cooked in a flavorful sauce rich with pistachios and apricots, are a wonderful dish.

1 pound lean ground chicken
2 tablespoons vegetable oil

FOR THE SAUCE
2 tablespoons vegetable oil
½ teaspoon cumin seeds
1 garlic clove, grated
¼-inch piece of ginger, grated
1¼ cups finely chopped onions
1 cup diced tomatoes, fresh or canned
2 tablespoons sour cream
Salt to taste
¼ teaspoon cayenne pepper
¼ teaspoon ground black pepper
½ teaspoon turmeric
1 teaspoon ground coriander seeds
½ teaspoon ground cumin seeds
1 teaspoon garam masala
1 teaspoon kasoori methi
   (dried fenugreek leaves)
10 dried apricots, finely chopped
1 tablespoon raw pistachios
1½ cups water

- In a food processor, mince the onions, garlic, and ginger. Add the fresh coriander, salt, pepper, powdered almonds, egg, and bread, and mince again. Add the ground chicken and process until everything is well blended. Transfer to a mixing bowl. You can prepare this mixture a day ahead of time and let it marinate, covered, in the refrigerator.

- Wetting your hands whenever necessary, make lime-size balls of the ground chicken mixture. You should have about 25 meatballs in all. Warm the oil in a nonstick frying pan over medium heat and gently place some of the meatballs in a single layer. Brown lightly for about 2 minutes per side, turning once or twice and shaking the pan lightly for even cooking. Drain on paper towels and set aside. You can make these up to 3 days ahead of time.

- To make the sauce, warm the oil in a nonstick skillet over medium-high heat and add the cumin seeds, then, after a few seconds, the grated garlic and ginger. Sauté for 30 seconds, then add the onions and sauté for 5 minutes, until the onions are lightly browned. Reduce heat to medium and stir in the tomatoes, mashing them well with the back of your spoon. Cook for 5 minutes, until the moisture evaporates and the oil appears around the edges. Mix in the sour cream and stir-fry for 3 minutes. Add salt, all the spices, the apricots, pistachios, and water, then bring to a boil. Gently slide in the browned meatballs, cover, and reduce the heat to low. Cook for about 30 minutes or until the meatballs are cooked through. Stir occasionally, taking care not to break up the meatballs. This dish tastes better if cooked a day in advance.

• SERVES 3 TO 4 WITH OTHER DISHES

Bhindi Jhinga Masala

Shrimp stir-fried with okra and spices

1 tablespoon anardana
  (dried pomegranate seeds)
10 raw almonds
1 teaspoon fennel seeds
½ teaspoon black mustard seeds
1 teaspoon white poppy seeds
Salt to taste
½ teaspoon ground black pepper
½ teaspoon turmeric
½ teaspoon ground coriander seeds
½ teaspoon ground cumin seeds
½ teaspoon garam masala
2 tablespoons vegetable oil
½ teaspoon cumin seeds
2 garlic cloves, finely chopped
1 hot green chili, thinly sliced
1¼ cups thinly sliced onions
½ cup diced tomatoes, fresh or canned
1 pound small fresh okra, washed,
  ends trimmed, and halved

 Muslims believe that the Shab-e-Barat or "night of record," is the time of year when the sins and virtues of humanity are recorded in heaven. People fast all day and in the evening eat halwa, a sweet made with flour, clarified butter, sugar, almonds, and raisins. Homes and ancestral tombs are illuminated with tiny clay lamps. The names of deceased family members are recited, along with prayers for their well-being in the next world. Emperor Jahangir, never very devout, celebrated the event in his own inimitable manner:

I held the celebration in one of the pavilions occupied by Nur Jahan Begam in the middle of a large lake. The amirs and intimates were invited to the assembly arranged by the begam and I ordered wine bowls and all sorts of intoxicants given to whoever wished. Many chose wine bowls. . . . All sorts of roasted meats and fruits were placed before everyone as relishes. It was a really good party. As night fell . . . all the torches and lanterns were reflected in the water and made it look as though the entire surface of the water was a field of flame.

Jahangir, who was very fond of seafood, would have enjoyed this shrimp dish at his banquet. I have cooked the shrimp with fresh okra in a sautéed onion–tomato–nut sauce. You can make the recipe without the shrimp for an all-vegetarian dish, or you can omit the okra and double the quantity of shrimp instead. Since the dish has no sauce, it would go well with an Indian bread and Paneer Makhani Masala (cottage cheese, cashews, and mushrooms in a creamy, buttery tomato sauce, page 95).

½ pound raw jumbo shrimp, about 20, peeled, deveined, and washed
1 tablespoon heavy cream
1 tablespoon lemon juice
2 tablespoons chopped fresh coriander leaves

- In a clean coffee or spice grinder, powder the dried pomegranate seeds, almonds, fennel seeds, mustard seeds, and poppy seeds. Transfer to a small bowl and mix in the salt, black pepper, turmeric, ground coriander, ground cumin seeds, and the garam masala. Set aside.
- Warm the oil in a nonstick skillet over medium-high heat. Add the cumin seeds and, after a few seconds, the chopped garlic and green chili. Sauté for about 30 seconds, then stir in the onions and sauté, stirring, for about 5 minutes. Reduce heat to medium and add the tomatoes, mashing with the back of your spoon; cook for 5 minutes. Add all the powdered spices and cook for 1 minute. Gently stir in the okra, then cover, reduce heat to medium-low, and cook for 20 minutes, stirring occasionally.
- Now mix in the shrimp, cover, and cook again for 10 minutes. Stir very gently so as not to break the okra. When the shrimp and okra are cooked through, turn off the heat and gently fold in the cream, lemon juice, and fresh coriander leaves. The sauce should be cooked off when done.
  - SERVES 3 TO 4 WITH OTHER DISHES

Machali ke Tikke

**Fish fillets marinated in yogurt, nuts, and spices,
grilled on the barbecue**

When I lift the veil from my face, a cry rises from the rose; if
I put the comb to my tress, a moan comes forth from the
hyacinth.

When I pass through the garden in such beauty and per-
fection, a cry of "blessed" arises from the nightingale's souls.

—*Empress Nur Jahan, seventeenth century*

1 pound thick-cut salmon fillet or
  other firm-fleshed fish

Salt to taste

1 tablespoon lemon juice

½ cup plain yogurt, not low-fat

1 garlic clove, grated

¼-inch piece of ginger, grated

¼ teaspoon ground black pepper

¼ teaspoon ground coriander seeds

¼ teaspoon ground cumin seeds

¼ teaspoon garam masala

Tiny pinch of saffron (optional)

½ teaspoon kasoori methi
  (dried fenugreek leaves)

1 teaspoon melted butter

5 raw almonds

5 raw cashews

1 teaspoon desiccated
  unsweetened coconut

10 raw pistachios

1 teaspoon whole fennel seeds

3 tablespoons plain bread crumbs

Lemon juice to taste

Nur Jahan had no doubts about her own charms,
and why should she? Ravishingly beautiful, she
was an accomplished artist and architect, renowned poet, and famous hunter. As if this were not
enough, she was also a very successful businesswoman who
made a fortune in trade. She was married to Emperor
Jahangir, who was so deeply in love with his queen that the
English ambassador, Sir Thomas Roe, wrote that the king's
wife "governs him, and wynds him up at her pleasure." Her
influence was so great in the Moghul administration that
Jahangir made no decision without consulting her first. The
emperor's other wives did not share his fascination with Nur
Jahan; his second wife, Jodh Bai, was a bitter rival. When
Nur Jahan lovingly told Jahangir that his breath was sweeter
than other men's, Jodh Bai retorted that only someone who
had known many men intimately would be able to tell the
difference.

Of all Nur Jahan's talents, the one that endeared her most
to the emperor was her culinary skill. "Since I am very fond
of fish, all sorts of good fish are brought to me," said Jahangir,
a renowned gourmet. Nur Jahan constantly invented new
ways to serve fish for Jahangir, and today, four hundred years
later, many of the best-known dishes of Moghul cuisine are

still attributed to her. If she had served these fish tikkas, rich with spices, nuts, and saffron, even Jodh Bai would have conceded defeat.

- Wash the fish well and dry with paper towels. Lay it skin side down in a single layer in a large dish and sprinkle with salt and lemon juice. Set aside for 15 minutes. Line a fine mesh sieve with a double layer of cheesecloth or a coffee filter, set over a bowl, and pour in the yogurt. Let it drain for 15 minutes or longer.
- Scrape the yogurt into a small bowl. Add the grated garlic, ginger, black pepper, ground coriander, ground cumin, garam masala, saffron (if using), dried fenugreek leaves, and butter. Mix well. In a clean coffee or spice grinder, powder the almonds, cashews, coconut, pistachios, and fennel seeds. Mix into the spiced yogurt.
- Drain the liquid accumulated at the bottom of the fillets, then smear the spiced yogurt marinade all over the fleshy side of the fish. Cover and marinate in the refrigerator for at least 2 hours. Just before grilling, sprinkle the bread crumbs all over the fish and pat gently to hold in place.
- When ready to grill, place the fish skin side down in a covered barbecue over medium heat. Grill until the bottom is well cooked, about 10 minutes. Flip carefully and cook for another 10 minutes or until it is cooked through. Remove to a platter and sprinkle with lemon juice. Split the fillet down the center and serve.

  - SERVES 2

Khumani Kabab

Ground lamb kababs with sautéed onions, almonds, and spices,
stuffed with dried apricots and cottage cheese

1 pound lean ground lamb
2 tablespoons vegetable oil
½ teaspoon cumin seeds
1¼ cups chopped onions
4 garlic cloves, chopped
1-inch piece of ginger, chopped
15 raw almonds
1 large egg
1 slice of bread, broken up
1 teaspoon ground coriander seeds
1 teaspoon ground cumin seeds
1 tablespoon whole fennel seeds
1 teaspoon garam masala
¼ teaspoon ground black pepper
Salt to taste

FOR THE STUFFING
10 dried apricots, finely chopped
½ cup grated or crumbled paneer
(cottage cheese)
Salt to taste
¼ teaspoon roasted ground
cumin seeds
¼ teaspoon ground cardamom seeds
1 tablespoon sour cream
1 cup plain bread crumbs
Lemon juice to taste

François Bernier, personal physician to Emperor Aurangzeb, had been told that in Kashmir one could find "the finest brunettes in all *Indies,* justly renowned for their fine and slender shapes." But when Monsieur Bernier traveled to Kashmir, his enjoyment of all this loveliness was hampered by the women's veils. Ever resourceful, Bernier enlisted the aid of an elderly Kashmiri who was teaching him Persian. Bearing gift baskets loaded with delicacies, the pair visited every household known to have eligible daughters. The old man announced that his guest was a "kinsman lately arrived from *Persia,* rich and eager to marry." Many a pleasant dalliance later, Bernier announced that there was "left no doubt on my mind that there were as handsome faces in *Kachemire* as in any part of *Europe.*"

François Bernier didn't marry any of the Kashmiri damsels, which was his loss. He would have discovered that the beauty of Kashmiri women extends to their cooking; this dish from Kashmir is an example of the culinary pleasures he missed out on: ground lamb is flavored with nuts and spices, stuffed with creamy cottage cheese and chopped dried apricots, rolled in bread crumbs, and then grilled. The bread crumbs form a delicious crust on the outside while the meat remains moist inside. You can substitute chopped hard-boiled eggs or sautéed mushrooms for the dried apricots and paneer (cottage cheese). Serve with lettuce and tomatoes in a hamburger bun, topped with a little chutney.

- Wrap the ground lamb in 3 layers of paper towels to absorb the juices and set aside. Warm the oil in a nonstick skillet on high heat. Add the cumin seeds and, after a few seconds, the chopped onions, garlic, ginger, and almonds. Sauté, stirring frequently, for about 4 minutes, until lightly browned. Cool slightly and transfer to a food processor, leaving behind as much oil as possible. Mince well, then add the egg, bread, all the spices, and salt. Whirl to mix again, then add the ground lamb. Process until everything is well blended, then transfer to a bowl. Cover and refrigerate for an hour.

- To prepare the stuffing, combine all ingredients except the bread crumbs and lemon juice and mix well. To make the kababs, divide the lamb mixture into 12 equal-size balls, flattening each slightly. Divide the stuffing into 6 equal portions and place in the center of 6 of the lamb patties. Now cover with the remaining patties and press the edges together to seal. Spread the bread crumbs in a flat dish and roll the stuffed lamb patties through, patting gently to hold the bread crumbs in place. Up to this point, you can make the kababs ahead of time and keep them covered in the refrigerator until cooking.

- You can either grill the patties in a covered barbecue on low heat for 15 to 20 minutes, turning occasionally, or shallow-fry in a stovetop skillet on low heat until done to your liking. If you wish, brush each side of the patties lightly with oil or butter about 5 minutes before they are done grilling. Serve with a sprinkling of lemon juice.

- MAKES 6 KABABS

Dhaniwal Roghan Josh

Lamb cooked with onions, yogurt, almonds, and fresh coriander

 Every important occasion in Kashmir is celebrated with a *mishani*, a meal that traditionally consists of seven dishes—all of them made from lamb. It includes roast leg of lamb; cubes of lamb spiced with cardamom, cumin seeds, and cinnamon; grilled lamb kababs;

2 tablespoons vegetable oil
½ teaspoon cumin seeds
1¼ cups chopped onions
2 garlic cloves, chopped
½-inch piece of ginger, chopped

10 raw almonds

1 cup plain yogurt, not low-fat

1 cup diced tomatoes, fresh or canned

1 tablespoon whole fennel seeds

10 whole cardamom

Salt to taste

½ teaspoon paprika

¼ teaspoon ground black pepper

1 teaspoon ground coriander seeds

½ teaspoon garam masala

*2 pounds bone-in lamb, washed and
    drained, cut into 2-inch cubes*

1 bay leaf

1 whole cardamom

1 whole clove

½-inch cinnamon stick

½ cup water

*1 cup packed fresh coriander leaves
    and tender upper stems,
    finely chopped*

spiced lamb liver; lamb kidneys; shoulder of lamb; and delicate lamb meatballs pounded with yogurt and spices. At a Kashmiri wedding, the bride's family welcomes the groom by serving a mishani to all the wedding guests. The following day, when the bride goes to her husband's home, his family serves a second mishani to mark the occasion.

The bride knows her new family has accepted her when they reveal their most closely guarded secret: the family recipe for ver. This is a spice mixture that Kashmiris use in all their food, giving it a characteristic flavor and red color. Ver is usually a combination of Kashmiri red chilies, turmeric, coriander, dried ginger, cumin, cloves, and cardamom. Muslims add garlic and onions, while Hindus use asafetida and fenugreek seeds. The spices are ground, shaped into small discs with a hole in the center, and left to dry for a few days; these cakes are then strung together and suspended from the ceiling. Pieces are broken off and sprinkled over food as it cooks.

In this recipe, a variation of the classic Kashmiri Roghan Josh, I have combined the fresh fragrance of coriander with the richness of lamb and almonds. Since ver is not readily available, all the spices are added separately to achieve much the same taste. I find that Hungarian paprika is a good substitute for Kashmiri chilies and colors the food just the right shade of red. This dish is best made with bone-in meat, as it is stewed for a long time, but if you find that to be a problem you can substitute boneless lamb. If you would rather not serve seven lamb dishes all at once, pair Dhaniwal Roghan Josh with Kashmiri Dum Alu (baby potatoes served in a sautéed onion, tomato, and yogurt sauce, page 90).

- Warm the oil in a nonstick skillet over medium-high heat, then add the cumin seeds. After a few seconds, add the chopped onions, garlic, ginger, and almonds. Sauté, stirring, for about 5 minutes, until lightly browned. Allow to cool slightly, then lift them out of the oil, leaving behind as much oil as possible. Set the skillet aside; you will need it again later.

- In a food processor or blender, combine the sautéed onions, garlic, ginger, and almonds with the yogurt and tomatoes and mince well. In a clean coffee or spice grinder, powder the whole fennel seeds and cardamom pods. Add to the minced onions in the food processor along with the salt, paprika, black pepper, ground coriander seeds, and garam masala. Whirl again to mix, then transfer to a large mixing bowl. Toss in the pieces of lamb and coat with the marinade. At this point, you can either cover and refrigerate for a day, or you can proceed with cooking.

- Warm the leftover oil in the skillet over medium-high heat and add the bay leaf, whole cardamom, clove, and cinnamon stick. After a few seconds, add the lamb and all its marinade. Stir-fry for about 10 minutes, until the sauce browns lightly, then mix in the water. You can pressure-cook the meat at this point for quicker results, or continue cooking in the skillet until it is tender.

- If pressure-cooking: transfer the meat and all its sauce to a pressure cooker and bring to full pressure over high heat. Immediately reduce the heat to low and cook for 20 minutes. Switch off the heat and let the pressure dissipate before opening the pan. On medium-high heat, boil off some of the liquid, stirring constantly, which will take about 5 minutes. The sauce should be fairly thick when the dish is done.

- If cooking in the skillet: make sure to add more water (about 1 cup in all) and stir occasionally to prevent burning. Cook on low heat for about 1½ hours, or until the meat is tender.

- Add the fresh coriander just before you take the lamb off the heat, fold gently into the sauce, and serve. You can make this dish up to 2 days ahead of time.

  - SERVES 3 TO 4 WITH OTHER DISHES

Mookal

Cooked shredded lamb stir-fried with onions, yogurt, and spices

1 pound boneless lamb

3 cups water

2 tablespoons vegetable oil

1 bay leaf

1 whole cardamom

1 whole clove

½-inch cinnamon stick

1 large plus 1 medium onion,
  finely chopped separately

2 garlic cloves, finely chopped

3 tablespoons plain yogurt,
  not low-fat

Salt to taste

¼ to ½ teaspoon cayenne pepper

½ teaspoon turmeric

1 teaspoon ground coriander seeds

¼-inch piece of ginger, grated

½ teaspoon garam masala

1 cup loosely packed fresh coriander
  leaves, washed and finely
  chopped

 The day had come for Princess Sanyogita to choose her husband. All the great Rajput princes were assembled, eager to be picked by the beautiful princess. But the only man she truly desired, Prithvi Raj Chauhan, was not there. Her father, King Jaichand, detested Prithvi Raj, the ruler of the rival kingdom of Ajmer, and refused to let Sanyogita marry him. To show his contempt, the king had a mannequin of Prithvi Raj made and placed in the position by the door normally occupied by a humble doorman. When it was time for the princess to indicate her choice by hanging a garland of flowers around the neck of her future husband, she walked past the ranks of Rajput nobles and placed the garland on the mannequin. Prithvi Raj, who had been observing from a hiding place, immediately sprang forward and lifted Sanyogita onto his horse. Together they galloped away to the safety of his kingdom, where they were married.

The Rajputs are descendants of Central Asian migrants who came to India long after the Aryans, possibly in the fourth or fifth century. They were eventually assimilated into Hindu society, but retain some old tribal customs. At a Rajput wedding, the groom rides on horseback to his bride's home, sword at his side, just as Prithvi Raj did centuries ago. Rajput food also provides evidence of non-Hindu origins: the cuisine includes many chicken, lamb, and even pork dishes.

In this unusual dish from Rajasthan, the lamb is first cooked in water until tender, then shredded and stir-fried with onions, spices, and yogurt until dry and lightly browned. My cousin Atul Trivedi, a gourmet cook who lives in Rajasthan, gave this recipe to me, and I have never come across a more delectable way to prepare lamb. I like to serve it with Indian bread and Chane ki Dal Laukiwali (yellow split peas cooked with zucchini, tomatoes, and spices, page 94).

- In a heavy-bottomed pan or pressure cooker, cook the lamb in the water, covered until very tender. If pressure cooking, it will take about 15 minutes; if cooking in a saucepan, it should take about 1 hour. Lift the lamb out of the broth and cool, reserving the broth. Using a sharp knife, remove any fat from the lamb and cut the meat into thin long shreds. Set aside.

- Warm the oil in a nonstick skillet over medium-high heat and add the bay leaf, cardamom, clove, and cinnamon. After a few seconds, add the large chopped onion and half of the chopped garlic. Sauté for about 10 minutes, until the onions are soft and lightly browned.

- Meanwhile, combine the yogurt in a bowl with the remaining garlic, salt, cayenne, turmeric, ground coriander seeds, and grated ginger. Reduce the heat under the skillet to medium and add the spiced yogurt. Stir constantly for 5 minutes, until all the moisture has evaporated and the oil appears around the edges.

- Add the lamb and ½ cup of the reserved broth to the skillet. Stir-fry uncovered on medium heat for 5 minutes. Mix in the medium chopped onion and cook uncovered for 10 minutes, stirring occasionally. Add the garam masala and the fresh coriander and stir-fry for another 5 minutes, until the oil appears again and the lamb has browned lightly. There should be no sauce left at the end of cooking. You can make this dish up to 3 days ahead of time.

- SERVES 3 TO 4 WITH OTHER DISHES

Saag Kofte

Spicy meatballs served in a sautéed spinach and yogurt sauce

FOR THE KOFTAS (MEATBALLS)

1 pound lean ground lamb

1 cup fresh coriander leaves and
    tender upper stems, washed and
    well drained

1 garlic clove, chopped

¼-inch piece of ginger, chopped

Salt to taste

¼ teaspoon ground black pepper

½ teaspoon garam masala

1 teaspoon fennel seeds

1 egg

2 slices of white bread, broken up

2 to 3 tablespoons vegetable oil

FOR THE SPINACH SAUCE

8 ounces fresh spinach leaves,
    trimmed

1¾ cups water

2 tablespoons vegetable oil

½ teaspoon cumin seeds

¼ teaspoon cayenne pepper

½ teaspoon turmeric

½ teaspoon ground coriander seeds

½ teaspoon ground cumin seeds

Salt to taste

1 garlic clove, grated

¼-inch piece of ginger, grated

4 tablespoons plain yogurt, not low-
    fat, beaten briefly with a spoon

½ teaspoon garam masala

"Before meals it is right to wash your hands openly, even though you have no need to do so, in order that those who dip their fingers in the same dish as yourself may know for certain that you have cleaned them." This advice was offered by Giovanni della Casa to sixteenth-century diners who were sharing a platter of food with other guests, as was the custom in medieval Europe.

Table manners take on added importance when several people eat from the same plate. It is still the tradition in Kashmir for food to be served in *tramis*, large plates around which four people sit. Before the meal begins, attendants bring pitchers of water and basins so diners can wash their hands. Then the tramis are brought in and uncovered. In their center is a mound of rice divided into quarters by four skewers of grilled meat. Each section contains an assortment of meats. The diners carefully pick and eat portions of rice and meat with their fingertips. Elaborate rules of etiquette govern each person's territory.

This is a good dish to eat with your fingers; whether you want to share a plate with your guests is up to you. This recipe combines two popular Kashmiri dishes: koftas, meatballs cooked in a yogurt-based sauce, and saag, made with spicy spinach greens. You can also serve the koftas in any other sauce of your choice from this book. The spinach can be cooked with stir-fried cubes of paneer (cottage cheese) for an all-vegetarian dish.

- Wrap the lamb in 3 layers of paper towels to absorb all the juices. Set aside. In a food processor, mince the fresh coriander, garlic, and ginger. Add the salt, pepper, garam masala, fennel seeds, egg, and bread. Whirl to mix, then add the ground lamb. Process until everything is well mixed with the lamb. Transfer to a large mixing bowl.

- Wetting your hands lightly whenever necessary, make small walnut-size meatballs from the lamb mixture. Warm the oil in a nonstick frying pan over medium heat, and in small batches lightly brown the meatballs on all sides for a few minutes. The object here is not to cook them but to seal in the flavor. Drain on paper towels.

- In a microwave-safe bowl, combine the spinach with ¼ cup of water, cover tightly with plastic wrap, and microwave on high for 6 minutes. (You can also cook the spinach in a saucepan with water until it is tender.) Lift the spinach out of its cooking liquid and mash it well with a fork on a chopping board, then transfer to a small bowl.

- Warm the oil in a nonstick skillet over medium heat. Add the cumin seeds and, after a few seconds, the cayenne pepper, turmeric, ground coriander seeds, ground cumin seeds, and salt. As soon as the mixture starts foaming—this will take just a few seconds—add the grated garlic and ginger. Stir to mix, then add the yogurt. Stir continuously for 5 minutes, until the moisture has evaporated and the oil appears on the edges.

- Add the spinach and 1½ cups water to the skillet. Mix well, then stir in the meatballs. Cover and bring to a boil. Reduce the heat to low and cook for 30 minutes, stirring once in a while. The sauce should be quite thick and the meatballs cooked through. Mix in the garam masala and serve. You can make this dish up to 3 days ahead of time.

- SERVES 3 TO 4 WITH OTHER DISHES

Keema Guchchi

Portobello mushrooms stuffed with spicy ground lamb and peas

1 pound lean ground lamb
6 small portobello mushrooms
2 tablespoons vegetable oil
1 teaspoon whole fennel seeds
2 garlic cloves, grated
½-inch piece of ginger, grated
1 cup finely chopped onions
Salt to taste
1 teaspoon ground coriander seeds
½ teaspoon ground cumin seeds
½ teaspoon turmeric
¼ to ½ teaspoon Kashmiri chili
  powder or ¼ teaspoon paprika
  plus ¼ teaspoon ground black
  pepper
½ teaspoon garam masala
1 cup plain yogurt, not low-fat
1 cup frozen peas

 To the Moghuls, Kashmir was the most beautiful place in the world. Emperor Jahangir's love for Kashmir shines through in his lyrical description of a meadow:

> What can one write in praise of it? As far as the eye could see, there were all sorts of flowers in bloom, and flowing through the midst of the greenery and flowers were streams of the purest water. You'd think it was a picture drawn by the master painter of destiny. Seeing it caused the bud of the heart to burst into blossom.

In these beautiful Kashmiri pastures, morel mushrooms grow plentifully, the only place in India where they are found. They are prized for their earthy flavor and musky aroma and used in many delectable ways in Kashmiri cooking.

In this recipe I have used portobello mushrooms, which are easier to find than morel mushrooms. The ground lamb stuffing is cooked in typical Kashmiri fashion with fennel seeds and yogurt. If you have leftover ground lamb mixture, freeze for later use or eat with rice or bread. You can also use it to stuff other vegetables such as tomatoes, eggplant, or sweet green peppers. I find it makes great samosas when encased in a puff pastry shell and baked.

- In a fine mesh sieve, wash the lamb under running water, breaking up all the lumps. Set aside to drain. Cut off the muddy ends from the stems of the mushrooms and wash mushrooms quickly under running water. Slice off the stems at the base, keeping the mushroom caps intact. Set the caps aside and coarsely chop the stems.

- Warm the oil in a heavy-bottomed skillet over medium-high heat, then add the fennel seeds and, after a few seconds, the grated garlic and ginger. Sauté for 30 seconds, then mix in the chopped onions. Sauté, stirring occasionally for about 5 minutes, until lightly browned. Add the chopped mushroom stems and cook for 2 minutes, then add and stir-fry the drained minced lamb for about 8 minutes, until all liquid has evaporated and oil appears around the edges. Add salt and all the spices and cook for 1 minute. Stirring constantly, add the yogurt to the skillet; then, after a minute, when it has all been incorporated, stir in the peas. Cover and bring to a boil. Reduce the heat to medium-low and cook for 30 minutes, stirring occasionally. The sauce should be very thick (almost dry) and clinging to the meat when the dish is done. Cool to room temperature. You can prepare up to 3 days ahead of time and fill the mushroom caps just before baking.
- Preheat the oven to 400°F. In an ungreased ovenproof dish, stuff the reserved mushroom caps generously with the ground lamb mixture and bake uncovered for 15 to 20 minutes. You can stuff a variety of other vegetables—such as sweet peppers, tomatoes, or eggplant—with this ground meat mixture (adjust baking times accordingly).

- SERVES 3 TO 4

Gosht Yakhni Biryani

Fennel-scented lamb curry, layered and baked with rice

 When Sir Thomas Roe, English Ambassador at the Moghul Court, was invited to dinner by Asaf Khan (brother of Empress Nur Jahan and the grandest of all nobles at Emperor Jahangir's court) his chaplain, the Reverend Edward Terry, described the meal:

FOR THE SAUCE

1 pound bone-in lamb, cut into
*   chunks, washed*

1½ cups water

1 whole clove

1 whole cardamom

½-inch cinnamon stick

1 bay leaf

Salt to taste

¼ teaspoon ground black pepper

½ cup plain yogurt, not low-fat

½ teaspoon dried powdered ginger
   (optional)

1 tablespoon fennel seeds,
   powdered fine

½ teaspoon garam masala

¼ teaspoon cayenne pepper

2 tablespoons chopped fresh
   coriander leaves

FOR THE RICE

1 cup Basmati rice, washed

1 cup 2% milk

1 whole cardamom

1 whole clove

½-inch cinnamon stick

1 bay leaf

Salt to taste

FOR THE GARNISH

2 tablespoons vegetable oil

1 cup thinly sliced onions

10 raw almonds

1 tablespoon golden raisins

1 hard-boiled egg (optional)

The Asaph Chan entertained my Lord Ambassador in a very spacious and very beautiful tent. . . . The Ambassador had more dishes by ten, and I less by ten, than our entertainer had; yet for my part I had fifty dishes. They were all set before us at once . . . so that I tasted of all set before me, and of most did but taste, though all of them tasted very well.

Now of the provision itself; for our larger dishes, they were filled with rice . . . ; and this rice was presented to us, some of it white, in its own proper colour, some of it made yellow with saffron, some of it was made green, and some of it put into a purple colour; but by what ingredient I know not; but this I am sure, that it all tasted very well: And with rice thus ordered, several of our dishes were furnished; and very many more of them with flesh of several kinds, and with hens and other sorts of fowl cut in pieces.

At this entertainment we sat long, and much longer than we could with ease cross-legged; but all considered, our feast in that place was better than Apicius, that famous Epicure of Rome, . . . could have made with all provisions had from the earth, air, and sea.

Asaf Khan's banquet centered on elaborate rice biryanis, as was the custom in Moghul times; Kashmiri banquets, still strongly influenced by Moghul customs, also give pride of place to a biryani. In this Kashmiri biryani I have first cooked the lamb curry, then layered it with rice and nuts to create a fragrant, delicate dish. It would go well with Kashmiri Dum Alu (baby potatoes served in a sautéed onion, tomato, and yogurt sauce, page 90) or Dhaniwal Roghan Josh (lamb cooked with onions, yogurt, almonds, and fresh coriander, page 123).

- In a pressure cooker, combine the lamb, water, whole clove, cardamom, cinnamon, bay leaf, salt, and pepper. Bring to full pressure over high heat. Immediately reduce the heat to medium-low and cook for 15 minutes. Let it cool a little before you open the cooker. The lamb should be just tender, not falling off the bone. (You can also cook the lamb in a saucepan with the water and spices, cooking it longer and with more water.) You should be left with about 1¼ cups of sauce when the curry is done.

- Lift the lamb out of the broth and remove the fat and bones. Divide the meat into 1-inch pieces and set aside in a small bowl. Whisk the yogurt, ginger if using, powdered fennel seeds, garam masala, and cayenne pepper into the broth. Bring back to a boil over medium heat, stirring to prevent the yogurt from curdling. Add the lamb, cover, and cook on medium-low heat for 15 minutes. Remove from the heat and add the chopped fresh coriander leaves.

- In a heavy-bottomed pan, combine all the ingredients for the rice. Cover and bring to a boil, then immediately reduce heat to low and cook for 10 minutes. The rice should have absorbed all the milk by now. Stir gently with a slotted spoon.

- Warm the oil in a small nonstick frying pan over medium-high heat. Add the sliced onions, almonds, and raisins. Stir-fry for 5 minutes, until lightly browned. Drain on paper towels. Peel the egg, if using, and divide into 8 pieces.

- To assemble the biryani, preheat the oven to 250°F. Take a square ovenproof dish and spread in half the rice. Now lift out the lamb with a slotted spoon and arrange over the rice. Spread the remaining rice on top and drizzle all the curry sauce over. Arrange the fried onions, almonds, raisins, and boiled egg evenly on top. Cover tightly with foil and bake for 45 minutes. Mix the biryani gently with a spoon and serve. You can make this biryani up to 3 days ahead of time.

  - SERVES 3 TO 4 WITH OTHER DISHES

Shahi Kofte ki Biryani

Rice layered and baked with a spicy meatball curry

2 cups Basmati rice, washed

1 cup water

½ cup 2% milk

1 bay leaf

1 whole clove

1 whole cardamom

½-inch cinnamon stick

Salt to taste

1 recipe Shahi Kofte (page 116)

2 tablespoons chopped fresh mint

*2 tablespoons chopped fresh
   coriander leaves*

2 tablespoons vegetable oil

1 cup thinly sliced onions

The noblest women in the land were playing at being shopkeepers for a day. It was the *Meena Bazaar:* a marketplace set up in the royal palace to celebrate the New Year. Aristocratic ladies sold brocades, silks, and jewelry from stalls, amid which the king and his queens strolled looking for bargains. Haggling was fierce; the king disputed every penny demanded, and the sellers were equally adamant. Finally a bargain was struck. The king promptly paid the amount settled upon, but dropped, as if by accident, gold coins instead of the silver requested.

The Meena Bazaar was the only occasion when flirtations were sanctioned and women went unveiled at the Moghul court. It was at such a gathering on New Year's day in 1611 that Emperor Jahangir's eye fell upon the exquisite beauty of Mihrunnisa, lady-in-waiting to the Queen Mother. He was so captivated that he immediately resolved to marry her, and they were wed within two months. Jahangir gave his queen the title "Nur Jahan"—Light of the World—and remained deeply devoted to her for the rest of his life.

Great celebrations and feasts, at which enormous platters of biryani and pulaos were served, marked the wedding of Jahangir and Nur Jahan. To the uninitiated, these dishes may appear similar, but connoisseurs hotly debate their merits. A biryani is an elaborate preparation of meat curry layered with partially cooked rice, garnished with fried onions, nuts, and sliced boiled eggs. The rice softens as it absorbs sauce and flavor from the meat curry. Pulaos are simpler, mildly spiced dishes––rice cooked with meat or vegetables. Those who champion the superiority of pulao claim that biryanis are overspiced and lack the subtle flavors of a well-cooked pulao.

This book contains recipes for both biryanis and pulaos, and I will let you be the judge of which is better. You can start with this biryani, which is easily made if you have some leftover Shahi Kofte (chicken balls cooked in a sauce of tomatoes, onions, and sour cream with pistachios and apricots, page 116). You can also make the koftas ahead and assemble the biryani later.

- In a heavy-bottomed pan, combine the rice, water, milk, bay leaf, clove, cardamom, cinnamon, and salt. Bring to a boil, then immediately reduce the heat to low, cover, and cook for 10 minutes. Let it sit covered for 5 minutes after cooking, then remove and discard the whole spices.
- Preheat the oven to 250°F. Take a large flat ovenproof dish and spread a thin layer of rice at the bottom. Lift half the meatballs out of their sauce and place them evenly over the rice. Now layer on the remaining rice and meatballs. Drizzle the sauce over and spread on the chopped mint and coriander. Cover the dish tightly with foil and bake for 45 minutes.
- Meanwhile, warm the oil in a nonstick frying pan over medium-high heat. Sauté the onions until golden brown, 8 to 10 minutes. When the biryani is done, sprinkle the fried onions on top and mix in gently with a fork.
  - SERVES 3 TO 4 WITH OTHER DISHES

Aam ki Kulfi

Ice cream made with thickened, sweetened milk, flavored with mangoes and pistachios

 Horse-drawn carriages sped through the night without stopping. Every second of delay meant losing more of the precious cargo—ice for the Moghul emperor's table. The only source of ice during the scorching northern Indian summer was several hundred miles away from Delhi, on the Himalayan peaks that remained snowbound all year. A relay of boats and horses carried ice to

6 cups whole milk

13-ounce can evaporated milk

½ cup sugar

Tiny pinch of saffron

15 whole cardamom

¼ cup raw pistachios

1 cup sweetened canned mango pulp

the royal palace every day, where it was used for sherbets and frozen desserts.

A favorite dessert of the Moghuls was kulfi—ice cream made with thickened, sweetened milk. A recipe from 1590 describes how it was made in Emperor Akbar's kitchen: a mixture of condensed milk, pistachio nuts, and saffron was filled in conical metal containers, whose lids were sealed with dough. These containers were packed in large, ice-filled earthenware vats. This recipe is so good that it has remained unchanged over the centuries, and in India you can still buy traditional kulfi. Connoisseurs swear that authentic kulfi has to be frozen in earthenware vats, but you will probably find a freezer more convenient. Traditional conical kulfi containers are widely available in Indian stores, but you can substitute an ice tray. In this recipe I have mixed mango pulp into the thickened milk, which adds its own wonderful flavor. You can also make this dessert without the mango.

- In a very large microwave-safe bowl, microwave the milk uncovered on high for 15 minutes. Stir well, scraping down sides. Cook again for 15 minutes, then repeat stirring and scraping. Cook for another 15 minutes, stir and scrape again, then cook for a final 10 minutes. Add the evaporated milk and sugar and mix well. Cook for 10 minutes on high, then scrape down the sides of the bowl. Add the saffron.
- Pound the cardamom in a mortar a few times to crack the skins. Discard skins and reserve seeds. Put the seeds back in the mortar and powder coarsely. (You can also do this with two sheets of wax paper and a rolling pin.)
- Coarsely crush the pistachios or pulse a few times in a food processor. Add the pistachios and cardamom to the thickened milk. Let it cool for 10 minutes before you add the mango pulp. Stir well to mix, then pour into a kulfi container or ice cube tray. Freeze overnight. Remove the ice cream and serve.

- SERVES 6

Decline of the Moghul Empire: Flowering of Regional Cuisines

It was deplorably careless of the Moghul Empire to mislay its ruler. Jahandar Shah, dissolute grandson of the mighty Emperor Aurangzeb, was the unfortunate occupant of the throne subjected to this indignity in 1711. Remembered today mostly for debauchery, his favorite pastime was to carouse in the taverns of Delhi with his mistress Lal Kunwar. Once, when the two were returning from a late-night jaunt, he fell into a drunken stupor in the coach. On reaching the palace, his mistress staggered off to bed, too inebriated to realize she was alone. The coachman did not notice that his master was still sleeping in the coach and left after parking the vehicle. Panic ensued the next morning when the emperor was nowhere to be found. Lal Kunwar, sure that her paramour had been abducted, erupted into loud wails and could not be consoled. Finally, after a thorough search, Jahandar Shah was found slumbering peacefully in the coach house. In retrospect, this absurd little farce marked the beginning of the end for the Moghul Empire—a kingdom that loses its own monarch is unlikely to survive long.

Cracks in the foundation of the empire had become visible even while Aurangzeb was alive. His oppression of Hindus, which reversed the tradition of

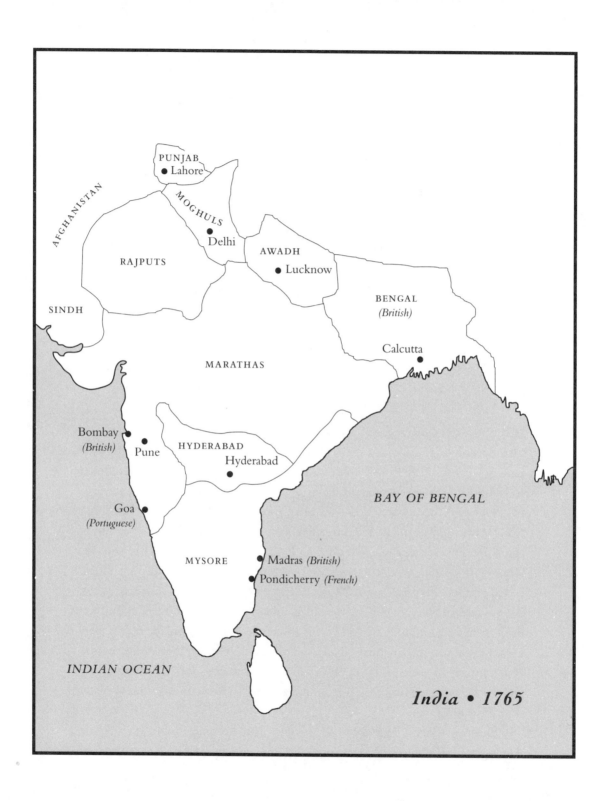

India • 1765

religious toleration established by Akbar, had led to several rebellions. The most successful was that of the Marathas, the hardy natives of Maharashtra in southwestern India; Shivaji, the rebel leader, is still revered for the élan with which he defied the Moghuls. Aurangzeb spent his last two decades in futile attempts to stamp out the rebellion, almost bankrupting the Moghul treasury in the process. After Aurangzeb's death, the Marathas threw off Moghul rule, founded an independent kingdom, and created an army that threatened the imperial capital of Delhi itself.

The Maratha court reflected the ascetic tastes of its ruler. Shivaji disdained the extravagance of the Moghul palaces and ate only one meal a day. The simplicity of Maharashtrian food also contrasts with the elaborate preparations of the Moghuls. Maharashtrian banquets are served in *thalis*—circular metal platters. Convention dictates the arrangement of food: the left half is reserved for condiments, relishes, pickles, pappadums, and salads. On the right side are small bowls of curries, vegetable stir-fries, and sweets. Just below the center is a small mound of steaming white rice, topped with a dollop of yellow dal (lentils). Within Maharashtra there are regional variations in food. Food eaten by Brahmins, the priestly caste, is simple, vegetarian, and sparing with spices. Maratha warriors from the city of Kolhapur developed fiery curries with lamb browned in clarified butter and cooked in coconut-based sauces. The coastal fishing villages cooked fish in lots of herbs, green chilies, onions, garlic, and coconut.

The disintegration of the Moghul Empire gathered momentum when the Sikhs wrested control of Punjab. The Sikhs were a small religious group, devotees of the teachings of Guru Nanak, a preacher in fifteenth-century Punjab. The Sikhs remained an obscure, peaceful sect for two centuries, until Moghul persecution drove them to gather a group of volunteers known as the Khalsa to defend their faith. This small company of soldiers grew into a formidable force capable of defeating the best armies that the Moghuls could muster. By the early eighteenth century, the Moghul administration retained only a very tenuous grip on Punjab. The province was plunged into anarchy, for the Sikhs remained disunited, clustering in several independent bands with no central authority. Restoring order took the forcefulness and organizational skills of Ranjit Singh, leader of one of the Sikh clans, who in 1801 made himself ruler of the independent kingdom of Punjab with his capital in the city of Lahore.

Ranjit Singh was a bundle of contradictions. He made himself a king but remained simple and unassuming in his habits. Though illiterate, he possessed a voraciously inquisitive mind. A renowned warrior, he was a warm and kind-hearted man who hated to punish even his enemies and was adored by his subjects. He surrounded himself with beautiful women though he was famously disfigured himself, with one blind eye and a scarred face. "Where were you when God was giving out good looks?" one of his wives is said to have asked him. "Busy seeking power," replied the king.

Ranjit Singh's lusty approach to life bewildered English visitors, who were taken aback by his troupe of dancing girls and choked on the fiery liquor he pressed on his guests. Emily Eden, visiting Punjab with her brother, the governor general of India, did not quite know what to make of the king:

> Another of Runjeet's topics was his constant praise of drinking, and he said he understood that there were books which contained objections to drunkenness, and he thought it better that there should be no books at all, than that they should contain such foolish notions. He is a very drunken old profligate, neither more nor less. Still he has made himself a great king; he has conquered a great many powerful enemies; he is remarkably just in his government; he has disciplined a large army; he hardly ever takes away life, which is wonderful in a despot; and he is excessively beloved by his people.
>
> I certainly should not guess any part of this by looking at him.

The hearty food served at Ranjit Singh's table was that of the Punjabi peasants he grew up with. Most of Punjab is farm country and still yields some of the best wheat, corn, and dairy products in India. All of these form the foundation of Punjabi food. *Saag,* freshly harvested greens cooked in clarified butter, is served with *makki ki roti,* corn flatbread, and dollops of butter on the side. *Paneer ki bhurji* is soft cottage cheese stir-fried with sautéed onions and tomatoes. Chicken and lamb are browned in clarified butter before being cooked in spicy sauces, then topped with cream. *Lobhiya* (black-eyed peas), *rajma* (red kidney beans), or *chole* (chickpeas) are simmered in spicy tomato-based sauces. Desserts such as *kheer* and *phirni,* made with milk and sugar, are rich with cream, raisins, and nuts. Every meal includes *lassi,* a drink made from sweetened yogurt, crushed cardamom seeds, and thick cream or *badaam doodh,* sweetened milk and powdered almonds.

As rebellions sapped the strength of the Moghul Empire, its outlying provinces began to assert their autonomy. Sadat Khan had been appointed governor of the province of Awadh in 1720, at a time when the Moghul emperor's authority was slowly ebbing away. Awadh did not formally secede from the Moghul Empire, and its rulers were always careful to use the title of *Nawab,* meaning viceroy, implying that they ruled in the name of the emperor. But the descendants of Sadat Khan remained free of any control from Delhi and reigned as virtually independent kings for more than a century. The Awadh court in the city of Lucknow was modeled after that of the Moghuls in Delhi, and soon outshone the original. As the eighteenth century wound to a close, the fortunes of the two cities diverged: Lucknow flourished while Delhi sank into a tragic decline from which it took many years to recover.

The glittering court of Awadh offered patronage to artists, musicians, and craftsmen, who led an exodus from Delhi to Lucknow. Among the first to move were the chefs: though good cooking had been valued at the Moghul court, in Awadh it was raised to fine art. They refined the beloved Moghul recipes, creating dishes unique to Awadhi cuisine. Some of the more exotic examples of Awadhi cooking include *mutanjan,* a sweet and spicy lamb and rice pilaf; *zamin doz,* whole fish stuffed with spices and nuts, sealed in an earthen pot and cooked in the ground under live charcoal; *kakori kababs,* boneless leg of lamb minced with spices and thickened milk, grilled on skewers; and *kundan kaliya,* chunks of lamb individually wrapped in edible gold leaf and served in a spicy sauce.

A skilled chef in Awadh was called a *rakabdar* and valued much more than a mere *bawarchi*—a cook who prepared food in large quantities. A rakabdar considered it beneath his dignity to prepare food for big gatherings. Salar Jang, brother-in-law of Nawab Shuja ud Daula, was reputed to pay his rakabdar a salary of twelve hundred rupees a month, more than any cook in Indian history had ever received. Reports of his skill reached the Nawab, who asked to taste some of the pulaos he was famous for. The chef refused the royal command, declaring that he only worked for his employer.

Awadhi chefs were reluctant to cook in large quantities because the presentation of a dish was considered as important as its taste. Dishes were decorated with edible silver and gold foil or dried fruits carved into flowers. The true artistry of a chef was displayed by making dishes that deceived the eye, and no effort was spared in achieving a truly startling effect. An especially famed cook made *khichadi,* a dish usually made from a mixture of rice and lentils, considered peasants' food. But this khichadi was made from pistachio nuts and almonds, with the almonds painstakingly carved into the shape of rice grains and the pistachios made to look like lentils. Then there was rice pulao in which each rice grain resembled a pomegranate seed—half of each grain was dyed red, with the remainder left white. Another pulao was made from rice colored to look like different gems, so that it appeared to be a platter of glittering jewels. The famed chef Pir Ali created sweets that seemed to be fresh pomegranates, but were in fact made of sugar and filled with imitation seeds fashioned from almonds covered with dried pear juice. Great skill was required to cook vegetables while leaving them unblemished: pumpkins and gourds cooked in spicy sauces arrived on the table looking freshly plucked.

The art of disguising food led to elaborate pranks. When Nawab Wajid Ali Shah entertained a visiting nobleman from Delhi who was a great connoisseur of food, what appeared to be a fruit conserve was placed on the table. His guest was amazed to find that the conserve was actually made from meat. When the Nawab was invited to dinner a few days later, he went prepared for tricks but saw nothing suspicious in the table loaded with platters of meat, rice, breads, chutneys, and pickles. It was only when he tasted the food that he realized that everything on the table was made from sugar—even the plates, cups, and bowls!

Indian cooks trained in the Awadhi arts of food presentation were to delight—or exasperate, depending on taste—their British employers in later centuries. Flora Annie Steel, who wrote *The Complete Indian Housekeeper and Cook* in 1898, objected to the practice of sculpting butter into elaborate shapes. The cook, she cautioned, "should be generally discouraged from making it the medium for a display of his powers in plastic art; it is doubtless gratifying to observe such yearning for beauty, even in butter, but it is suggestive of too much handling to be pleasant." We can only conjecture what she would have thought of dinner at the home of Brigadier and Mrs. Comet-Dane in the 1930s, as described by one of the guests, Elizabeth Crawford Wilkins:

> . . . we were led to the dining room where we were confronted by a long table in the centre of which was a fantastic arrangement of coloured rice. Thousands of small grains, dyed the most flagrant hues conceivable, were laid on the white cloth in the pattern of a flower basket, from which sprang in ricey splendour exotic blue roses, green zinnias, black corn flowers and pink golden rod. . . .
>
> By the time I had eaten purple carrots and red brussels sprouts I felt prepared for any eventuality, but the arrival of the iced pudding left me shaken and

exhausted of surprise. It was served on a tray in what appeared to be a large blue Wedgwood china bowl of the most delicate texture and exquisite colouring. To my alarm Mrs Comet-Dane took a fork and spoon and, raising them simultaneously a few inches into the air, brought them smartly down into the sides of the bowl breaking it into several pieces. That it was made of spun sugar had not occurred to me!

Everyone in Lucknow loved good food, and some of the best examples were found in marketplace stalls. The fame of the men who ran these shops has survived over the years; people still talk of the delicacy of Shahid's pulao, the flavor of Jhumman's chicken, and the skill with which Mirza Kababia made kababs, said to be better than the royal kitchen's. Mahumdu served such exquisite *nahari*—a spicy slow-simmered lamb stew—that the greatest nobles flocked to his little stand. Even today you'll see a luxurious car pull up in front of a nondescript shop in the heart of Lucknow and find that the stall is famed for the best kababs in the city.

While Awadh prospered, its claim to being the cultural capital of Muslim India did not go unchallenged. Another kingdom had risen from the rubble of the Moghul Empire—Hyderabad, in southern India. Nizam ul Mulk, prime minister of the Moghul Empire, sought refuge from the intrigue that tore apart the court at Delhi after the death of Aurangzeb. He withdrew to Hyderabad, where he became governor in 1724. Though Nizam ul Mulk carefully maintained the fiction that he was a servant of the emperor, in reality he was the ruler of an independent kingdom that increased in wealth and power.

To fill posts in his government, Nizam ul Mulk took with him an entire army, military officers, administrative clerks, scholars, and priests. Following behind were families, servants, shopkeepers, and anyone who scented an opportunity to make quick money in a rapidly growing city. News of its prosperity reached Delhi and attracted many Moghul nobles, who formed the nucleus of a new aristocracy. Hyderabadi society recreated the etiquette and style of the Moghul court but added a refinement and dignity all its own. Exquisite courtesies and flowery forms of address marked even the simplest conversations, and this politeness still characterizes everyday language in Hyderabad.

Incoming chefs brought recipes for the pulaos, kormas, and biryanis they had served the Moghuls, but incorporated the flavors of southern India, such as coconuts, tamarind, curry leaves, hot chili peppers, mustard seeds, peanuts, and cinnamon. Hyderabadi cooks created combinations the Moghuls had never dreamed of: *baghare baingan,* eggplant stuffed with coconut and spices cooked in a thick tamarind-peanut sauce; *dalcha,* yellow split peas cooked with lamb, coconut, tamarind, and curry leaves; *lukmi,* small squares of dough filled with spicy ground meat and deep-fried. Many of the best cooks of Awadh were also attracted to Hyderabad, including Pir Ali, renowned for creating a pie containing several live birds, which flew out as the pie was cut open. This is said to have delighted English visitors, perhaps because it reminded them of childhood nursery rhymes.

The nineteenth century dawned on a political landscape that was entirely different from what it had been a hundred years earlier. The Moghul Empire, ruled by an increasingly irrelevant emperor, had shrunk to a small area around Delhi. Real power lay with the kingdoms of the Marathas, Punjab, Awadh, and Hyderabad, all of them hoping to succeed the Moghuls as masters of all India. But even as they faced off, they were nervously glancing over their shoulders at a new and growing force in Indian affairs—the British.

English merchants, who two hundred years earlier had begged for an audience with Emperor Jahangir, were now well established in their coastal settlements of Bombay, Madras, and Calcutta. The British governor general of India, living in his capital city of Calcutta, administered a rapidly expanding colony and commanded the most powerful army in India. British political ambitions inevitably led to clashes with the Indian states. A century of complex political maneuvering punctuated by wars with the Marathas and Sikhs ended with a British victory. Their empire engulfed Punjab and Awadh by 1860, and Hyderabad and the Maratha kingdoms became British protectorates, independent only in name.

The decline of the Moghul Empire did not mean the end of their great cuisine. The palace cooks of Hyderabad and Awadh preserved the culinary legacy of the Moghuls, with creative twists. The rustic fare of the Marathas and the Punjabis was very different from that of the Moghuls; it originated in villages, not royal kitchens. The establishment of independent kingdoms in these regions, whose rulers employed skilled chefs, gave their food much greater sophistication and produced the dishes we are now familiar with.

The kingdoms built on the debris of the Moghul Empire produced wonderful new styles of cooking that still flourish in India. Talented chefs in Hyderabad and Lucknow keep alive the culinary traditions of these cities. Punjabi entrepreneurs who opened restaurants all over the world have done much to make their food popular. Indian restaurants in most Western cities typically feature a mixture of Punjabi and Moghlai dishes. Maharashtrian food is not as well known outside India, but these recipes will introduce you to this cuisine if it's new to you. In this chapter you will experience a variety of cooking styles from four very different regions of India.

Baghare Baingan • Stuffed eggplant cooked in a spicy nutty sauce

Dhingri ka Dulma • Portobello mushrooms stuffed with spicy sautéed cottage cheese

Bharvan Dum Lauki • Zucchini stuffed with spicy cottage cheese baked in a sautéed onion-tomato sauce

Gobhi Mussallam • Spicy baked cauliflower topped with cottage cheese, bread crumbs, and nuts

Paneer ki Bhurji • Crumbled cottage cheese stir-fried with sautéed onions, tomatoes, and spices

Bhindi ki Sabzi • Okra stir-fried with onions, garlic, and spices

Ande ki Kari • Hard-boiled eggs cooked in a sautéed onion-tomato sauce with cream

Kabab Nawabi • Chicken breast marinated in herbs, cream, and cashews, grilled with onions and tomatoes

Hyderabadi Kabab • Boneless grilled chicken thighs marinated in sautéed onions, yogurt, cream, toasted spices, and almonds

Murgh Dumdaar • Chicken marinated and grilled in vinegar and spices, baked in a sauce of onions, tomatoes, and cream

Masala Murgh • Marinated spicy chicken stir-fried till crisp, served in a sautéed onion, tomato, and yogurt sauce

Murgh Nizami • Chicken cooked with sautéed onions, tomatoes, yogurt, nuts, and spices, with mint and raisins

Dhaniye aur Kaju wala Murgh • Chicken cooked with cashews and fresh coriander

Murgh Paneer Anardaana • Chicken and cottage cheese cooked with sautéed onions, tomatoes, and dried pomegranate seeds

Murgh Tamatari • Chicken cooked with onions, tomatoes, and spices

Dum Machali • Grilled marinated fish baked in a sauce of sautéed onions, sun-dried tomatoes, and yogurt

Chutney Fish Curry • Fish fillets marinated in a fresh herb chutney, grilled and cooked in a sauce of sautéed onions, tomatoes, and spices

Hariyali Keema • Ground lamb cooked with spinach and sour cream and a fresh herb chutney

Shahi Gosht Korma • Lamb cooked in a rich sauce of onions, yogurt, and nuts

Gosht ka Salan • Lamb curry with sautéed onions, tomatoes, yogurt, and baby potatoes

Chatni Gosht • Lamb cooked with sautéed onions, yogurt, tomatoes, and a fresh herb chutney

Kolhapuri Mutton Curry • Lamb cooked with sautéed onions, tomatoes, coconut, and poppy seeds

Saag Gosht Do Pyaza • Dry lamb curry folded with spinach, sautéed onions, and mushrooms

Subz Gosht • Lamb stewed with onions, tomatoes, yogurt, and mixed vegetables

Methi Gosht • Lamb cubes cooked with onions, tomatoes, and spices, folded with sautéed fenugreek leaves

Murgh Korma Biryani • Rice layered and baked with spicy chicken, cream, and nuts

Jhinga Subz Pulao • A delicate rice pilaf with shrimp, sweet red pepper, asparagus, and fresh dill

Saadey Naan • Broiled pizza dough bread

Paneerwale Kulche • Pan-fried bread stuffed with cottage cheese

Malai ki Puri • Deep-fried balls of cream and flour served in a cardamom-flavored syrup

Baghare Baingan

Stuffed eggplant cooked in a spicy nutty sauce

It was the year 1697 and Edward Barlow, captain of the East India Company ship *Sceptre,* had just returned from dinner at an Indian Muslim merchant's home. "He provided a great deal of good victuals," the captain wrote, "but they used no tables but spread a carpet and sat all round on their heels, which we could not very well do, being not used to such fashions." The traditional Muslim custom of serving food on the *dastarkhwan,* a cloth spread on the floor around which all the diners sat, was a trial for many a European. But for Muslims it symbolized a sense of family and togetherness, and to invite guests to share a meal was to welcome them into the bosom of the family. Europeans who lived in the country learned to eat Indian fashion. John Ovington commented that the English merchants, "when they eat at Home, do it after the *English* manner, but abroad they imitate the Customs of the *East* in lying round the Banquet upon the *Persian* Carpets which are spread upon the Ground."

This recipe from Hyderabad would have pride of place on the dastarkhwan. The eggplant are first stuffed with a sweet, spicy, nutty mixture, then sautéed lightly in oil and finally cooked in a tart onion-tamarind sauce. It is an elaborate dish, great for dinner parties. You can cook it in stages by sautéing the stuffed eggplant ahead of time and cooking it in the sauce the next day. The entire dish can be assembled up to two days ahead of time. Serve with Indian bread such as naan or puris.

- In a microwave-safe bowl, microwave the tamarind and water on high for 2 minutes. Mash well with a fork and let cool for 10 minutes. (If you prefer, you can soak the tamarind in the water for 2 hours instead.) Set a fine mesh

Walnut-size piece of seedless tamarind (2 ounces)

½ cup hot water

1¼ pounds (about 4) long thin purple eggplant, washed, dried, and stemmed

3 tablespoons grated coconut, preferably fresh, or desiccated unsweetened

1 teaspoon white sesame seeds

1 teaspoon white poppy seeds

1 bay leaf

¼ teaspoon fenugreek seeds

1 teaspoon whole coriander seeds

1 teaspoon cumin seeds

2 whole dried red chilies

2 whole cloves

½-inch cinnamon stick

2 whole cardamom

½ teaspoon fennel seeds

¼ cup roasted peanuts

2 teaspoons brown sugar

Salt to taste

3 tablespoons vegetable oil

½ teaspoon black mustard seeds

10 to 15 curry leaves, preferably fresh

½-inch piece of ginger, grated

2 garlic cloves, grated

1¼ cups finely chopped onions

Salt to taste

½ teaspoon turmeric

1 tablespoon chopped fresh
  coriander leaves

sieve over a bowl and pour the tamarind and all its liquid through, squeezing out the pulp and discarding the fibrous residue. You should have about ½ cup of tamarind extract; if not, add enough water to make up the difference.

- Slit the eggplant down the center, leaving a ½-inch piece intact at the bottom. Set aside. Warm a nonstick skillet over medium heat, then add the coconut, sesame seeds, poppy seeds, bay leaf, fenugreek seeds, coriander seeds, cumin seeds, red chilies, cloves, cinnamon, cardamom, and fennel seeds. Toast for 8 to 10 minutes, until all the coconut water has evaporated and the spices are lightly browned. Stir in the peanuts and let the pan cool on the stove, then powder the spice and peanut mixture in a clean coffee or spice grinder. You may have to do this in two batches. Transfer to a bowl and mix in the brown sugar and salt to taste. Stuff each eggplant with about 2 teaspoons of this mixture, secure with a toothpick, and set aside. Reserve the remaining spice mixture.

- Warm the oil in a nonstick skillet over medium-high heat. Add the eggplant one by one, laying them side by side. Cover and cook for about 10 minutes, occasionally turning the eggplant gently to brown evenly. When all the eggplant are lightly sautéed, remove to a covered platter.

- To the remaining oil in the skillet, add the mustard seeds and curry leaves, then, after a second, the grated ginger and garlic, and sauté for 30 seconds. Now stir in the chopped onions and sauté, stirring for 5 minutes, until lightly browned. Add the reserved spice powder and cook for 2 minutes. Mix in the tamarind extract, salt, and turmeric, reduce the heat to low, and gently add the eggplant. Coat well with the sauce, cover, and cook for 10 minutes, stirring gently once in a while. Transfer to a serving dish, remove the toothpicks, and garnish with the chopped fresh coriander leaves.

- SERVES 3 TO 4 WITH OTHER DISHES

Dhingri ka Dulma

Portobello mushrooms stuffed with spicy sautéed cottage cheese

The arrival of George Eden, governor general of India, was a momentous occasion for the kingdom of Awadh in 1837, for its survival depended on the goodwill of the British government. The Nawab of Awadh offered the greatest honor possible to his English visitors: he sent a contingent of chefs from his own kitchen. This magnanimous gesture was wasted on the governor general's sister, Fanny Eden, who disliked all Indian food. She poured out her woes in letters home:

> That Oude cook will be the death of me. He sends in about twelve dishes every day at breakfast and stands by with his satellites to see that we eat them. I happen to hold Hindoostanee cookery in horror. George tastes them all handsomely as a Governor-General should do and the old khansama (butler) always insists upon my taking some and chuckles behind his long white beard in most inhuman manner as he sees my sufferings.

The Eden family's French chef, St. Cloup, was furious at having these new associates thrust upon him. The only member of the party who truly enjoyed the food was young Prince Henry from Holland, who was traveling with the governor general. Miss Eden did not like him very much either:

> He is invaluable during the Oude cook visitation, for he will eat to any amount, but of all the heavy ingenuous boys of seventeen that have ever been created, he is the most heavy and ingenuous. . . . The Oude cooks silver some of their dishes and gild others. He is always happy when he is eating, but the

6 large portobello mushrooms
2 tablespoons vegetable oil
½ teaspoon cumin seeds
1 cup finely chopped onions
1 garlic clove, finely chopped
1 large plum tomato, diced
½ teaspoon turmeric
¼ to ½ teaspoon cayenne pepper
½ teaspoon garam masala
Salt to taste
2 cups grated or crumbled paneer
  (cottage cheese)
½ cup water
2 tablespoons heavy cream
2 tablespoons chopped fresh
  coriander leaves

deep and intellectual happiness he enjoys when he is eating rice which looks like silver, it is beyond words to express . . .

Ignore Fanny's criticisms, for Awadh cuisine is a delight to eat, as you will see from this recipe. Traditionally, this dish is made with white mushrooms chopped and sautéed with meat or cottage cheese. Here, I have stuffed portobello mushrooms with cottage cheese. The filling can also be used to stuff tomatoes, eggplant, and green peppers. You can also make wonderful samosas: stuff leftover filling into puff pastry pouches and bake.

- Snip off the muddy ends of the mushroom stems and wipe the mushrooms clean with a damp paper towel. Carefully slice off the stems and finely chop. Set the mushroom caps aside.
- Warm the oil in a nonstick skillet over medium-high heat. Add the cumin seeds and, as soon as they sputter, the chopped onions and garlic. Sauté for about 4 minutes, until the onions are lightly browned. Add the chopped mushroom stems and sauté for 2 minutes.
- Reduce the heat to medium and stir in in the diced tomato, all the spices, and salt. Sauté for about 5 minutes, mashing the tomato lightly with the back of your spoon. Mix in the cottage cheese and the water. Reduce the heat to medium-low and cook covered for 10 minutes, stirring once in a while. Remove the skillet from the heat, cool for 5 minutes, then mix in the cream and chopped coriander leaves. You can make this stuffing up to 2 days ahead of time.
- Preheat the oven to 350°F. Stuff the cottage cheese mixture generously into the reserved mushroom caps, pressing down gently to hold in place, then put them in a lightly greased baking dish. Bake uncovered for 20 minutes, or until the mushrooms are tender and just beginning to release their liquid.

- SERVES 3 TO 4

Bharvan Dum Lauki

Zucchini stuffed with spicy cottage cheese baked in a
sautéed onion-tomato sauce

Jenab Aulea Begam, queen of Awadh, rose at ten or
eleven in the morning. Attendants bathed and
dressed her, after which she was ready to listen to
a passage from the holy Koran, read by a priest sitting behind
a screen. Servers brought her a cooling fruit drink with dissolved pearls—believed to have great restorative powers. At
noon a cannon was fired, a signal for the first meal of the day,
cooked by women in her private kitchen.

The king, Amjad Ali Shah, had his own apartments and a
separate kitchen, where men did all the cooking. If the king
dined with the queen, his food was brought from his kitchen
on silver platters. The meal was laid on the *dastarkhwan*—an
embroidered cloth spread on the carpeted floor—around
which the diners reclined on cushions. Twenty to thirty dishes
were served: pulaos of three kinds, kormas, kababs, curried
meats, vegetables, and sweets. *Hookahs* were carried in with
great ceremony at the end of the meal; and the queen had
special servers whose only job was to prepare these smoking
pipes.

In the afternoon the queen received women from all over
the country bearing petitions for assistance. Later she would
stroll or ride in her carriage through the extensive palace
grounds, which were laid out with fountains, pools, flower
gardens, and fruit orchards. After sunset a second meal was
served, even more elaborate than the first. When the queen
was ready to retire, a storyteller would entertain her until she
fell asleep, which could be late into the night if the tale was
amusing.

This dish, a classic from Awadhi cuisine, would often grace
the queen's dastarkhwan. The zucchini, lightly sautéed and

1 pound yellow or green zucchini
  (1 large or 2 medium)
2 tablespoons vegetable oil

FOR THE STUFFING

1 cup crumbled or grated paneer
  (cottage cheese)
Salt to taste
¼ teaspoon garam masala
¼ teaspoon roasted ground cumin
  seeds
¼ teaspoon dried ground ginger
  (optional)
¼ teaspoon ground black pepper
1 tablespoon chopped fresh coriander
  leaves, plus 2 tablespoons for
  garnish (optional)

FOR THE SAUCE

1 tablespoon vegetable oil
½ teaspoon cumin seeds
1¼ cups onions, chopped
2 garlic cloves, chopped
½-inch piece of ginger, chopped
1 cup diced tomatoes
½ cup plain yogurt,
  not low-fat
Salt to taste
¼ teaspoon cayenne pepper
½ teaspoon turmeric

½ teaspoon ground cumin seeds
½ teaspoon ground coriander seeds
½ teaspoon garam masala

stuffed with creamy cottage cheese, is baked in a sauce of sautéed onions, tomatoes, and yogurt. It is an impressive dish and not too difficult to make. Serve with Shahi Gosht Korma (lamb cooked in a rich sauce of onions, yogurt, and nuts, page 182).

- Peel the zucchini and halve it lengthwise. Using a sharp knife, scoop out the seeds and insides, leaving a ½-inch-thick shell. Warm the oil in a nonstick skillet over medium-high heat. Sear the zucchini halves, covered, for 2 minutes per side. Remove and set aside on a plate, reserving skillet and oil.
- Combine all the stuffing ingredients and generously fill half of the seared zucchini. Cover the stuffed halves with the reserved zucchini halves and secure well with toothpicks. Set aside.
- To make the sauce, preheat the oven to 250°F. Warm 1 tablespoon of vegetable oil in the reserved skillet (do not discard any leftover oil) and add the cumin seeds. After a few seconds, add the chopped onions, garlic, and ginger. Sauté, stirring frequently over medium-high heat until the onions are lightly browned, about 5 minutes. Cool and transfer to a food processor or blender. Add the diced tomatoes and yogurt, salt, and all the spices. Mince or blend till smooth.
- Pour half of the sautéed-minced mixture in an ovenproof dish. Place the stuffed zucchini carefully on top and pour the remaining mixture over. Seal tightly with foil and bake for 30 minutes. Garnish with fresh coriander leaves if desired.
  - SERVES 3 TO 4 WITH OTHER DISHES

Gobhi Mussallam

Spicy baked cauliflower topped with cottage cheese,
bread crumbs, and nuts

Nauroz, the Persian New Year, was celebrated all over Awadh, but nowhere were the festivities more lavish than at the king's palace. The king, his principal wife, and his eldest son arrived early in the morning to greet the queen mother. After the king had offered his mother presents, the rest of his wives—numbering over a hundred—came to pay their respects. The queen mother sprinkled a few drops of red coloring on each person who approached, a custom adapted from the Hindu festival of Holi. The palace servants celebrated in the courtyards with music and dancing, smearing colored powders on one another and passing around platters of sweets.

A great banquet was served in the evening. The largest hall in the palace was prepared with dastarkhwans—long strips of embroidered cloth on which food was placed—laid on the floor. The king and his mother, brothers, and heir sat on cushions in the place of honor at the end of the room. Arrayed on all sides were the royal women, attired in brocade, silks, and jewels. The food was brought in, heaping platters of biryani topped with silver and gold leaf, steaming tureens of kormas (meat cooked with nuts and cream), skewers of kababs, and trays of stuffed vegetables.

Gobhi Mussalam, a classic dish from Awadh, is served at all festive occasions. Usually the whole cauliflower is lightly steamed, stuffed with a sautéed onion-tomato paste and shallow-fried or baked. I have simplified the recipe by cutting up the florets and tossing them in the sautéed spice paste, instead of stuffing the paste between the florets, which is a tedious task. When I make this dish, I top it with cottage cheese, nuts, and bread crumbs, which form a nice crunchy crust when baked.

1¼ cups finely chopped onions

½ cup diced tomatoes, fresh or canned

½ cup plain yogurt, not low-fat

1 teaspoon kasoori methi
   (dried fenugreek leaves)

¾ teaspoon garam masala

1 teaspoon powdered fennel seeds

2 tablespoons vegetable oil

½ teaspoon cumin seeds

¼-inch piece of ginger, finely chopped

1 garlic clove, finely chopped

½ teaspoon turmeric

¼ to ½ teaspoon cayenne pepper

Salt to taste

½ teaspoon ground coriander seeds

½ teaspoon ground cumin seeds

1 pound cauliflower, cut into 1-inch
   florets

2 medium potatoes (about ½ pound),
   peeled and diced into 1-inch cubes

2 slices of white bread or
   ½ cup store-bought plain
   bread crumbs

10 raw cashews

10 raw almonds

½ cup crumbled paneer
   (cottage cheese)

½ cup grated cheddar cheese

¼ teaspoon roasted ground
   cumin seeds

The more traditional recipe does not have this topping—you can try it both ways. Serve with Shahi Gosht Korma (lamb cooked in a rich sauce of onions, yogurt, and nuts, page 182).

- In a food processor or blender, puree the onions, tomatoes, yogurt, dried fenugreek leaves, ½ teaspoon of the garam masala, and the powdered fennel seeds. Set aside.
- Warm the oil in a nonstick skillet over medium heat. Add the cumin seeds and, after a few seconds, the chopped ginger and garlic. Sauté for 30 seconds, then mix in the turmeric, cayenne, salt, ground coriander, and ground cumin seeds. Stir-fry for a few seconds, then stir in the cauliflower and potatoes, cover, and cook for 5 minutes, stirring once or twice—the object is to slightly sear and soften the vegetables. Turn off the stove, leaving the skillet on the burner, then pour the onion-tomato mixture over. Mix well and transfer to a flat-bottomed ovenproof dish. (If you prefer, you can divide the cauliflower mixture into 4 portions and transfer to individual au gratin dishes.)
- Preheat the oven to 350°F. Put the bread on a paper towel and microwave on high for 1 minute per side, then break into smaller pieces. In a food processor, whirl to crumb consistency, then transfer to a mixing bowl. In a clean coffee or spice grinder, powder the cashews and almonds, then mix into the bread crumbs.
- In a mixing bowl, combine the crumbled cottage cheese, grated cheddar cheese, roasted ground cumin seeds, and remaining ¼ teaspoon garam masala.
- Bake the cauliflower, covered tightly with foil, for 15 minutes. Remove from the oven and spread the cottage cheese mixture over. Bake uncovered for 10 minutes, then sprinkle the bread crumb–nut mixture over. Bake for 10 minutes, until the top is lightly browned. If you are not going to serve the dish right away, cover with foil to prevent drying out and keep warm in the oven.

- SERVES 4 WITH OTHER DISHES

Paneer ki Bhurji

Crumbled cottage cheese stir-fried with sautéed onions, tomatoes, and spices

Visit a *Gurudwara*—a Sikh temple—and you will be invited to eat in the attached community kitchen known as a *langar*, where volunteers cook as an act of devotion. Guru Nanak, who founded the Sikh religion in the fifteenth century, established the langar to remind his followers of the equality of all humans: sitting together on the floor to eat is a powerful illustration. Later Sikh leaders promoted the langar by insisting that those who came to meet them first eat there. This custom became such a well-recognized part of the Sikh faith that Banda, leader of the Sikh rebellion in the early eighteenth century, inscribed on his seal a cauldron symbolic of the langar.

This ancient tradition of communal dining still thrives in the modern world, and in any city in the world where there is a sizable Sikh population, you will find a Gurudwara with a langar. Stop by and eat; no questions are ever asked about your faith, no payment is expected, and the food is delicious. Meals are always vegetarian and reflect the simple, wholesome diet of the rural Punjabis who were the first followers of Guru Nanak. Punjabi farms produce large quantities of milk, butter, and cottage cheese, and they are all used freely in cooking.

This is a quick and delicious cottage cheese stir-fry that is commonly served in Punjabi homes. The sweet peppers and mushrooms that I have added to the recipe enhance the taste and aroma of this dish. It is usually served with parathas (shallow-fried wheat bread).

2 cups crumbled pressed paneer (cottage cheese)

½ cup frozen peas

3 tablespoons vegetable oil

½ teaspoon cumin seeds

½-inch piece of ginger, grated

2 garlic cloves, grated

1¼ cups finely chopped onions

1 small sweet green or red pepper, diced fine

10 mushrooms, quartered

1 cup peeled, diced tomatoes, fresh or canned

Salt to taste

1 teaspoon garam masala

¼ to ½ teaspoon cayenne pepper

½ teaspoon turmeric

1 teaspoon ground coriander seeds

1 teaspoon ground cumin seeds

½ teaspoon kasoori methi (dried fenugreek leaves) (optional)

2 tablespoons chopped fresh coriander leaves

- Mash the cottage cheese in a bowl with a fork. Put the peas in a microwave-safe bowl and cover with water. Seal tightly with plastic wrap and microwave on high for 5 minutes. (You can also cook them in a saucepan with enough water to cover until tender.) Drain in a sieve.

- Warm the oil in a nonstick skillet over medium-high heat and add the cumin seeds. As soon as they sputter, add the ginger and garlic. Sauté for 30 seconds, then stir in the onions. Sauté for about 5 minutes, until the onions are lightly browned. Mix in the sweet pepper and sauté for 2 minutes, then add the mushrooms. Sauté for 4 minutes, just until they begin to release their liquid, then add the tomatoes, salt, and all the spices. Mix gently and cook for 5 minutes, stirring occasionally. Now stir in the cottage cheese and peas and cook covered on medium-low heat for 10 minutes. Stir occasionally. Mix in the chopped fresh coriander leaves. You can make this dish up to 3 days ahead of time.

- SERVES 3 TO 4 WITH OTHER DISHES

Bhindi ki Sabzi

Okra stir-fried with onions, garlic, and spices

2 tablespoons vegetable oil

¼ teaspoon cumin seeds

1 cup thinly sliced onions

2 garlic cloves, chopped

1 hot green chili, sliced (optional)

1 pound fresh small okra,
    washed, ends trimmed,
    halved lengthwise

Salt to taste

½ teaspoon turmeric

¼ to ½ teaspoon cayenne pepper

½ teaspoon ground coriander seeds

¼ teaspoon garam masala

 Holi is an Indian harvest festival, celebrated with much feasting, drinking, and raucous music. It is the one time in the year when all social barriers collapse: people douse one another with colored water and sprinkle red, green, yellow, and purple powders on anyone they meet. Holi at the court of the king of Punjab, Ranjit Singh, was a riotous occasion. Sir Henry Fane—commander-in-chief of the British Army and a most dignified gentleman—was the guest of honor at a celebration in 1837. Sir Henry's aide, among those present, described the revelry:

In front of every chair were small baskets, heaped one above another, full of small, brittle balls, filled with red powder, and alongside them large bowls of thick yellow saffron, and long golden squirts, with which each one of us armed ourselves. As soon as we were all seated, the Rajah took a large butter-boat kind of article, filled with the said saffron and poured it on Sir Henry's bald head; while, at the same time, the prime minister rubbed him over with gold and silver leaf, mixed with red powder.

An Afghan ambassador, just arrived . . . from Candahar . . . was dressed in his best. . . . Never before having seen the festival of the Holi, he had not the smallest idea what he had to expect, and his look of astonishment of a ball of red dust being shied in his eye, and his horror when his beard was turned to a bright saffron colour, I shall long remember.

This is a pretty fair description of modern-day Holi celebrations, except that nowadays nobody can afford to throw perfectly good saffron around. In the evening, when everybody has finally calmed down and cleaned up, the feasting starts. Traditionally, no meat is served; there are several kinds of vegetable dishes, raitas (yogurt relish), pilafs, and puris (deep-fried wheat bread). Fresh okra, cooked in simple Punjabi style, is a favorite at this occasion.

- Warm the oil in a nonstick skillet over medium-high heat. Add the cumin seeds and, after a few seconds, the onions, garlic, and chili (if using). Sauté for 3 to 4 minutes, until the onions are softened but not browned. Add the okra, salt, and all spices except for the garam masala. Stir gently to mix, cover, and cook the okra on medium-low for about 20 minutes. They should be just done but not mushy. Sprinkle the garam masala on top and serve. You can make this dish up to 3 days ahead of time.
  - SERVES 3 TO 4 WITH OTHER DISHES

Ande ki Kari

Hard-boiled eggs cooked in a sautéed onion-tomato sauce with cream

2 tablespoons vegetable oil

½ teaspoon cumin seeds

1½ cups finely chopped onions

1 garlic clove, finely chopped

1 cup diced tomatoes, fresh or canned

Salt to taste

½ teaspoon turmeric

¾ teaspoon ground coriander seeds

½ teaspoon ground cumin seeds

½ teaspoon garam masala

¼ to ½ teaspoon cayenne pepper

1 teaspoon kasoori methi
  (dried fenugreek leaves)

1 cup water

8 hard-boiled eggs, peeled

1 tablespoon lemon juice

2 tablespoons chopped fresh
  coriander leaves

2 tablespoons heavy cream

 "*Carîl* is a name which in *India* they give to certain Broths made with Butter, the Pulp of Indian Nuts, and all sorts of Spices, particularly Cardamoms and Ginger, besides herbs, fruits and a thousand other condiments." When Pietro della Valle, an Italian traveler in India, wrote this in 1623, the term "curry" was already in common use by Europeans. The origin of the word is unclear—it is not found in any Indian language—but it may derive from the Tamil *kari,* which refers to meat or vegetables cooked in a sauce.

The seventeenth-century Portuguese cookbook *Arte de Cozinha* had a curry recipe, as did the English *Art of Cookery,* published in 1747. London coffeehouses soon listed curry on their menus, and two Indian cooks were employed in Queen Victoria's kitchens to prepare curry, served every day at lunch. Prince Albert instructed his French chef to learn how to make authentic curry but unfortunately found that "the French intelligence, fine and keen as it is, does not penetrate the depths of curry lore."

Ready-made curry powders, which cooks in India don't use, have made curries popular all over the world and spawned some strange offspring. I have encountered curried goat from the Caribbean, curried noodles from Singapore, curried chicken from China, curried sausage from Germany, and curried turkey from America. Purists in India are infuriated by any mention of curry, viewing it as a caricature of a great cuisine. I try to avoid either extreme of the great curry debate and use the term curry in the sense that it is widely accepted in India today: any dish that has been cooked in a sauce. I don't use curry powder in my cooking, because the essence of Indian cooking lies in its creative use of freshly prepared spice mixtures and pastes.

In this delicious egg curry from Punjab, the sauce is made from fresh sautéed ingredients such as onions, garlic, and tomatoes combined with spices. Hard-boiled eggs are simmered in this sauce to absorb the flavors. You can also cook chicken, meat, fish, or vegetables in this basic sauce and serve with plain cooked rice.

- Warm the oil in a nonstick skillet over medium-high heat. Add the cumin seeds and, after a few seconds, the chopped onions and garlic. Sauté, stirring for about 5 minutes, until lightly browned. Reduce heat to medium and add the tomatoes. Cook for 5 minutes, mashing them into the sauce with the back of your spoon. When the oil appears around the edges, add salt and all the spices. Cook for 1 minute, then add the water and the whole eggs.
- Cover and bring to a boil. Immediately reduce the heat to medium-low and cook for 30 minutes. Turn off the heat and mix in the lemon juice and fresh coriander. Let the curry cool for a few minutes before mixing in the cream. Just before serving, lift the eggs out of the sauce and transfer to a serving bowl. Halve them and pour the sauce over. You can make this dish up to 3 days ahead of time; reheat on low heat so as not to curdle the cream.

- SERVES 3 TO 4 WITH OTHER DISHES

Kabab Nawabi

Chicken breast marinated in herbs, cream, and cashews,
grilled with onions and tomatoes

FOR THE MARINADE

¾-inch piece of ginger, chopped

3 garlic cloves, chopped

1 cup fresh coriander leaves and
    tender stems, washed and drained

1 cup fresh mint leaves,
    washed and drained

2 hot green chilies, deseeded if desired

¾ teaspoon cumin seeds

6 tablespoons heavy cream

4 tablespoons lemon juice

Salt to taste

½ teaspoon garam masala

½ cup raw cashews, powdered finely
    in spice or coffee grinder

1 pound boneless, skinless chicken
    breast, washed, dried, and cut into
    1-inch cubes

FOR THE VEGETABLES

1 medium onion, cut into 1-inch cubes

2 medium plum tomatoes, cut into
    1-inch cubes

Salt to taste

¼ teaspoon ground black pepper

1 tablespoon lemon juice

"They took us in in England, when they talked about the quantities of curry we were to eat. The natives eat it but I hardly ever see Europeans touch it," wrote Fanny Eden in 1838. But earlier generations of English people living in India had been far more adventurous in trying the local cuisine. John Ovington, chaplain of the English settlement at Surat in 1689, found that the merchants employed English, Portuguese, and Indian cooks to cater to all tastes. The food served at dinner was much like that eaten in wealthy Muslim homes at the time:

> Palau, that is Rice boil'd so artificially, that every grain lies singly without being clodded together, with Spices intermixt, and a boil'd Fowl in the middle, is the most common *Indian* Dish; and a dumpoked Fowl, that is, boil'd with Butter in any small Vessel, and stuft with Raisons and Almonds, is another. Cabob, that is Bief or Mutton cut into small pieces, sprinkled with Salt and Pepper, and dipt with Oil and Garlick, which have been mixt together in a Dish, and then roasted on a Spit, with sweet Herbs put between every piece, and stuft in them, and basted with Oil and Garlick all the while, is another *Indian* Savory Dish.

These kababs from Hyderabad are similar to the ones described above, but in addition to the sweet herbs, the marinade contains nuts and cream. I like to intersperse with onions and tomatoes before grilling and then serve wrapped in Mexican flour tortillas with a fresh herb chutney on the side.

- In a food processor or blender, mince the ginger, garlic, fresh coriander, fresh mint, and green chilies. Add the cumin, cream, lemon juice, salt, garam masala, and cashews and whirl again to mix. Pour this marinade over the chicken, toss well to mix, then cover and refrigerate for 4 hours.

- Just before you are ready to grill, toss together the onion, tomatoes, salt, pepper, and lemon juice. Thread the marinated chicken cubes on skewers, interspersing with marinated onions and tomatoes. Grill, covered, for about 5 minutes per side on medium heat. Uncover, turn up the heat slightly, and char the skewers for 2 minutes. To serve, you can either slide the chicken and vegetables off the skewers and heap them onto a plate, or serve the skewers as they come off the grill. You can also wrap them up in tortillas.

- SERVES 3 TO 4 WITH OTHER DISHES

Hyderabadi Kabab

Boneless grilled chicken thighs marinated in sautéed onions, yogurt, cream, toasted spices, and almonds

 Lancelot Canning and Robert Trully, two seventeenth-century English musicians, were men with a mission—to teach Indians the wonders of Western music. Permitted to perform at Emperor Jahangir's court, Mr. Canning went first, playing the virginals—a small harpsichord popular at that time. To his great embarrassment, the audience soon became restless. Fortunately Mr. Trully, who followed on the cornet, proved to be a huge success. The emperor himself tried out the cornet and ordered all his court musicians to learn how to play it. The royal bandmaster, jealous of this attention shown to a foreign rival, blew so hard on the instrument that he grievously injured himself internally and died. Sadly for the English musicians, the emperor soon tired of their music. Robert Trully decided to try his

FIRST MARINADE

1 garlic clove, grated

¼-inch piece of ginger, grated

4 tablespoons plain yogurt, not low-fat

Salt to taste

¼ teaspoon ground black pepper

1¼ pounds boneless, skinless chicken thighs (about 8 pieces), washed and drained

SECOND MARINADE

2 tablespoons vegetable oil

¼ teaspoon cumin seeds

1¼ cups chopped onions

1 garlic clove, chopped

¼-inch piece of ginger, chopped

2 tablespoons grated coconut,
    preferably fresh, or desiccated
    unsweetened

2 tablespoons heavy cream

1 tablespoon chickpea flour or
    1 teaspoon cornstarch

10 raw almonds

1 teaspoon cumin seeds

¼ teaspoon whole black pepper

2 whole cardamom

2 whole cloves

½-inch cinnamon stick

1 dried red chili (optional)

1 teaspoon white poppy seeds

Salt to taste

Lemon juice to taste

luck elsewhere and traveled to the southern kingdom of Golconda (later known as Hyderabad). There he found his fortune by becoming a great favorite of the king. He settled in Golconda, became a Muslim, and adopted an Indian name. But he never did succeed in making Western music popular in India.

As the power of the Moghul Empire waned and the court in Delhi languished, many others followed Robert Trully to Hyderabad. Several of the most famous chefs of Delhi went to Hyderabad, bringing with them generations of Moghlai cooking traditions. They incorporated the new ingredients they found in South India, such as coconuts and tamarind, and gave birth to a new Hyderabadi cuisine.

These kababs from Hyderabad are great as appetizers with a little chutney or dip on the side. If you want to serve them as a main dish, grill ahead of time, then lightly cook in any sauce from this book.

- Combine the ingredients of the first marinade and rub all over the chicken. Cover and marinate while you prepare the second marinade.
- Warm the oil in a skillet over medium heat. Add the cumin seeds. As soon as they begin to sputter (this will only take a few seconds), stir in the chopped onions, garlic, and ginger. Sauté, stirring for about 5 minutes, until lightly browned. Cool slightly and transfer to a food processor or blender. Add the coconut, cream, and chickpea flour and mince well.
- Warm a small, heavy skillet over medium heat. Toast the almonds, cumin seeds, black pepper, cardamom, cloves, cinnamon, red chili, and poppy seeds for 2 to 3 minutes, until they change color and smell roasted; then powder them in a clean coffee or spice grinder. Add this powder, and salt to taste, to the minced onion mixture in the food processor and whirl again to mix well, scraping down the sides. Mix this marinade into the chicken, tossing well to coat thoroughly. Cover and refrigerate for at least 4 hours.

- When you are ready to grill, lift the chicken pieces out of the marinade and place on a medium-hot barbecue grill. Cover and cook for about 25 minutes, or until the chicken is tender. Turn the pieces occasionally for even cooking and baste with the leftover marinade. Serve with a dash of lemon juice.

- SERVES 3 TO 4 WITH OTHER DISHES

Murgh Dumdaar

Chicken marinated and grilled in vinegar and spices,
baked in a sauce of onions, tomatoes, and cream

The kingdom of Awadh lay in the relentless grip of famine in the year 1784, and its ruler Asaf ud Daula was concerned about the suffering of his people. Rather than offering them charity, he employed them to work on the construction of a mosque. It is said that he ensured work for all by ordering the walls that had been built during the day to be destroyed during the night. To feed this multitude of workers, meat, vegetables, and seasonings were sealed in huge cauldrons that were slow-cooked on glowing coals all night. This technique came to be known as "dum pukht," and was so good that the royal cooks began to use it in the palace kitchens.

Though people in Awadh recount this story and claim that the dum pukht method originated in their region, this cooking style existed long before Asaf ud Daula. John Fryer described the Indian food he ate during his visit in 1673, and wrote that they "Eat highly of all Flesh *Dumpoked,* which is Baked with Spice in Butter."

In this recipe, I have adapted the dum pukht technique to the oven, first grilling the marinated chicken for a smoked aroma and then baking it on low heat. I like to serve this dish

2 pounds skinned chicken, drumsticks and/or thighs, washed

FOR THE MARINADE
2 garlic cloves, grated
½-inch piece of ginger, grated
Salt to taste
½ teaspoon garam masala
4 tablespoons white vinegar
½ teaspoon ground black pepper
1 tablespoon vegetable oil

FOR THE SAUCE
1 cup chopped onions
1 garlic clove, chopped
¼-inch piece of ginger, chopped
2 tablespoons vegetable oil
½ teaspoon cumin seeds
1 bay leaf
1 whole cardamom
1 whole clove

½-inch cinnamon stick

1 cup diced tomatoes, fresh or canned

½ cup plain yogurt, not low-fat

½ teaspoon turmeric

¼ to ½ teaspoon cayenne pepper

½ teaspoon ground coriander seeds

½ teaspoon ground cumin seeds

½ teaspoon garam masala

15 raw almonds, powdered in a spice
    or coffee grinder

Salt to taste

2 tablespoons heavy cream

½ cup water

2 tablespoons chopped fresh coriander
    leaves (optional)

with a rice pilaf and Dhingri ka Dulma (portobello mushrooms stuffed with spicy sautéed cottage cheese, page 151).

- Make a few deep gashes in each piece of chicken and set aside. In a large mixing bowl, combine the grated garlic and ginger, salt, garam masala, vinegar, black pepper, and oil. Toss in the chicken pieces and coat well with the marinade. Cover and refrigerate for at least 2 hours.

- While the chicken is marinating, you can prepare the sauce, which can be made and refrigerated up to 2 days ahead of time. In a food processor, mince the onions, garlic, and ginger.

- Warm the oil in a nonstick skillet over medium-high heat. Add the cumin seeds, bay leaf, cardamom, cinnamon, and clove. After a few seconds, stir in the minced onions and sauté for about 10 minutes, until the onions are lightly browned, stirring once in a while.

- Meanwhile, whirl the tomatoes to a puree in the food processor. Reduce heat to medium, add the tomatoes to the skillet, and cook, stirring for about 5 minutes, until well incorporated. Now add the yogurt, stirring all the while for 5 minutes to prevent curdling. Add the turmeric, cayenne, ground coriander, ground cumin, garam masala, almond powder, and salt to taste. Stir-fry for 2 minutes, then turn off the heat. When ready to grill, lift the chicken out of its marinade and place on a medium-hot barbecue. Cook covered for about 20 to 25 minutes, until tender and lightly browned.

- Preheat the oven to 250°F.

- Now stir the grilled chicken, cream, and ½ cup of water into the sauce. Transfer to a large flat ovenproof dish, cover tightly with foil, and bake for 30 minutes. To serve, tear off the foil and garnish with fresh coriander leaves if desired.

    • SERVES 3 TO 4 WITH OTHER DISHES

Masala Murgh

Marinated spicy chicken stir-fried till crisp, served in a sautéed onion,
tomato, and yogurt sauce

 "What a mean and vulgar thing does the tobacco
pipe seem, when compared with this," exclaimed
an English traveler when he first saw a *hookah*.
After a meal in rich Indian households, stewards would carry
in magnificent silver and gold hookahs—pipes in which
tobacco smoke was drawn through a long, coiled tube and
passed through an urn of water to cool it. Smoking hookahs
became fashionable for Europeans in early eighteenth-century
India and had its own elaborate etiquette:

> The rage of smoking extends even to the ladies; and the high-
> est compliment they can pay a man is to give him preference
> for smoking his hookah. In this case it is a point of politeness
> to take off a mouthpiece he is using and substitute a fresh
> one, which he presents to the lady with his hookah, who soon
> returns it.

Later English settlers were much more reluctant to adopt
Indian habits. General Sir Alured Clarke, soon after arriving
in Calcutta in 1797, was confounded by the sight of his
nephew smoking a hookah at the dinner table:

> Sir Alured, with considerable asperity, looking at his nephew,
> who sat nearly opposite to him, said, "Pray, sir, give me leave
> to ask what that may be?" "A hookah," bluntly replied Cap-
> tain Griffith. "A hookah," echoed the General, "it is a useless
> if not an offensive thing."

A meal in Awadh usually concluded with a hookah, which
was maintained by a skilled attendant employed solely for

FOR THE CHICKEN

*1 pound boneless, skinless chicken
    breast or thighs, washed and cut
    into 1-inch pieces*
Salt to taste
¼ teaspoon ground black pepper
½ teaspoon garam masala
¼ teaspoon whole cumin seeds
1 tablespoon lemon juice
*2 tablespoons chopped fresh
    coriander leaves*
1 garlic clove, grated
¼-inch piece of ginger, grated
1 teaspoon fennel seeds, powdered fine
1 bay leaf, crushed fine
*3 tablespoons besan (chickpea flour)
    or 3 tablespoons cornstarch*
2 tablespoons vegetable oil

FOR THE SAUCE

½ cup yogurt, not low-fat
2 tablespoons vegetable oil
½ teaspoon whole fennel seeds
1¼ cups chopped onions
½ cup diced tomatoes
1 bay leaf
1 whole clove
1 whole cardamom
¼-inch cinnamon stick
10 raw almonds, powdered fine

Salt to taste

¼ teaspoon ground black pepper

¼ teaspoon cayenne pepper

½ teaspoon turmeric

½ teaspoon ground coriander seeds

½ teaspoon ground cumin seeds

½ teaspoon garam masala

1 teaspoon kasoori methi
   (dried fenugreek leaves)

1 cup water

this purpose. Few people in Indian cities today have the time or leisure required for preparing and smoking hookahs. In villages, where the pace of life is slower, the old practice still survives. In the evening, after dinner, men congregate in the shade of a large tree to talk and share a hookah.

Masala Murgh is a chicken dish from Awadh that would go well with naan and Gobhi Mussallam (spicy baked cauliflower topped with cottage cheese, bread crumbs, and nuts, page 155)—and perhaps a hookah afterward!

- Combine all ingredients for the chicken (except the chickpea flour and oil) in a large mixing bowl. Toss well, cover, and refrigerate for at least 15 minutes.
- To make the sauce, first thicken the yogurt. Line a fine mesh sieve with a coffee filter or 2 layers of cheesecloth, set it over a bowl, and pour in the yogurt. Let it drain for 2 hours or overnight in the refrigerator.
- Warm the oil in a nonstick skillet over medium-high heat. Add the fennel seeds and, after a few seconds, the chopped onions. Sauté for about 5 minutes, until the onions are lightly touched with brown. Lift them out of the oil, leaving behind as much oil as possible. Combine with the tomatoes in a food processor or blender and mince well.
- Warm the remaining oil in the skillet over medium heat. Add the bay leaf, clove, cardamom, and cinnamon. After a few seconds, add the powdered almonds. Stir for 30 seconds, then add the onion-tomato mixture and cook, stirring occasionally for about 5 minutes, until all the moisture has evaporated. Add salt and all the spices and cook for 1 minute. Stir in the thickened yogurt and cook for 5 minutes, until the oil appears around the edges. Now pour in the water, cover, and bring to a boil. Immediately reduce heat to low and cook for 15 minutes. This sauce can be made up to 2 days in advance and refrigerated until needed.
- To cook the chicken, sprinkle the chickpea flour or cornstarch over the marinated chicken and mix in with a spoon.

Warm 2 tablespoons of oil in a nonstick skillet over medium-high heat. Stir-fry the chicken until cooked through, crisp, and golden—about 5 minutes for breasts, 8 for thighs. Drain on paper towels, then fold gently into the warmed-up sauce. Serve immediately.

• SERVES 3 TO 4 WITH OTHER DISHES

Murgh Nizami

Chicken cooked with sautéed onions, tomatoes, yogurt, nuts, and spices, with mint and raisins

 When Niccolò Manucci—an Italian who spent most of his life in India—disembarked from his ship in 1656, his first sight of Indians horrified him:

I was much surprised to see that almost everybody was spitting something as red as blood. I imagined it must be due to some complaint of the country, or that their teeth have become broken. I asked an English lady what was the matter, and whether it was the practice in this country for the inhabitants to have their teeth extracted. When she understood my question, she answered that it was not any disease, but [due to] a certain aromatic leaf, called in the language of the country, *pan,* or in Portuguese, *betele.* She ordered some leaves to be brought, ate some herself, and gave me some to eat. Having taken them, my head swam to such an extent that I feared I was dying. It caused me to fall down, I lost my colour, and endured agonies, but she poured into my mouth a little salt, and brought me to my senses. The lady assured me that everyone who ate it for the first time felt the same effects.

Visitors to India quickly become accustomed to the sight of people chewing paan, which is a betel leaf wrapped around a

2 tablespoons vegetable oil

½ teaspoon cumin seeds

2 cups finely chopped onions

4 garlic cloves, chopped

½-inch piece of ginger, chopped

10 raw almonds

10 raw cashews

1 teaspoon whole fennel seeds

1 cup plain yogurt, not low-fat

½ cup diced plum tomatoes, canned or fresh

Salt to taste

¼ teaspoon ground black pepper

¼ teaspoon cayenne pepper

½ teaspoon turmeric

1 teaspoon ground coriander seeds

¾ teaspoon ground cumin seeds

½ teaspoon garam masala

3 pounds skinned chicken thighs and/or drumsticks, washed and drained

1 tablespoon raw pistachios

2 tablespoons golden raisins

2 tablespoons chopped fresh mint leaves

2 tablespoons chopped fresh coriander leaves

2 tablespoons heavy cream (optional)

1 tablespoon lemon juice

mixture of ingredients that include sliced betel nut, lime paste, cardamom, and cloves. Paan acts as a breath freshener, but has the unfortunate effect of temporarily turning the mouth bright red.

A meal in Hyderabad always concludes with paan. As contented diners lean back after a satisfying repast, a good paan is all that is required to complete their sense of well-being. Parents arranging the marriage of their son are always careful to first inquire about the skill of the prospective bride in making paan.

This wonderful dish from Hyderabad is redolent with coconut and raisins. Serve it with plain cooked rice and Baghare Baingan (stuffed eggplant cooked in a spicy nutty sauce, page 149). If you want an authentic Hyderabadi dinner, offer your guests a platter of paan after the meal. Go ahead, it's quite safe—I have never heard of anyone besides Manucci collapsing in agony after eating paan!

- Warm the oil in a nonstick skillet over medium-high heat. Add the cumin seeds and, after a few seconds, the chopped onions, garlic, and ginger. Sauté, stirring occasionally for 8–10 minutes, until lightly browned. Cool slightly and lift them out of the oil, leaving behind as much oil as possible. Put them in the container of a food processor or blender.

- In a clean coffee or spice grinder, powder the almonds, cashews, and fennel seeds. Add this powder to the onions in the food processor, along with the yogurt, tomatoes, salt, pepper, cayenne, turmeric, ground coriander, ground cumin, and garam masala. Process until smooth.

- Warm the leftover oil in the skillet over medium-high heat and add the onion mixture. Stir constantly for 5 minutes, then reduce heat to medium and stir for another 5 minutes, until the mixture has thickened and the oil appears around the edges. Add the chicken, the whole pistachios, and the raisins, then cover and bring to a boil. Immediately reduce the heat to medium-low and cook for 30 minutes, or until the chicken is tender, stirring occasionally. The sauce should be very thick at the end of cooking. Gently fold in the chopped mint, coriander, cream, and lemon juice and serve hot. This dish can be made up to 3 days ahead of time; reheat gently so as not to curdle the cream.

• SERVES 4 TO 6

Dhaniye aur Kaju wala Murgh

Chicken cooked with cashews and fresh coriander

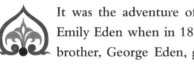 It was the adventure of a lifetime for Fanny and Emily Eden when in 1838 they accompanied their brother, George Eden, governor general of India, on a visit to the court of Ranjit Singh, king of Punjab. The English visitors were met by an army of Sikh horsemen who formed a four-mile line on either side of the road. The soldiers were a magnificent sight, in uniforms of gold and silver brocade and orange turbans topped by black heron's plumes, with beards flowing down to their waists. To ensure that the governor general camped in salubrious surroundings, Ranjit Singh sent six hundred gardeners to set up a splendid garden around his tent in just one day.

Ranjit Singh's feasts were equally lavish. Fanny described a banquet he gave to welcome the Eden family:

The table was covered with gold bottles and cups and some specimens of Sikh cookery—spiced balls of meat, or rather essence of meat, of very strong composition, pomegranate seeds etc. . . . The composition he calls wine is like burning fire, much stronger than brandy, and his great delight when he sets in to be gay is to make people drink it. . . . I got on very well for some time, pretending to drink it and passing it to his cup-bearer. But he grew suspicious, put it up to his one eye,

FOR THE MARINADE
¼ cup raw cashews
1 teaspoon ground coriander seeds
¾ teaspoon ground cumin seeds
½ teaspoon cayenne pepper
¼ to ½ teaspoon ground
  black pepper
Salt to taste
½ teaspoon garam masala
½ teaspoon turmeric
1 cup plain yogurt, not low-fat
2 garlic cloves, chopped
½-inch piece of ginger, chopped
1 cup packed fresh coriander leaves
  and upper stems, washed and
  drained
1 hot green chili, stemmed
8 skinless chicken thighs, bone-in,
  washed and drained

FOR THE GARNISH
2 tablespoons vegetable oil
½ teaspoon cumin seeds

2 medium onions, peeled and
  thinly sliced
¼ cup raw cashews
½ cup fresh coriander leaves, chopped
1 tablespoon lemon juice

looked well into the cup, shook his head and gave it me back again. The next time he put his finger into the cup to see how much was gone. I made Major Wade explain to him that ladies did not drink so much in England, upon which he watched till George's head was turned away and passed a cup to me under his arm, thinking George was the horrid tyrant who prevented me.

Fanny was far too preoccupied to sample much "Sikh cookery," but this recipe, a fine example, is easy to make. The chicken can be marinated in the yogurt, nuts, and spices a day in advance. The next day, cook it till tender and fold in sautéed onions and cashews. The sauce is rich, nutty, and imbued with the fragrance of coriander leaves. I like to serve it with rice and Bhindi ki Sabzi (page 158).

- In a coffee or spice grinder, powder the cashews. Transfer to a mixing bowl and add the ground coriander seeds, ground cumin seeds, cayenne pepper, black pepper, salt, garam masala, turmeric, and yogurt. In a food processor, mince the garlic, ginger, coriander, and green chili. Mix into the yogurt and spices, then toss in the chicken and coat well. Refrigerate for at least 2 hours, or overnight if possible.
- To cook, warm oil in a nonstick skillet over medium-high heat and add the cumin seeds. After a few seconds, add the onions and cashews. Sauté for about 10 minutes, until the onions are golden. Transfer to a small bowl, leaving behind as much oil as possible. Keep the skillet on medium-high heat and add the chicken and its marinade. Stir well, cover, and bring to a boil. Reduce heat to medium-low and cook for 40 minutes or until tender, stirring occasionally. Fold in the onions, cashews, chopped coriander leaves, and lemon juice. Cook for 5 minutes, then serve hot. This dish can be made up to 3 days ahead of time.

  - SERVES 3 TO 4 WITH OTHER DISHES

Murgh Paneer Anardaana

Chicken and cottage cheese cooked with sautéed onions, tomatoes, and dried pomegranate seeds

 "He is exactly like an old mouse, with grey whiskers and one eye" was how Emily Eden described Ranjit Singh, king of Punjab. She met him in 1838, only a year before he died, but age had not dimmed the old autocrat's zest for life. At a dinner for his English visitors, the king was shocked to discover that Englishmen were allowed only one wife, and that Emily's brother, Governor General George Eden, did not have even this minimal number. Sikhs were allowed twenty-five wives, explained Ranjit Singh. An excellent custom, agreed the governor general, and one he would try to introduce when he returned home to England.

An unstinting host, the king insisted on piling far more food than Emily could eat onto her plate. She got rid of it unobtrusively:

> That carpet must have presented a horrible scene when we went. I know that under my own chair I deposited two broiled quails, an apple, a pear, a great lump of sweetmeat, and some pomegranate seeds, which Runjeet gave me with his dirty fingers into my hand, which, of course, became equally dirty at last.

Fresh pomegranate seeds, which Emily dropped under her chair, are very popular in India. Dried pomegranate seeds are used in Punjabi cooking to add a tart flavor. In this recipe, I have cooked boneless chicken thighs and cubes of cottage cheese in a deliciously piquant sauce of sautéed onions and dried powdered pomegranate seeds. The addition of chopped

1½ cups finely chopped onions, plus 1 small onion, finely chopped

4 garlic cloves, chopped

½-inch piece of ginger, chopped

2 tablespoons vegetable oil

½ teaspoon cumin seeds

1 bay leaf

1 whole cardamom

1 whole clove

½-inch cinnamon stick

8 ounces paneer (cottage cheese), cut into 1-inch pieces

1 cup diced tomatoes, fresh or canned

3 tablespoons dried whole pomegranate seeds or 3 tablespoons powdered seeds

Salt to taste

½ teaspoon ground black pepper

1 teaspoon ground coriander seeds

¾ teaspoon ground cumin seeds

1 teaspoon garam masala

½ cup water

6 boneless, skinless chicken thighs, washed and halved

1 tablespoon lemon juice

1 medium tomato, finely chopped

*1 hot green chili, stemmed and finely
  chopped*
*½ cup chopped fresh
  coriander leaves*

fresh onions and tomatoes, which are folded in when the dish is done, makes Murgh Paneer Anardaana special. Serve it with an Indian bread.

- In a food processor, mince the 1½ cups chopped onions, garlic, and ginger.
- Warm the oil in a nonstick skillet over medium-high heat. Add the cumin seeds, bay leaf, cardamom, clove, and cinnamon and, after a few seconds, the minced onion mixture. Sauté, stirring, for 10 minutes. Reduce the heat to medium and add the pieces of cottage cheese. Sauté for another 5 minutes, stirring gently once or twice in between.
- Puree the diced tomatoes in the food processor, then stir into the onions in the pan and cook for 5 minutes, stirring very gently now and then. In a clean coffee or spice grinder, powder the dried pomegranate seeds. Add them to the skillet along with the salt, pepper, ground coriander, ground cumin, and ¾ teaspoon of the garam masala. Sauté for 1 minute, then mix in the water. Add the halved chicken thighs, coating well with sauce. Cover and bring to a boil, then immediately reduce heat to medium-low and cook for 30 minutes or until the chicken is tender and the sauce clings thickly. If you have a soupy sauce, uncover and boil off some of the excess liquid.
- When the chicken is done, gently fold in the lemon juice, the reserved ¼ teaspoon garam masala, and the chopped remaining onion, the tomato, chili, and fresh coriander, and serve. This dish can be made up to 3 days ahead of time, but mix in the fresh onion, tomato, chili, and coriander just before serving.
- SERVES 3 TO 4 WITH OTHER DISHES

Murgh Tamatari

Chicken cooked with onions, tomatoes, and spices

Baisakhi is a harvest festival marking the end of winter in northern India, when crops are gathered before the summer sun parches the fields. People of all religions celebrate the festival, but for Sikhs it has a special significance. It was on Baisakhi Day in 1699 that Guru Gobind Singh founded the order of the Khalsa—the Pure—to defend the Sikh faith against Moghul persecution. The Guru asked for a volunteer who was willing to lay down his life. He led the man who came forward into a tent, from which he emerged alone a few minutes later carrying a bloody sword in his hand. Four more brave souls stepped forward, and each disappeared by turn into the tent. Finally, with the crowd increasingly frantic, the Guru revealed that it had just been a test of their resolution: he had only slaughtered a goat. The five "beloved ones," as they were henceforth called, became the core of the Khalsa, the army of Sikhs, which one day conquered the entire Punjab.

Baisakhi is celebrated by Sikhs with a procession led by five men carrying drawn swords. Men dance the lively *Bhangra*, while women perform the *Gidda* dance. Above all, though, Baisakhi is an occasion for feasting, and a time to give thanks for a bountiful harvest. It is the season when tomatoes are plentiful, and they are used in many dishes for the Baisakhi feast.

This simple, delicious chicken dish is cooked in typical Punjabi style with lots of tomatoes; you can use either canned or fresh. Serve with rice and Bhindi ki Sabzi (okra stir-fried with onions, garlic, and spices, page 158).

- Warm the oil in a nonstick skillet over medium-high heat. Add the cumin seeds and after a few seconds, the grated

2 tablespoons vegetable oil
½ teaspoon cumin seeds
2 garlic cloves, grated
1-inch piece of ginger, grated
1½ cups finely chopped onions
2 cups diced tomatoes, fresh or canned
Salt to taste
½ teaspoon turmeric
¼ to ½ teaspoon cayenne pepper
1 teaspoon ground coriander seeds
½ teaspoon ground cumin seeds
½ teaspoon garam masala
*2 pounds chicken drumsticks
    and/or thighs, skinned, washed,
    and patted dry*
1 tablespoon lemon juice
*2 tablespoons chopped fresh
    coriander leaves*

garlic and ginger. Sauté for 1 minute, then add the onions. Sauté for about 5 minutes, stirring occasionally, until lightly browned. Reduce heat to medium-low and mix in the tomatoes. Cook for another 8 to 10 minutes, mashing with the back of your spoon until the oil appears around the edges. Add the salt and all the spices and stir for another minute. Now add the chicken and mix well with the sautéed spice paste. Cover and bring to a boil, then reduce heat to low and cook for about 25 minutes, stirring occasionally, until the chicken is tender. Mix in the lemon juice and fresh coriander leaves. This dish can be made up to 3 days ahead of time.

• SERVES 3 TO 4 WITH OTHER DISHES

Dum Machali

Grilled marinated fish baked in a sauce of sautéed onions, sun-dried tomatoes, and yogurt

1 pound thick-cut firm-fleshed fish
   fillet, such as rainbow trout or
   salmon

FOR THE MARINADE
1 tablespoon lemon juice
Salt to taste
½ teaspoon turmeric
¼ teaspoon cayenne pepper
¼ teaspoon ground black pepper

FOR THE SAUCE
2 tablespoons vegetable oil
¼ teaspoon cumin seeds

 Asaf ud Daula, ruler of Awadh, was interviewing a new cook who was being unusually difficult. The new employee presented a long list of demands: he wanted a monthly salary of 500 rupees—a princely sum; he would prepare nothing but dal (lentils); he had to be informed a day in advance when his services were required; and when the dal was ready, it had to be eaten without delay. The king, who appreciated the value of a good cook, willingly agreed to all these conditions. But the chef's debut proved to be a disaster, for when the meal was ready, Asaf ud Daula was deep in conversation with a visitor. Three reminders later, he still had not appeared at the table. The infuriated cook hurled the bowl of dal out of a window, where it fell at the foot of a withered old tree, and departed in a huff. People in Awadh still describe, in awed whispers, how the dead tree burst into blossom the next morning.

The great chefs of Awadh were indulged in their idiosyncrasies because they were considered great artists of culinary masterpieces. Much of their creativity went into preparing fish caught in the rivers that flow through Awadh. This lightly grilled fish is baked in a sauce of sautéed onions, yogurt, sun-dried tomatoes, and fresh herbs. It is delicious with naan, and I guarantee you won't have to remind your guests three times to come and eat it.

1¼ cups finely chopped onions
1 garlic clove, chopped
¼-inch piece of ginger, chopped
1 cup plain yogurt, not low-fat
10 sun- or oven-dried tomato halves
½ cup fresh coriander leaves and
   tender upper stems, washed and
   drained well
Salt to taste
½ teaspoon garam masala
½ teaspoon ground cumin seeds
½ teaspoon ground coriander seeds

- Wash the fish and pat it dry with paper towels. Place in a single layer in a large dish and sprinkle evenly with the lemon juice, salt, turmeric, cayenne, and ground black pepper. Cover and refrigerate for 1 hour. Preheat the oven broiler. Line a large ovenproof dish with foil and place a grilling rack on top. Lift the fillets out of their marinade and put them side by side on the rack with the skin side down. Grill them in the oven for 5 minutes, without turning. Cool slightly and remove the skin, dividing the fish into chunks as you do so. Remove the foil from the baking dish and put the fish chunks in the dish.

- Warm the oil in a nonstick pan over medium-high heat. Add the cumin seeds and, after a few seconds, the chopped onions, garlic, and ginger. Sauté, stirring occasionally, for about 5 minutes, until lightly browned. Lift the sautéed vegetables out of the oil and combine in a food processor or blender with the yogurt, sun-dried tomatoes, fresh coriander, salt, garam masala, ground cumin, and ground coriander seeds. Mince well and pour this sauce over the fish. Preheat the oven to 250°F. Seal the dish tightly with foil and bake for 45 minutes.

  - SERVES 3 TO 4 WITH OTHER DISHES

Chutney Fish Curry

Fish fillets marinated in a fresh herb chutney, grilled and
cooked in a sauce of sautéed onions, tomatoes, and spices

1½ pounds thick-cut rainbow trout
    or other firm fish fillet

FOR THE MARINADE

1 cup fresh coriander leaves and
    tender stems, washed

½ cup fresh mint leaves, washed

1 green chili, stemmed

3 tablespoons plain yogurt,
    not low-fat

2 tablespoons lemon juice

Salt to taste

¼ teaspoon turmeric

FOR THE SAUCE

2 tablespoons vegetable oil

¼ teaspoon ajwain (carom seeds)
    or ¼ teaspoon cumin seeds

2 garlic cloves, finely chopped

¼-inch piece of ginger, grated or
    minced

1¼ cups finely chopped onions

1 cup diced tomatoes, canned
    or fresh

Salt to taste

½ teaspoon ground coriander seeds

¼ teaspoon ground cumin seeds

¼ teaspoon garam masala

¼ teaspoon turmeric

¼ teaspoon cayenne pepper

 The Maratha rebellion seemed doomed in 1666. Outnumbered by the immense Moghul army, the rebel leader, Shivaji, was forced to surrender. Shivaji was taken to the imperial court at Agra and placed under house arrest while Emperor Aurangzeb considered his fate. Surprisingly, Shivaji tried to ingratiate himself with the Moghul nobles, sending them food prepared by his cooks in the Maharashtrian style. The courtiers felt obliged to respond to his generosity and sent him enormous platters of rich Moghul food. Every day huge baskets of food, each so big it had to be carried by two porters, went in and out of Shivaji's house. The guards at first diligently searched every container, but soon became so accustomed to these comings and goings that they waved the porters through with only a perfunctory glance.

Then Shivaji fell ill and retired to his bedchamber, complaining that he was not used to eating so much rich food. When the guards finally got suspicious and burst into his room, they found it empty—Shivaji was long gone, smuggled out in one of the immense food baskets. Shivaji's daring escape galvanized the Marathas, and they rose up in a rebellion that eventually brought down the mighty Moghul Empire.

This delicate fish curry is a good example of the Maharashtrian delicacies that Shivaji used to tempt his captors. Maharashtrian cooks use spices with a light hand so as not to overpower the natural flavor, color, and texture of the main ingredient. Here, the fish is first marinated in a fresh herb chutney, then grilled, and finally cooked in a spicy, slightly sweet sauce of sautéed onions and tomatoes. The flavors of the chutney, the sauce, and the fish blend wonderfully.

- Wash the fish and dry with paper towels. Place in a single layer, skin side down, in a large flat dish. In a blender, combine all marinade ingredients and puree till smooth. Pour this marinade over the fish, cover, and refrigerate for at least an hour.

- When ready to cook, line an ovenproof dish with foil and put a grilling rack over it. Lift the fillets out of their marinade and arrange them skin side down side by side on the rack. If your grilling rack is not large enough to accommodate all the fillets, you may have to grill in batches. (You can also grill on an outdoor barbecue.) Place the oven rack on the second rung from the top in your oven and preheat the broiler. Broil the fillets for about 10 minutes, until grilled just enough to loosen their skins and achieve a roasted aroma. Remove from the oven, and when they are cool enough to handle, remove the skins and divide the meat into bite-size chunks. Set aside in a bowl.

- To make the sauce, warm the oil in a nonstick skillet over medium-high heat. Add the carom or cumin seeds. As soon as they begin to sputter, add the garlic and ginger. Sauté for about 30 seconds, then stir in the onions. Sauté, stirring occasionally for about 5 minutes, until the onions are lightly browned. Reduce heat to medium and add the tomatoes. Cook for 5 minutes, blending them in with the back of your spoon. Then add salt, all the spices, and sugar, and cook for 1 minute. Add the water and bring to a boil, then mix in the grilled fish, spooning the sauce gently over. Cover and cook on medium-low heat for 12 to 15 minutes. You can grill the fish ahead of time, or make the entire dish up to 3 days ahead of time.

  - SERVES 4 WITH OTHER DISHES

¼ teaspoon ground black pepper

1 teaspoon sugar

1 cup water

Hariyali Keema

Ground lamb cooked with spinach and sour cream and a fresh herb chutney

8 ounces fresh spinach, washed,
   with woody stems trimmed

2 tablespoons vegetable oil

½ teaspoon cumin seeds

1½ cups finely chopped onions

4 garlic cloves, finely chopped

1 cup diced tomatoes, canned or fresh

3 tablespoons sour cream

Salt to taste

¼ teaspoon cayenne pepper

¼ teaspoon ground black pepper

½ teaspoon turmeric

1 teaspoon ground coriander seeds

½ teaspoon ground cumin seeds

1 pound lean ground lamb, washed
   and drained in fine mesh sieve

1 cup frozen peas

FOR THE CHUTNEY

1 cup packed fresh coriander leaves
   and tender upper stems, washed

½ cup packed fresh mint leaves,
   washed

½-inch piece of ginger, chopped

1 hot green chili, stemmed

1 ripe tomato, quartered

1 tablespoon lemon juice

½ teaspoon ground roasted
   cumin seeds

½ teaspoon garam masala

When a Hyderabadi noble sat down to breakfast, it was no rushed affair. The entire extended family—including children, grandchildren, aunts, uncles, and cousins—ate together; there were usually more than fifty people at a meal. Everyone sat cross-legged on the carpet with the food on a cloth spread before them: covered dishes of parathas (pan-fried flatbread), keema (spiced ground lamb), eggs, and khichadi (rice and lentils cooked together). Trays of fresh fruit followed: mangoes, papayas, peaches, grapes, and bananas. The meal ended with hot, sweetened, milky tea.

An enormous kitchen functioned continuously to produce these vast quantities of food. There was a strict hierarchy of kitchen servants: the most trusted servants, who had served the family for generations, supervised. Cooking was done by women known as *bua*s or aunts, each of whom specialized in just a few dishes. Each of the buas was assisted by four girls whom they trained in the art of cooking. Finally, there was an army of women to do laborious chores such as pounding spices, cleaning rice and lentils, chopping vegetables, and washing the dishes.

Keema can be served at any meal. This unusual keema from Hyderabad is fragrant with fresh herbs, which are folded in after cooking to retain their aroma. The herbs and spinach add a delicate green color to the dish, which is aptly named Hariyali Keema, or green keema. Serve with plain cooked rice and have leftovers with parathas for breakfast.

- In a microwave-safe bowl, covered tightly with plastic wrap, microwave the spinach on high for 6 minutes. (You can also

Women in the kitchen, nineteenth century

cook the spinach in water in a saucepan for 6 to 8 minutes till soft.) Lift the spinach out of its liquid and mash well on a chopping board with a fork. Transfer to a bowl and set aside.

- Warm the oil in a nonstick skillet over medium-high heat. Add the cumin seeds and, after a few seconds, the chopped onions and garlic. Sauté for about 5 minutes, until the onions are lightly browned. Reduce heat to medium and add the tomatoes. Cook for 5 to 8 minutes, blending them in with the back of your spoon. Add the sour cream and stir for 2 minutes. Mix in the salt, cayenne pepper, black pepper, turmeric, ground coriander, and ground cumin seeds. Now add the lamb and stir-fry for 5 minutes, taking care to break up all the lumps. Stir in the peas and 1 cup of water, cover, and bring to a boil. Reduce heat to medium-low and cook for 20 minutes. Then add the spinach, mix well, and re-cover. Cook for another 10 minutes, or until the lamb is tender.

- While the lamb is cooking, in a blender, combine the coriander, mint, ginger, chili, tomato, lemon juice, and roasted cumin seeds. Blend to a smooth paste, adding a tablespoonful or two of water if necessary. Fold this chutney into the lamb along with the garam masala and mix well. Remove the skillet from the heat. You can make this dish up to 3 days ahead of time; reheat gently to preserve the fresh flavor of the herbs.

- SERVES 3 TO 4 WITH OTHER DISHES

Shahi Gosht Korma

Lamb cooked in a rich sauce of onions, yogurt, and nuts

1 cup plain yogurt, not low-fat
3 tablespoons vegetable oil
½ teaspoon cumin seeds
1¼ cups finely chopped onions
2 garlic cloves, chopped
½-inch piece of ginger, chopped
¼ cup raw cashews
1 teaspoon white poppy seeds
   (optional)
1 tablespoon desiccated unsweetened
   coconut
1 teaspoon whole fennel seeds
1 bay leaf
¼ teaspoon ajwain (carom seeds)
   (optional)
½ teaspoon ground coriander seeds
½ teaspoon ground cumin seeds
½ teaspoon garam masala

 An Englishwoman, after living for several years in India during the 1830s, was asked what she had seen of the country and its people. "Oh, nothing!" said she, "thank goodness, I know nothing at all about them, nor I don't wish to: really I think the less one sees and knows of them the better!"

Sadly, this attitude was only too typical of the British who colonized India. But then there was Fanny Parks, who accompanied her husband, who was a government official, to India in 1822 and lived there for the next twenty-four years. Insatiably curious, she delved deep into Indian life and meticulously recorded everything in her journals. She befriended the Begam (queen) of Awadh and was a guest at a royal wedding. She described dinner:

Of course, according to Asiatic custom, we all sat on the ground. The Begam said, "What shall we do? We have no knives and forks for the bibi sahiba." I assured her my fingers were more useful than forks. She sent me a large dish, well filled and well silvered. . . . After holding forth my right hand to have water poured upon it, I boldly dipped my fingers into the dish, and contrived to appease my hunger very comfortably, much to the amusement of the Asiatic ladies.

When eating this dish, I recommend that you follow the example of the adventurous Mrs. Parks and eat with your fingers. It is a much easier way to eat this korma than using a fork and knife, as the meat contains bones and the sauce is cooked until thick, so it can be scooped up with pieces of naan.

Salt to taste
Small pinch of saffron
¼ teaspoon cayenne pepper
1 pound bone-in lamb, cut into 1-inch
    pieces, washed, and drained
1 whole cardamom
1 whole clove
½-inch cinnamon stick
1 cup water
10 raw almonds
1 tablespoon heavy cream

- Line a fine mesh sieve with 2 layers of cheesecloth or a coffee filter and place over a bowl. Pour in the yogurt, cover, and refrigerate overnight.
- Warm the oil in a nonstick skillet over medium-high heat and add the cumin seeds, then, after a second, the chopped onions, garlic, and ginger. Sauté for about 5 minutes, until the onions are lightly brown. Lift them out of the oil, leaving as much oil behind as possible, and put them in a food processor or blender. Scrape the thickened yogurt into the food processor as well.
- Warm a small frying pan over medium heat and add the cashews, poppy seeds, coconut, fennel seeds, bay leaf, and ajwain, if using. Toast for a few minutes until they change color and smell roasted. Transfer to a clean coffee or spice grinder and powder finely. Add this powder to the food processor, along with the ground coriander, ground cumin, garam masala, salt, saffron, and cayenne pepper, and mince well, then transfer to a large mixing bowl. Mix in the cubed lamb and coat well. At this point, you can either marinate the meat for a few hours (or overnight in the refrigerator) or you can cook it right away.
- Warm leftover oil in the nonstick skillet over medium-high heat. Add the whole cardamom, clove, and cinnamon. Pour

in the lamb with all its marinade and stir-fry continuously for 10 minutes. Reduce the heat to medium and stir-fry for another 10 minutes. By this time the moisture should have evaporated and the oil should be floating on top. Stir in 1 cup of water and transfer the meat to a pressure cooker. Bring to high pressure, then reduce the heat to low and cook for 10 to 12 minutes. Let the pressure drop before you open the cooker and boil off the excess liquid. (You can also cook it in a saucepan or the skillet if you don't have a pressure cooker: Cook for 1 hour or until the lamb is tender, stirring occasionally.) The sauce should be very thick at the end of the cooking time. Cool for 5 minutes. Powder the almonds in a clean coffee or spice grinder and mix them into the lamb curry along with the heavy cream. This dish can be prepared up to 3 days ahead of time.

• SERVES 3 TO 4 WITH OTHER DISHES

Gosht ka Salan

Lamb curry with sautéed onions, tomatoes, yogurt, and baby potatoes

1 pound small new white potatoes
   (12 to 14)
1¼ cups finely chopped onions
2 garlic cloves, chopped
½-inch piece of ginger, chopped
3 tablespoons vegetable oil
½ teaspoon cumin seeds
1 cup diced tomatoes, canned or fresh
½ cup plain yogurt, not low-fat
1 teaspoon ground coriander seeds
½ teaspoon ground cumin seeds
½ teaspoon turmeric
¼ teaspoon cayenne pepper

It is written in the Koran that God tested the faith of Ibrahim by asking him to sacrifice his son Ismail. Without hesitation Ibrahim prepared to do as commanded, but blindfolded himself so that his hand would not falter. When the sacrifice was over and he uncovered his eyes, Ismail stood before him, for an angel had saved his son and placed a ram on the sacrificial altar instead.

To honor the devotion of Ibrahim, Muslims celebrate the festival of Baqr-Id. A goat is ceremoniously sacrificed and the meat is distributed. People congregate in mosques to offer prayers. Then it is time for a feast, and cooks vie with one another to create delicious dishes from the goat meat.

Salan refers to any meat dish cooked with vegetables. In this recipe from Hyderabad, I have cooked lamb with small new potatoes, which absorb the flavor of the sauce. Cooked with goat, this dish would be ideal for a Baqr-Id feast. Serve with rice or Indian bread and Baghare Baingan (stuffed eggplant cooked in a spicy nutty sauce, page 149).

1 teaspoon kasoori methi
(dried fenugreek leaves)
Salt to taste
¾ teaspoon garam masala
1 pound bone-in lamb, cubed,
washed, and drained
2 cups water

- Boil the potatoes until they are just tender but not mushy. Cool and peel, then halve the larger ones. In a food processor, mince the onions, garlic, and ginger.
- Warm the oil in a nonstick skillet over medium-high heat. Gently slide in the potatoes and stir-fry for 8 to 10 minutes, until lightly browned all over. Drain on paper towels and set aside. Put the cumin seeds in the same oil, set over medium-high heat. After a few seconds, add the minced onion mixture and stir-fry for about 8 minutes, until the onions are lightly brown. Meanwhile, puree the diced tomatoes in the food processor or blender. Reduce the heat to medium and add the pureed tomatoes to the skillet. Cook for 5 minutes, until all the moisture has evaporated and the oil appears around the edges. Add the yogurt, stirring all the while, and cook for 5 minutes. Now add all the spices and salt, reserving ¼ teaspoon of the garam masala for later. Toss in the cubed lamb and stir-fry for 10 minutes.
- At this point, you can either cook the lamb in a pressure cooker or continue cooking it in the skillet. Add 2 cups of water, stir well to mix, and bring to a boil. Reduce the heat to low and cook until the lamb is tender—15 minutes in the pressure cooker or 1 hour in the skillet. Stir the lamb occasionally if using the skillet, and check the water levels to make sure the curry does not burn. Uncover, add the potatoes, and continue cooking covered on medium-low heat, without pressure, for 15 minutes. Mix in the reserved ¼ teaspoon garam masala and serve. This curry can be made several days in advance and refrigerated until needed.

- SERVES 3 TO 4 WITH OTHER DISHES

Chatni Gosht

Lamb cooked with sautéed onions, yogurt, tomatoes,
and a fresh herb chutney

2 tablespoons vegetable oil

½ teaspoon cumin seeds

1 cup chopped onions

2 garlic cloves, chopped

½-inch piece of ginger, chopped

½ cup plain yogurt, not low-fat

½ cup canned crushed tomatoes

1 cup packed fresh coriander leaves
    and tender stems, washed

½ cup packed fresh mint leaves,
    washed

1 to 2 green chilies, stemmed

Salt to taste

½ teaspoon turmeric

¼ teaspoon ground black pepper

¼ teaspoon cayenne pepper (optional)

1 teaspoon ground coriander seeds

½ teaspoon ground cumin seeds

½ teaspoon garam masala

1½ pounds bone-in lamb, cubed,
    washed, and drained

½ cup water

2 tablespoons lemon juice

When John Ovington visited India in 1689, he observed that when mangoes "are Green, they are Pickl'd there and sent abroad, and make that Mango Achar, which we taste in *England*." The first samples of Indian food to reach English shores were pickles, and the Hindi word for pickle, *achar*, was well known. Chutneys and pickles could be shipped long distances without spoiling since they were preserved in oil, vinegar, and spices. Like pickles, Indian chutneys were immensely popular in England and inspired a number of locally produced varieties, including, most famously, those of Major Grey. Their renown led John F. Mackay to ponder:

> All things chickeney and mutt'ny
> Taste better far when served with chutney
> This is the mystery eternal:
> Why didn't Major Grey make Colonel?

Major Grey might not have recognized the chutney used here, which is made fresh rather than preserved and bottled. The lamb is first marinated in a sautéed onion and fresh herb chutney, then cooked until the sauce is very thick. The wonderful aroma of the chutney permeates the lamb, giving it a fresh minty flavor. Any kind of Indian bread would go well with this dish.

- Warm the oil in a large nonstick skillet over medium-high heat. Add the cumin seeds and, after a few seconds, the chopped onions, garlic, and ginger. Sauté, stirring for about 5 minutes, until the onions are lightly browned. Lift them out of the oil, leaving behind as much oil as possible, and put into a food processor or blender. Add the yogurt, tomatoes, fresh coriander, mint, green chilies, salt, and all the spices and process until everything is smooth. Transfer to a large bowl and toss in the lamb, coating well with marinade. At this point, you can either put the lamb in the refrigerator to marinate for a while (even overnight) or proceed with the recipe.

- Warm the leftover oil in the skillet over high heat and carefully add the lamb and its marinade, then mix in ½ cup of water. Cover and bring to a boil. Reduce the heat to medium-low and cook, stirring occasionally, for 1 hour or until the lamb is tender and done to your liking; the sauce should be quite thick. Mix in the lemon juice and serve. This dish can be made up to 3 days ahead of time.

- SERVES 3 TO 4 WITH OTHER DISHES

Kolhapuri Mutton Curry

Lamb cooked with sautéed onions, tomatoes, coconut, and poppy seeds

 Indians, reported John Ovington in 1689, are "struck with astonishment at the voratious Appetites of the Christians, who . . . sacrifice whole Hecatombs of Animals to their Gluttony." Other Englishmen in India might have been eating well, but not the ambassadors sent to the Maratha court. To their dismay, they were offered "only *Cutchery*, a sort of Pulse and Rice mixed together, and boiled in Butter." This seemed no great hardship to Shivaji, king of the Marathas, whose only meal of the day was a bowl of rice and lentils. But the English ambassadors who "had been used to Feed on good Flesh" craved meat, which had to be roasted and not "stew'd, bak'd or made into Pottage." Goat's meat—

2 tablespoons vegetable oil

½ teaspoon cumin seeds

3 garlic cloves, chopped

½-inch piece of ginger, chopped

2 cups chopped onions

1 teaspoon white poppy seeds

1 tablespoon white sesame seeds

4 tablespoons desiccated unsweetened coconut

1 cup diced tomatoes, canned or fresh

Salt to taste

½ teaspoon turmeric

¼ to ½ teaspoon cayenne pepper

1 teaspoon ground coriander seeds

½ cup water

1½ pounds bone-in lamb, cubed, washed, and drained

½ teaspoon garam masala

the only kind available—was brought for the Englishmen, who consumed half a goat every day, to the amazement of the Marathas. When it was time for the English diplomats to leave, an old man requested a meeting with them. He stood gazing at them in silent wonder. He was the butcher who had been supplying the Englishmen with their daily half goat, and he explained that he just wanted to see those astounding men who in a few days had eaten more meat than he had sold in years!

Had the Englishmen eaten this popular lamb curry, they would have reconsidered their insistence on roasted meats. It is named after the city of Kolhapur, where it is said to have originated. The lamb is stewed in a rich sauce until very tender. The coconut, poppy seeds, and sesame seeds add a pleasant nutty flavor. Serve with Indian bread and Chatniwale Alu Gobhi (page 12).

- Warm the oil in a nonstick skillet over medium-high heat and add the cumin seeds, then after a few seconds, the chopped garlic, ginger, and onions. Sauté for about 5 minutes, until the onions are translucent. Add the poppy seeds, sesame seeds, and coconut. Sauté for 2 minutes, then add the tomatoes. Cook for 5 minutes, until some of their liquid has evaporated. Turn off the heat and add the salt, turmeric, cayenne, and ground coriander. Cool slightly, then transfer everything to a food processor or blender. Add the water and blend until smooth. Transfer to the same skillet, set over medium-high heat. Mix in the lamb, cover, and cook on medium-low heat for 1½ hours or until the lamb is done to your liking. The sauce should be very thick and clinging to the meat when the lamb is done. Mix in the garam masala and serve. You can make this dish up to 3 days ahead of time.

- SERVES 4 TO 6

Saag Gosht Do Pyaza

Dry lamb curry folded with spinach, sautéed onions, and mushrooms

Do Pyaza, literally translated, means "two kinds of onions." It is a traditional technique in which the meat is first cooked with onions and then mixed with sautéed onions. The Reverend Edward Terry, chaplain to the English ambassador at the Moghul court in 1615, was captivated by his first taste of Do Pyaza (referring to it as *Deu Pario*), which he described in these words:

> They have not many roast or baked meats, but stew most of their flesh. Among many dishes of this kinde Ile take notice but of one they call *Deu Pario,* made of venison cut in slices, to which they put onions and herbs, some rootes, with a little spice and butter: the most savorie meate I ever tasted, and doe almost thinke it that very dish which Jacob made ready for his father, when he got the blessing.

Here, in my version of Do Pyaza, I have added spinach and mushrooms to the meat. The sautéed onions folded in at the very end still impart their unique aroma to the dish.

- In a microwave-safe bowl, sealed tightly with plastic wrap, microwave the spinach on high for 6 minutes. (You can also cook the spinach and ½ cup water in a saucepan until it is tender.) Lift the spinach out of its cooking liquid and mash well with a fork on a chopping board, then transfer to a bowl and set aside.
- Peel and coarsely chop one of the onions. In a food processor or blender, mince the onion, garlic, and ginger, then add the tomatoes and yogurt and blend again. Add the salt and all the spices and mix again. Transfer to a pressure cooker or

8 ounces fresh spinach, washed,
   with woody stems trimmed

3 medium onions

3 garlic cloves, chopped

½-inch piece of ginger, chopped

½ cup diced tomatoes, canned or fresh

½ cup plain yogurt, not low-fat

Salt to taste

¼ teaspoon cayenne pepper

¼ teaspoon ground black pepper

½ teaspoon turmeric

½ teaspoon garam masala

1 teaspoon ground coriander seeds

¾ teaspoon ground cumin seeds

1 teaspoon kasoori methi
   (dried fenugreek leaves)

1 pound bone-in lamb, cubed,
   washed, and drained

½ cup water

15 medium white mushrooms,
   washed and halved

2 tablespoons vegetable oil

¼ teaspoon cumin seeds

1 tablespoon lemon juice

a heavy-bottomed saucepan and stir in the lamb and water (the lamb should take about 1 hour or slightly more to cook in a saucepan). If using a pressure cooker, build up the pressure, turn the heat to medium-low, and cook the lamb for 15 minutes. Switch off the stove and let the cooker cool down enough to open it. At this point you can debone the lamb, though this is optional. Add the spinach and cook covered without pressure on medium-low heat for 15 minutes, stirring occasionally. The sauce should be very thick and clinging to the meat when done.

- While the lamb is cooking, prepare the sautéed onions and mushrooms. Peel and thinly slice the remaining onions into half rings. Warm the oil in a nonstick skillet over medium-high heat. Add the cumin seeds and, after a few seconds, the sliced onions. Sauté for 10 to 12 minutes until the onions are golden-brown. Add the mushrooms to the onions and cook for 5 minutes, just until they release their liquid. Stir into the lamb and cook on medium-low heat for 5 minutes. Mix in the lemon juice. This dish can be prepared up to 3 days ahead of time.

- SERVES 3 TO 4 WITH OTHER DISHES

Subz Gosht

Lamb stewed with onions, tomatoes, yogurt, and mixed vegetables

"They roast innocent kids and call them lamb; that I detected for myself," wrote an indignant Fanny Eden in 1837. "I wonder nobody has thought of eating a young camel. They look tender and good." *Mrs. Beeton's Household Management*, considered the final authority on domestic matters in Victorian homes, sniffed that goat "is anything but pleasant to English tastes." A "mutton club" was formed in every nineteenth-century English settlement in India, run cooperatively by its members to raise sheep for their own tables. George Atkinson was well pleased with the results:

> . . . high-caste sheep are ours, albeit they are black, and albeit they are diminutive; but encouraged by grain, their little plump carcasses yield us delicious mutton . . .

Indian cooks, who saw no great difference between goat and sheep meat, were mystified by all this fuss and continued to use both.

This dish would taste equally good with goat meat or lamb, or even camel for that matter (though I have never tried the latter). It is a traditional rustic dish from Punjab. Village women set it to simmer well before daybreak so that it is ready in time for farmers to eat before going off to the fields. The meat is stewed for a long time with vegetables and spices, so bone-in meat is preferable. The dish is done when the meat is so tender that it is literally falling off the bone and the vegetables are succulent enough to melt in your mouth. If you are pressed for time, you can substitute frozen mixed vegetables. Since I prefer not to rise before dawn, I usually don't serve Subz Gosht for breakfast, but I love to have it with plain rice on a cold winter evening.

2 tablespoons vegetable oil

½ teaspoon cumin seeds

2 garlic cloves, finely chopped

½-inch piece of ginger, grated or minced

1½ cups finely chopped onions

1 hot green chili, stemmed and finely sliced

1 cup diced tomatoes, fresh or canned

½ cup plain yogurt, not low-fat

Salt to taste

1 teaspoon ground coriander seeds

¾ teaspoon ground cumin seeds

¾ teaspoon garam masala

½ teaspoon turmeric

¼ to ½ teaspoon cayenne pepper

1 teaspoon kasoori methi (dried fenugreek leaves) (optional)

1¼ pounds bone-in lamb, cubed, washed, and drained

½ cup frozen peas

1 cup small cauliflower florets

1 medium carrot, scraped and diced into ¼-inch pieces

10 green beans, trimmed and cut into ½-inch pieces

5 baby potatoes, peeled and halved

10 small mushrooms, halved

2 cups water

1 tablespoon lemon juice

½ cup fresh coriander leaves, chopped

- Warm the oil in a nonstick skillet over medium-high heat. Add the cumin seeds and, after a few seconds, the chopped chili, garlic, and ginger. Sauté for 30 seconds, then add the chopped onions. Sauté, stirring, for about 5 minutes, then reduce the heat to medium and add the tomatoes. Cook for 5 minutes, softening them with the back of your spoon. Add the yogurt, stirring all the while for 5 minutes.

- Add the salt, ground coriander, ground cumin, ½ teaspoon of the garam masala, turmeric, cayenne, and fenugreek leaves. Cook for 1 minute, then add the lamb and stir-fry with the sauce for 10 minutes, then add all the vegetables and water. Cover and bring to a boil. Immediately reduce the heat to medium-low and cook the lamb and vegetables for 1 to 1½ hours, occasionally stirring gently, until they are very tender and the sauce is thin and soupy. Mix in the lemon juice, fresh coriander, and the remaining garam masala. This dish can be made up to 3 days ahead of time.

  - SERVES 4 WITH OTHER DISHES

Methi Gosht

Lamb cubes cooked with onions, tomatoes, and spices, folded with sautéed fenugreek leaves

FOR THE LAMB CURRY

1 cup finely chopped onions

2 garlic cloves, chopped

½-inch piece of ginger, chopped

1 cup diced tomatoes, canned or fresh

Salt to taste

1 teaspoon ground coriander seeds

½ teaspoon ground cumin seeds

½ teaspoon turmeric

¼ teaspoon cayenne pepper

 Muslims believe that their holy book, the Koran, was revealed to the Prophet Mohammed in the ninth month of the Islamic year. They commemorate this month, Ramzan, by fasting. They do not eat or drink—not even a sip of water—between dawn and dusk. The austerity of Ramzan ends with the joyous festival of Id ul Fitr. The entire family, dressed in new clothes, starts the celebrations with a dish of *sevian*—vermicelli cooked with milk, sugar, nuts, and saffron. After prayers at the mosque, they distribute alms to the poor, then head off to the Id fair, which children love, because the fair is full of toys, and parents are always indulgent on Id. The families return home to a feast that makes up for the entire month of fasting.

For Muslims, a feast is always an occasion to serve biryani, great platters of rice cooked with spiced meats, nuts, and saffron, alongside kababs and curries made with chicken, lamb, or beef. Several different kinds of flatbreads and many varieties of sweets are served. Methi Gosht, cooked in characteristic Hyderabadi fashion, is perfect for the Id feast.

Here, I have cooked the lamb curry separately until the lamb is tender and the sauce very thick, then folded it with fresh fenugreek leaves stir-fried with onions and spices. This method helps balance the very different flavors of the lamb and fenugreek. It is a dry dish and would be best served with an Indian bread. You can substitute spinach for the fenugreek and chicken for the lamb.

½ teaspoon garam masala
1 tablespoon vegetable oil
¼ teaspoon cumin seeds
1 pound boneless lamb, cubed and washed

FOR THE FENUGREEK LEAVES
2 tablespoons vegetable oil
¼ teaspoon cumin seeds
1 cup finely chopped onions
2 garlic cloves, chopped
2 cups tightly packed fresh fenugreek leaves, washed, drained, and chopped
Salt to taste
¼ teaspoon turmeric
¼ teaspoon cayenne pepper

- In a food processor or blender, mince the onions, garlic, ginger, and tomatoes. Add the salt, ground coriander seeds, ground cumin seeds, turmeric, cayenne pepper, and garam masala and process again.
- Warm the oil in a nonstick skillet over medium-high heat. Add the cumin seeds. After a few seconds, add the minced onion mixture, then toss in the lamb cubes. Stir to mix, cover, and bring to a boil. Reduce the heat to medium-low and cook the lamb for 1 to 1½ hours or until tender, stirring occasionally. The sauce should be clinging to the meat when the lamb is done. You can also cook the lamb in a pressure cooker without adding any water. Bring it to full pressure over high heat, then cook on low heat for 15 minutes. Uncover and boil off the excess liquid until the sauce is very thick and clings to the meat.
- Warm the oil in another nonstick skillet over medium-high heat and add ¼ teaspoon cumin seeds. After a few seconds, add the chopped onions and garlic. Sauté, stirring for 5 minutes, until the onions are lightly browned. Add the fenugreek

leaves, salt, turmeric, and cayenne. Stir to mix, cover, and reduce heat to medium-low. Cook for about 25 minutes, until the leaves are completely softened and dry.

- Gently fold the cooked fenugreek leaves into the lamb curry and cook for another 5 minutes, stirring occasionally. You can cook this dish up to 3 days ahead of time.

- SERVES 3 TO 4 WITH OTHER DISHES

Murgh Korma Biryani

Rice layered and baked with spicy chicken, cream, and nuts

FOR THE KORMA

10 raw almonds

2 tablespoons unsweetened desiccated
   coconut

1¼ cups chopped onions

2 garlic cloves, chopped

½-inch piece of ginger, chopped

2 tablespoons vegetable oil

½ teaspoon cumin seeds

1 bay leaf

1 whole clove

1 whole cardamom

½-inch cinnamon stick

½ cup peeled diced tomatoes,
   fresh or canned

3 tablespoons plain yogurt,
   not low-fat

Salt to taste

½ teaspoon ground black pepper

½ teaspoon ground cumin seeds

½ teaspoon ground coriander seeds

½ teaspoon garam masala

No banquet in Awadh was complete without a biryani—fragrant rice pilaf layered and baked with a spicy chicken or lamb curry, garnished with fried onions and nuts. Fanny Parks described the biryani served at a wedding dinner:

A white cloth was spread on the ground . . . upon which eight large round dishes of earthenware were placed. These were filled with boiled rice mixed with almonds and many good things, very pleasant food. These dishes are always prepared at Asiatic weddings, as bride-cake is always an attendant on the same ceremony in Europe. The rice was piled up high and silvered all over with silver leaf, and a tuft of silver ornamented on top. Silvered food is much used by natives; and in helping a dish, if you wish to pay a compliment, you send as much gold and silver leaf as you can.

This biryani is probably similar to the one that Fanny Parks ate, as it is rich with cream and nuts and suitable for serving at special occasions. You can dispense with the silver leaf—it looks grand but adds nothing to the flavor. You can also serve the korma as a main dish without layering it with the rice.

- In a small nonstick frying pan, toast the almonds and coconut over medium heat for a few minutes. The coconut should turn light brown and smell toasted when done. Cool and powder in a clean coffee or spice grinder. Put the onion, garlic, and ginger in a food processor and mince well.
- Warm the oil in a nonstick skillet over medium-high heat. Add the cumin seeds, bay leaf, clove, cardamom, and cinnamon. After a few seconds, add the minced onion mixture. Sauté for about 8 minutes, until lightly browned.
- Meanwhile, puree the diced tomatoes in the food processor. Add to the onions and cook for 5 minutes on medium heat until they thicken and the oil appears around the edges. Add the yogurt, stirring all the while, then put in the coconut-almond powder, the salt, all the remaining spices, and saffron (if using). Stir-fry for 5 minutes, until the oil appears again around the edges. Add the chicken thighs and coat well with sauce. Cover and bring to a boil. Reduce heat to low and cook the chicken for 30 minutes until tender. Cool slightly, mix in the coriander, mint leaves, and heavy cream.
- In a heavy-bottomed pot, combine rice, milk, water, peas, and salt. Cover and bring to a boil. Reduce the heat to low and cook for 10 minutes. Most of the liquid should be absorbed. Remove from heat and let the pan sit covered for 10 minutes.
- In a small nonstick frying pan, warm the oil over medium-high heat. Add the onion, sweet pepper rings, and almonds and sauté for 5 to 8 minutes, until lightly brown.
- Prcheat the oven to 250°F. Spread the fried onion mixture in an ovenproof dish. Stir the rice gently and spread a thin layer on top of the fried onions. Lift the chicken pieces out of the sauce and distribute them over the rice. Spread the last layer of rice on top. Drizzle the sauce from the chicken korma all over the rice. Cover tightly with foil and bake for 30 minutes. To serve, invert the dish onto a serving platter.
  - SERVES 3 TO 4 WITH OTHER DISHES

Few strands of saffron (optional)

1½ pounds skinless chicken thighs, bone-in, washed

2 tablespoons chopped fresh coriander leaves

2 tablespoons chopped fresh mint leaves

2 tablespoons heavy cream

FOR THE RICE

1¼ cups Basmati rice, washed and drained

¾ cup 2% milk

½ cup water

½ cup frozen peas

Salt to taste

2 tablespoons vegetable oil

1 medium onion, sliced into rings

1 small sweet green pepper, seeded and sliced into thin rings

10 raw almonds

Jhinga Subz Pulao

A delicate rice pilaf with shrimp, sweet red pepper,
asparagus, and fresh dill

½ pound raw shrimp

1 cup Basmati rice

2 cups water

1 medium onion

1 small sweet red pepper

10 fresh asparagus spears

2 tablespoons vegetable oil

1 bay leaf

1 whole cardamom

1 whole clove

½-inch cinnamon stick

½ teaspoon cumin seeds

2 tablespoons chopped fresh dill

Salt to taste

¼ teaspoon garam masala

 Few men have packed so much adventure into their lifetime as the Comte de Boigne. Born in 1751 in the kingdom of Sardinia, he fled to France at the age of seventeen after killing another nobleman in a duel. His wanderings took him to Russia, where he became the lover of Catherine the Great. His charms proved fleeting, so she sent him off to war in Turkey. There he was captured, sold as a slave in Istanbul, freed, shipwrecked in Palestine, and recaptured by Arabs. De Boigne so charmed his captors that they not only freed him but also paid his passage to Alexandria, from where he sailed to India. He found service with a Maratha prince, Scindia, whose army he trained in European methods. Wearing French uniforms, General de Boigne's forces defeated every other army in India and made Scindia the most powerful man in the country.

De Boigne married a Persian princess who became a Catholic and changed her name to Catherine (perhaps evoking memories of Russia!). He lived in great style and entertained lavishly in an enormous palace that he built for himself. A guest at his table described their meal:

Dinner was served at four. It was much in the Indian style; pillaws and curries, variously prepared, in abundance; fish, poultry and kid. The dishes were spread over the large table fixed in the middle of the hall, and were, in fact, a banquet for a dozen persons, although there was no one to partake of it but the general and myself.

This pulao uses fresh dill in its preparation, which is more common in Persian than Indian cooking. Though this recipe is my creation, I like to think that it might well have graced de Boigne's table and pleased his Persian wife with its fresh, sophisticated flavors. It goes well with a raita.

- Peel and devein the shrimp. Wash and set aside in a colander to drain. Wash the rice well, then soak it in 2 cups of water for the length of time it takes you to prepare the rest of the pulao. Peel and halve the onion. Now thinly slice each half into rings. Remove and discard the stem and seeds from the red pepper, then cut it into slim 1-inch lengths. Snip off the woody ends of the asparagus and cut it diagonally into 1-inch pieces.
- Warm the oil in a heavy-bottomed pan over medium–high heat. Add the bay leaf, whole cardamom, clove, cinnamon, and cumin seeds. After a few seconds, add the sliced onions. Sauté for about 4 minutes, until lightly brown. Add the sweet pepper and sauté for 2 minutes. Add the asparagus and cook for 2 minutes. Now add the shrimp and stir-fry for 1 minute. Add the dill, the rice, and all its soaking water. Mix in the salt and garam masala and cover, then bring to a boil. Immediately reduce heat to very low and cook for 30 minutes without uncovering. Let it sit covered for 5 minutes before you mix gently and serve.

  - SERVES 3 TO 4 WITH OTHER DISHES

Saadey Naan

Broiled pizza dough bread

1 package store-bought pizza dough, about 1 pound
Flour for rolling
Vegetable oil for greasing tray
Butter for spreading on naan (optional)

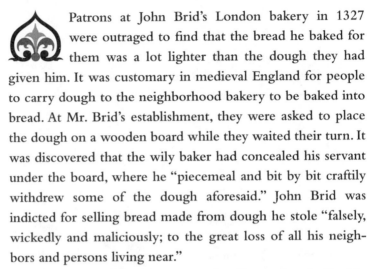 Patrons at John Brid's London bakery in 1327 were outraged to find that the bread he baked for them was a lot lighter than the dough they had given him. It was customary in medieval England for people to carry dough to the neighborhood bakery to be baked into bread. At Mr. Brid's establishment, they were asked to place the dough on a wooden board while they waited their turn. It was discovered that the wily baker had concealed his servant under the board, where he "piecemeal and bit by bit craftily withdrew some of the dough aforesaid." John Brid was indicted for selling bread made from dough he stole "falsely, wickedly and maliciously; to the great loss of all his neighbors and persons living near."

This custom of sharing an oven is still prevalent in Punjab, where villages maintain a communal *tandoor,* which resembles a large clay pot sunk into the ground, the bottom of which is lined with glowing coals. In the evenings women carry basins full of dough to the tandoor to be made into *naan*—leavened flatbread. The person maintaining the tandoor keeps a portion of the dough as payment, a more above-board arrangement than Baker Brid's!

You can make this naan in your oven. Make a stack of them, if you like, and refrigerate or freeze. They reheat very well in the microwave.

- Leave the pizza dough out on the counter for at least half an hour, which will make it easier to roll. Preheat the broiler. Divide the dough into 10 equal balls. Roll each ball lightly in flour. On a floured surface, roll out each ball to a disc about 6 inches in diameter and ⅛ inch thick. Grease an ovenproof tray or a cookie sheet lightly with oil and put the naans in a single layer. Place the cookie sheet with the naans on the oven rack set on the second rung from the top and broil for about 2 minutes. The naans will puff up and brown lightly. Now remove the tray from the oven, flip the naans, and broil until lightly brown on the other side, another 1 to 2 minutes. If the naans don't puff up after a minute or two, leave them under the broiler for another minute, taking care not to let them burn. Brush the tops of the naans lightly with butter if desired and serve.

• MAKES 10 NAANS

Paneerwale Kulche

Pan-fried bread stuffed with cottage cheese

Nizam ul Mulk, prime minister of the Moghul Empire, could no longer tolerate the corruption and depravity of the court at Delhi. Sorrowfully, he resigned from his post and went to live in Hyderabad, where he asked the emperor to appoint him governor in 1724. Before leaving Delhi, he sought the blessings of Niza-muddin, a famed holy man. Nizamuddin offered the departing minister a farewell present: seven kulchas (round flatbreads) wrapped in a yellow cloth. The gift was interpreted as a sign that seven generations of Nizam ul Mulk's descendants would reign in Hyderabad. Nizam ul Mulk's belief in this prediction was so deep that he chose as his banner a yellow flag on which was inscribed a kulcha. All seven rulers of the dynasty he founded—for the prophecy did come true—used the same banner.

Later kings of Hyderabad denied this tale, insisting that the symbol on their flag was a full moon. But I like to believe the

1 package store-bought pizza dough, about 1 pound

Flour for rolling the dough

¾ cup grated or crumbled paneer (cottage cheese)

Salt to taste

¼ teaspoon ground black pepper

¼ teaspoon garam masala

¼ teaspoon roasted ground cumin seeds

2 tablespoons chopped fresh coriander leaves

Vegetable oil or butter for shallow frying

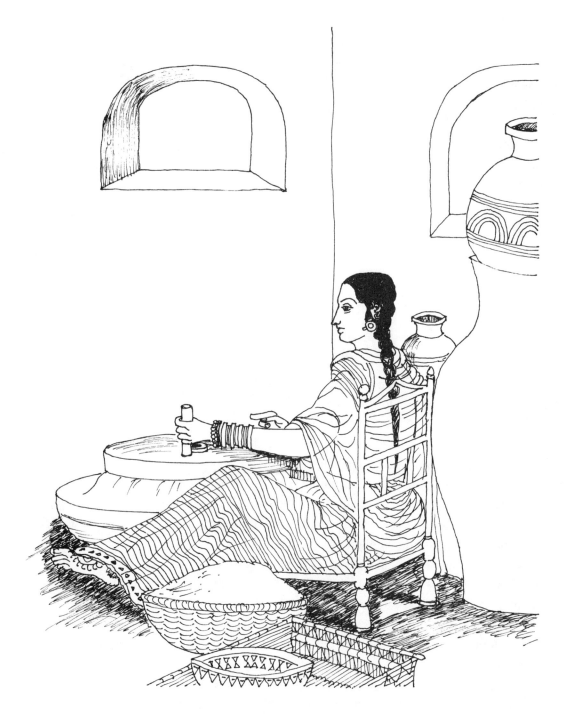

Woman grinding flour, nineteenth century

story of the saint and the kulchas, which is firmly entrenched in the folklore of Hyderabad, and to think that at one time a humble piece of bread fluttered on a royal standard.

Kulchas are one of the family of leavened flatbreads. The most common of these is naan, made from leavened flour and baked in a clay oven. Kulchas are very similar, except that ghee (clarified butter) is added to the dough to make it more elastic. A third variety, popular in Hyderabad and Awadh, is the sheermal, whose dough is slightly sweetened with milk.

This is a recipe for stuffed kulcha, but since it is made from store-bought pizza dough, you cannot add butter. Instead, I recommend shallow-frying it with butter on a griddle to get the authentic buttery flavor. The cottage-cheese stuffing is lightly spiced with garam masala and roasted ground cumin seeds. (As a variation, add 1 tablespoon kasoori methi [dried fenugreek leaves] to the stuffing.) The kulcha is quite delicious by itself, but you can also serve it with any chicken or lamb dish.

- Leave the pizza dough at room temperature for at least half an hour, which will make it easier to roll. Divide the dough into 8 equal portions, each about the size of a lemon. Roll each portion into a smooth ball. Lightly dust with flour and set aside at room temperature. In a bowl, combine the cottage cheese, salt, pepper, garam masala, roasted cumin, and fresh coriander and mix gently with a fork.
- You can either roll out all the kulchas and then fry them, or, with practice, fry them as you go along. Set a nonstick frying pan or a griddle over medium heat. Roll out a ball of pizza dough into a disc about 3 inches in diameter. Now put about 2 teaspoons of the cottage cheese filling in its center and gather up the ends to make a pouch, pinching the top firmly with your fingers to seal it. Dusting with flour whenever necessary, roll into a circle about ⅛ inch thick and 8 inches in diameter. Cook this kulcha on the griddle for a minute or until small bubbles appear on its surface. Flip

and cook on the other side. Now evenly spread about ¼ teaspoon of oil or butter on each side and cook till light brown on both sides. Cook all the remaining kulchas similarly. Leftovers can be wrapped tightly in foil, refrigerated, and reheated in the microwave.

• MAKES 8 KULCHAS

Malai ki Puri

Deep-fried balls of cream and flour served in a cardamom-flavored syrup

1 cup heavy cream
½ cup plus 3 tablespoons all-purpose white flour
½ cup milk
Vegetable oil for deep frying
3 cups water
3 cups sugar
Tiny pinch of saffron
10 to 15 whole cardamom
1 teaspoon powdered pistachios (optional)

 Refuse to eat sugar! The eighteenth-century Anti-Saccharite Society in England, which organized the first food boycott in history, was worried not about the health of the people eating sugar but about the welfare of slaves on Caribbean sugar plantations. They advocated that coffee should be drunk only with cream and no sugar. Those not willing to make such sacrifices could use sugar produced in India, where there was no slavery. Opponents of slavery made some remarkably precise calculations:

A family that uses 5 lbs. of sugar per week, will, by using East India instead of West India, for 21 months, prevent the slavery, or murder of one fellow-creature! Eight such families in 19 and a half years, will prevent the slavery or murder of one hundred.

People who wished to publicly display their support of the boycott could buy sugar pots prominently labeled "East India Sugar Not Made By Slaves" from Mrs. B. Henderson at the China Warehouse, Rye Lane, Peckham, London.

Malai ki Puri is a dessert that is simple to make and delicious, using copious amounts of sugar. My favorite sweet dish, it tastes much like the popular gulab jamuns (deep-fried thickened milk balls in syrup) but is easier to make.

- In a deep mixing bowl, combine the cream, flour, and milk. Stir well for a few minutes to obtain a smooth paste. Let this batter sit on the countertop for 15 to 20 minutes.
- Warm the oil for deep-frying in a wok or deep fryer over medium-high heat. Drop rounded tablespoonfuls of the batter into the hot oil. Do not overcrowd the wok; fry them in batches. Adjust the heat. If the oil is too hot, the balls will fry too quickly, and if it is not hot enough, they will disintegrate. They should take about 3 minutes to become golden brown on all sides. Try frying a test ball, and if it disintegrates, add one more tablespoonful of flour to the batter. Don't be in a hurry to flip the balls: spoon some hot oil over them to cook the tops and then turn gently after a few seconds. When you put the batter into the hot oil, it will soon spread and flatten a bit and rise to the top. When the balls are golden all over, drain them on many layers of paper towels and set aside.
- To make the syrup, combine the water and sugar in a large deep saucepan and bring to a boil over high heat, stirring occasionally. Reduce the heat to medium and simmer uncovered for 10 minutes. Remove from the heat and crush the saffron into the syrup. Cool to room temperature. Remove the skins from the cardamom and powder the seeds finely in a mortar and pestle, or between two sheets of wax paper with a rolling pin. Mix the crushed cardamom seeds into the syrup. Gently mix in the fried balls, making sure they are all immersed in syrup. Cover and let them soak for at least an hour. When ready to serve, lift them gently out of the syrup and lay them attractively in a serving dish. Sprinkle with powdered pistachios if desired. Refrigerate unused portions.
- SERVES 6

The Spice Traders:
European Influences on Indian Cuisine

Cinnamon, reported Herodotus, a Greek historian in the fifth century B.C., could be found only on a mountain in Arabia, where vicious birds of prey used it to build their nests. If you wanted some cinnamon, you had to lure the birds out with chunks of meat, then quickly seize their nests. Growing up in big cities in India, I never had the chance to personally test this theory, since it was easier to buy spices in a grocery store. Until I went to live in the southern state of Kerala, which produces the world's finest spices, I was almost as ignorant as Herodotus about where they came from.

The first time I saw pepper and cardamom growing was when my family moved from Delhi to Angamali, a little village near the Kerala coast. We rented an old rambling house with a huge backyard filled with banana, coconut, and palm trees. Pepper vines twined themselves around the trees, laden with dark peppercorns. Running water must have been a recent innovation in the house, for in the center of the yard, we found our very own well. My mother, delighted at the prospect of drawing fresh water, promptly went out to inspect it. To her consternation, several large frogs peered back at her from its depths. The landlord, when summoned, was baffled by our outrage. "Not enough frogs?" he asked, anxious to please. "I'll get some more tomorrow." We discovered that it was customary to keep a few frogs in the well, since they ate insects and kept the water clean. In spite of this perfectly sensible explanation, my mother never did get fresh water from the well. She did, however, make full use of the abundance of spices growing in the garden. I can still recall the wonderful flavor of freshly picked pepper and cardamom in her cooking.

We were not the first to discover the magic of fresh spices: their lure has been attracting traders from other countries for thousands of years. It was at Calicut, not far from where we lived, that the Portuguese explorer Vasco da Gama and his crew landed in 1498 shouting, "For Christ and spices." They soon realized that their missionary services would not be needed, since a large Christian community had flourished in Kerala for over a thousand years. But their struggle to control the spice trade was to profoundly change the history of India and to have a lasting impact on Indian cuisine.

Europeans always had an insatiable desire for spices, which they used for food, medicine, and perfumes. Roman and Greek spice ships regularly sailed to the Malabar Coast of Kerala, making it one of the greatest centers of trade in the ancient world. Direct trade links between Rome and India were severed in the seventh century by Arabs sweeping across North Africa, united under the banners of Islam by the prophet Mohammed, himself a spice merchant. For the next seven hundred years, Arabs were to control all shipping of spices, with merchants from Venice acting as their agents in Europe. The cost of spices soared, making them a luxury available only to wealthy Europeans. In the fourteenth century, a pound of nutmeg was worth seven oxen in Germany, and a pound of ginger sold for the price of a full-grown sheep in England. The enormous profits that accrued from this trade made Venice one of the wealthiest cities in the world and enabled the Arab Empire to expand until it stretched from Spain to India.

Seeking a share in the profits from spices, European explorers searched for a direct sea route to India, which would allow them to circumvent the Arab stranglehold on trade. Spain and Portugal, Europe's foremost maritime powers in the fifteenth century, led the way. The Spanish financed a venture by Christopher Columbus, who headed west and ran into a large, unexpected obstacle. He promptly declared his expedition a success, identified the natives as Indians, and sailed home with chilies that he labeled red pepper. Meanwhile, the Portuguese expedition led by Vasco da Gama was more profitable, sailing east and reaching India after a relatively uneventful journey. Their ships returned to Portugal laden with spices, and before long, pepper was selling in Lisbon at a fraction of the price in Venice. The Arab monopoly had been effectively shattered.

The Portuguese were soon fighting pitched battles against the Arabs—who were understandably upset about having to share their wealth—and then with the Dutch, who were aggressively building their own empire in the east. To establish a base from which they could defend their shipping lanes, a Portuguese army seized Goa in 1510. It was to remain in their possession for the next 450 years. The Portuguese tried to populate their colonies by encouraging marriage with local women. Immediately after the capture of Goa, the Portuguese commander arranged matches between his soldiers and the widows of the defeated Indian garrison. What the women thought about this arrangement is not known, but their weddings were the first of many that over the years produced a distinctive Goan population: Catholic, Portuguese-speaking, and with a unique culture. Goan cuisine shows the same medley of influences. Dishes frequently combine the Portuguese method of marinating meats in vinegar with distinctively Indian spicing. Goans who became Catholic had no religious objections to eating pork, and the cuisine has a lot of pork dishes rarely eaten elsewhere in India. *Chourisam* is a spicy sausage developed by monks in Goa, which is prepared from pork marinated in ginger, garlic, spices, and vinegar.

But the Portuguese impact on Indian food extended far beyond the confines of Goa. They brought hot chili peppers from the West Indies to India, which were soon grown all over the country and enthusiastically used in cooking. It is now hard to imagine Indian food without the bite of chili powder. If you ever find your mouth on fire after eating a curry, blame the Portuguese!

Seeing the Portuguese profits in the spice trade, almost every other country in Europe wanted a share. Soon Dutch, French, British, and Danish companies had established trading posts in India. Diplomats from each country constantly intrigued at the court of the Moghul emperor in Delhi to obtain favorable trade concessions, while rival ships clashed at sea. The fortunes of these companies fluctuated as wars were fought and treaties signed in Europe, with trading posts frequently changing hands. By the early eighteenth century, the most powerful trading company in India was the British East India Company, with forts at Bombay, Madras, and Calcutta.

The Moghul Empire was on the verge of disintegration by the middle of the eighteenth century, with each province virtually independent and the Moghul Emperor powerless to enforce his rule. Bengal, the largest and richest province, was ruled by Siraj ud Daula, who was young, headstrong, and not very bright. Eager to display his authority, he seized the British fort in Calcutta. A British relief force commanded by Robert Clive sailed from Madras and confronted the Bengal army near the village of Plassey in 1757. The British were outnumbered but better armed and better organized. They also had the foresight to bribe Siraj ud Daula's commander-in-chief, thereby ensuring that his forces would withdraw as soon as the battle began. After a brief, confused skirmish, the Bengal army hastily retreated. The British were victorious and, for the first time in history, had become the undisputed rulers of a large piece of India. The conquest of Bengal established a pattern of expansion that was to be repeated many times as one Indian prince after another was defeated, until by the mid-nineteenth century, the entire country lay under British control.

Early English traders who came to India did not expect to return home for a long time: travel was too slow, difficult, and dangerous. Many of them married Indian women and adopted Indian customs, dress, and eating habits. They probably did not find the food very exotic; seventeenth-century English food was as heavily spiced as any in India, making frequent use of mace, pepper, cinnamon, cloves, nutmeg, cumin, and ginger. The Indian custom of eating with one's fingers was also not strange to them. Forks were still uncommon in England and food was scooped up with pieces of bread, just as in India.

Many Englishmen were willing to leave home and brave the hazardous journey to India because a life of luxury awaited them. Even the humblest clerk employed by the East India Company could expect to live in a mansion attended by an army of servants. William Hickey, a fairly ordinary Calcutta businessman, listed sixty-three staff members, including eight to wait at his table, two bakers, two cooks, a hairdresser, nine valets, four grooms, one coachman, and three gardeners. With little other entertainment available, food became an obsession. A typical dinner in the home of the president of the English merchants in 1638 was described by a guest as consisting of fifteen or sixteen dishes of meat followed by dessert. Sunday and holiday feasts were even more elaborate and included platters of peacocks, partridges, hares, deer, and antelopes. Meals were often so long that diners took coffee breaks between courses. Gargantuan repasts were an enduring feature of British life in India.

Eliza Fay, the wife of a Calcutta lawyer, wrote home after arriving in India in 1780:

> We were very frequently told in England you know, that the heat in Bengal destroyed the appetite. I must own that I never yet saw any proof of that: on the contrary, I cannot help thinking that I never saw an equal quantity of victuals consumed. . . . I will give you our own bill of fare. . . . A soup, a roast fowl, curry and rice, a mutton pie, a fore quarter of lamb, a rice pudding, tarts, very good cheese, fresh churned butter, fine bread, excellent Madeira (that is expensive but eatables are very cheap).

It was quite usual to wash all this food down with three bottles of claret after dinner. Liver complaints and strokes were frequent among the English living in India, which they attributed to the hot weather.

The voyage to India became much shorter when the Suez Canal opened in 1869 and steamships were introduced. The ease with which people could travel transformed British society in India. Now the "fishing fleet" came from England each year—young single women hoping to find suitable husbands. Their arrival forever changed relations between the British and Indians: marriage with Indian women was no longer considered acceptable, and Indian attire was abandoned for the latest fashions from London, no matter how unsuitable they were for the Indian climate. English trends found their way to India, including the Victorian fad for French cuisine. Even the few Indian dishes that remained on dinner menus now had to have French names, straining the linguistic skills of English hostesses. Colonel Kenny-Herbert wrote in 1878:

> Our dinners of today would indeed astonish our Anglo Indian forefathers . . . dinners of sixteen or twenty, thoughtfully composed are de rigueur; our menu cards discourse of dainty fare in its native French.

Hapless Indian cooks struggled with primitive implements and charcoal stoves in futile attempts to prepare *haute cuisine* as described to them by English employers who had themselves never eaten real French food. The results would have made a French chef throw up his hands in despair.

British rule over India ended in 1947. Three and a half centuries of association with Britain taught Indians how to speak English, play cricket, and elect parliaments, but they never did learn to love English food. The British, on the other hand, were surprised to discover that the most enduring legacy of their empire was a tandoori restaurant in every English town.

This chapter starts with recipes from Goa, showing you how well Portuguese and Indian cuisines blend together. We next visit Bombay, which flourished under British rule and attracted people from all parts of the country, making it the most cosmopolitan city in India. I have included recipes from the kitchens of the Parsi and Sindhi communities, who are an important part of the mix that makes Bombay's population so vibrant and colorful. Our last stop will be Calcutta, which was the original capital of British India, and its most important trading port. Ships laden with tea from China filled Calcutta's harbor, and over the years, a large Chinese community settled in the city. Chinese restaurants created a unique cuisine, modifying traditional recipes to suit an Indian clientele accustomed to spicy fare. These recipes deserve to be better known outside India, and I present some of my favorites here. Finally, there are recipes from Calcutta's native Bengali population. Bengali cuisine is well known for its creative seafood preparations and distinctive spicing.

Five hundred years have passed since the first Europeans set sail for India. They left a lasting impression on its food, which you will taste in these recipes. I think you will find that their endeavors were worth it.

Sweet Corn Soup • Sweet corn soup with mixed vegetables and tofu, served with pickled green chilies in vinegar

Mushroom Spring Rolls • Spring rolls stuffed with onions and mushrooms in a chili-garlic-coriander sauce

Sweet and Sour Chili Potatoes • New potatoes smothered in a tamarind–red chili-garlic sauce

Breakfast Mushroom Spread • Sautéed mushrooms and onions, cooked with tomatoes and cheese

Dak Bungalow Omelet • Omelet made with chopped onions, tomatoes, chili, and fresh coriander

Bhindi Hariyali • Okra sautéed with onions, tomatoes, and fresh coriander

Grilled Hot Pepper Chicken • Chicken marinated in a paste of roasted spices, chilies, herbs, and vinegar

Grilled Chicken Curry • Grilled marinated chicken thighs in a spicy coconut milk–tamarind sauce

Hara Masala Murgh • Chicken cooked in a sauce of onions, tomatoes, coconut, cashews, and fennel seeds with fresh herbs

Murgh Masale Mein • Chicken marinated with sautéed onions, spices, and thickened yogurt, sautéed with tomatoes and cardamom

Jardaloo Murgh • Chicken and dried apricots cooked in a sweet-and-sour sauce of sautéed onions, tomatoes, spices, and vinegar

Chicken Curry • Chicken cooked with onions, tomatoes, yogurt, and spices

Chili Chicken • Chili chicken stir-fried with mushrooms and eggplant

Chicken Manchurian • Crisp morsels of chicken served in a garlic-flavored sauce with fresh coriander and scallions

Goan Shrimp Curry • Shrimp cooked in a sautéed onion, tomato, and coconut-milk sauce with almonds

Hot Garlic Shrimp • Crisp marinated shrimp served in a hot garlic sauce

Goan Fish Curry • Grilled salmon chunks served in a sauce of sautéed onions, tomatoes, coconut, and fresh coriander

Machali Patia • Fish cooked in a sweet-and-sour sautéed onion and tamarind sauce

Macher Jhol • Fillet of fish cooked with tomatoes and ground mustard seeds

Mangsho Jhol • Lamb cooked with tomatoes, yogurt, mustard seeds, baby potatoes, and shallots

Goan Lamb Curry • Lamb cooked in a sauce of sautéed onions, tomatoes, and coconut milk with vinegar and spices

Seyal Gosht • Lamb marinated and cooked in onions, yogurt, and fresh coriander, folded with sautéed onions, tomatoes, cardamom, and tamarind

Sweet Corn Soup

Sweet corn soup with mixed vegetables and tofu,
served with pickled green chilies in vinegar

One 14-ounce can creamed corn

3 cups water

1 teaspoon cornstarch

2 teaspoons water

½ teaspoon soy sauce

Salt to taste

¼ teaspoon ground black pepper

1 egg

1 teaspoon sesame oil

One 2-inch-thick block of tofu,
    cut into ½-inch-long,
    thinly slivered strips

2 tablespoons vegetable oil

½ medium onion, thinly sliced

½ medium carrot, peeled and thinly
    slivered in ½-inch strips

2 white mushrooms, washed and
    thinly sliced

½ cup shredded Napa cabbage

¼ cup tiny florets of cauliflower

1 green onion (including the green
    parts), finely chopped

 After spending many years in India, most English people became so accustomed to spicy food that they began to find soups bland. Their method of livening them up was to add a spoonful of green chilies pickled in vinegar, a bottle of which stood on every dining table. Now the only place where you can find this condiment is in Chinese restaurants, where you will always be offered a bowl.

In the days when I was growing up in India, Chinese restaurants had a very limited menu of soups. Sweet corn soup served either with vegetables or with shredded chicken was by far the most popular of those available. My friends and I would order brimming bowls of it and spike it liberally with hot chilies pickled in vinegar. This would invariably be followed by stir-fried noodles and shrimp in hot garlic sauce, and we would leave the restaurant feeling that all was well with the world.

I have adhered faithfully to the traditional recipe of sweet corn soup here, only taking the liberty of adding a few slivers of tofu. This is hearty soup to have for a cold winter's meal and is good accompanied with Mushroom Spring Rolls (spring rolls stuffed with onions and mushrooms in a chili-garlic-coriander sauce, page 214).

- In a large saucepan, combine the creamed corn and water and bring to a boil, stirring frequently. Meanwhile, mix the cornstarch with the water, soy, salt, and pepper. When the broth comes to a boil, reduce the heat to medium-low and add the cornstarch mixture, stirring well. Cook for 5 minutes. Beat the egg, and add the sesame oil to it. Pour the egg in a thin stream into the soup, stirring gently with a fork to separate the strands. Add the tofu and stir gently to mix. Remove the pot from heat.

- Warm the oil in a nonstick skillet over high heat. Add all the vegetables except the green onion and stir-fry for 3 to 4 minutes. Lift the vegetables out of the oil and stir them into the soup. Cook the soup on medium heat for 2 to 3 minutes. Fold in the chopped green onion. Serve hot with chilies in vinegar on the side.

NOTE: You can substitute ½ cup of milk for ½ cup of water to get a chowderlike effect. One half cup shredded crabmeat or cooked chicken can be added in place of some of the vegetables.

- SERVES 4 AS A STARTER

Green Chilies Pickled in Vinegar

- Combine all ingredients except the chilies in a heavy-bottomed saucepan set over high heat. Warm it until just ready to come to a boil. Remove from the heat and add the sliced green chilies. Cool to room temperature, then cover and refrigerate. This will keep in the refrigerator for at least 2 weeks or longer.

NOTE: The spiced vinegar is usually sprinkled over the food; the chilies are for flavor only and are generally not eaten.

1 cup white vinegar
½ teaspoon salt
¼ teaspoon ground black pepper
½ teaspoon sugar
¼-inch piece ginger, grated (optional)
1 small garlic clove, grated (optional)
1 teaspoon soy sauce
1 teaspoon sesame oil
6 hot green chilies, sliced

Mushroom Spring Rolls

Spring rolls stuffed with onions and mushrooms in a
chili-garlic-coriander sauce

FOR THE MUSHROOM STUFFING

2 hot green chilies, stemmed

1 garlic clove, chopped

¼-inch piece of ginger, chopped

1 teaspoon cornstarch

¼ cup water

1 tablespoon soy sauce

1 tablespoon rice vinegar

1 teaspoon sesame oil

¼ teaspoon ground black pepper

Salt to taste

¼ teaspoon red pepper flakes

½ teaspoon sugar

2 tablespoons vegetable oil

1 cup finely chopped onions

12 medium white mushrooms, washed
    and thinly sliced (about 2 cups)

½ cup loosely packed fresh coriander
    leaves, washed and drained

FOR THE SPRING ROLLS

8 wonton or spring roll wrappers

Vegetable oil for frying

Dr. Cornelius Decker of Amsterdam had great
faith in the beneficial effects of Chinese tea. Writing under the pseudonym of Dr. Bonteko ("good
tea") in 1693, he proclaimed:

It must be a considerable and obstinate fever that cannot be
cured by drinking every day forty to fifty cups of tea, about
twenty of which are strong and bitter. . . . We recommend in
particular the use of tea for all sorts of people of both sexes,
young and old, for all this nation, and all other peoples, and
we advise them to drink it every day, at all times, all hours, as
much as they can drink, beginning with eight to ten cups and
eventually augmenting the dose to whatever amounts the
stomach can hold. . . .

Cynics maintained that the good doctor was in the pay of the
Dutch East India Company, which was the chief European
importer of Chinese tea. Perhaps this harsh view did him an
injustice and he just really, really liked tea.

I, too, am very fond of Chinese tea, though I don't imbibe
quite as much as Dr. Decker advised. I especially like to drink
it while nibbling on these spring rolls. The mushrooms used
in this filling can also be left whole and served as a side dish.
If you find the dish too hot, just cut down on the number of
chilies used or deseed them before use.

- In a food processor, finely mince the chilies, garlic, and ginger. Dissolve the cornstarch with the water; add the soy,
  vinegar, sesame oil, black pepper, salt, red pepper flakes, and
  sugar. Mix well and set aside.

- Warm the oil in a nonstick skillet over medium-high heat. Add the minced chilies, garlic, and ginger. Sauté for 1 minute, then add the chopped onions. Stir for 2 minutes, then mix in the sliced mushrooms. Sauté for 2 to 3 minutes, just until they begin to release their juices. Add the chopped fresh coriander leaves, then the cornstarch mixture, stir quickly, and switch off the heat. The sauce will thicken immediately. Stir once again to mix, then remove from the heat. Set aside to cool slightly. This stuffing can be made up to 3 days ahead of time.
- When you are ready to make the spring rolls, have the mushroom stuffing and a small bowl of water nearby. Put 2 teaspoons or more of the mushroom mixture in the center of each wrapper and spread to fit the length of the wrapper. Now roll up the two ends of the wrapper and fold in the edges tightly like a jelly roll or a burrito. Seal the edges by moistening with a few drops of water. Complete all the spring rolls this way.
- Warm a nonstick skillet or frying pan over medium heat and add enough oil to come about halfway up the sides of the pan. Add a few rolls at a time and turn them around gently until they have cooked through and are lightly browned. Drain on absorbent paper and serve hot as appetizers.

- SERVES 3 TO 4 AS AN APPETIZER

Sweet and Sour Chili Potatoes

New potatoes smothered in a tamarind-red chili-garlic sauce

1½ pounds small new white potatoes,
    peeled

Salt to taste

½ teaspoon ground black pepper

1 tablespoon vegetable oil

1 tablespoon sesame oil

Walnut-size piece of seedless
    tamarind (2 ounces)

1 cup water

1 teaspoon cornstarch

1 teaspoon sesame oil

2 tablespoons soy sauce

1 tablespoon red chili sauce or
    chili paste

2 teaspoons sugar

1 tablespoon ketchup

2 tablespoons vegetable oil

2 whole dried red chilies

2 garlic cloves, grated

¼-inch piece of ginger, grated

1¼ cups finely chopped onions

 The discovery of tea growing wild in India in 1834 ended the Chinese monopoly of tea production. British planters who established tea gardens in India faced the problem of finding laborers who knew how to grow tea. There were complaints that skilled workers were being paid too much and that planters were "cutting their own throats by steadily increasing the rates of pay and bonus." The same writer added with heavy sarcasm, "laborers now arrive in red flannel jackets. Spurs will probably be added in due course!" Planters tried to solve their employment problems by importing Chinese laborers. Few of these workers remained on the tea plantations, gradually migrating to Calcutta and becoming part of the large Chinese community there.

The Hakka Chinese, who form most of Calcutta's Chinese population, are originally from China's southeastern provinces of Guangdong, Fujian, and Jiangxi. They brought with them the cuisine of this region, but cooks in Hakka Chinese restaurants were extremely inventive in adapting their menus to suit Indian tastes by spicing up their food. Hakka cuisine, in its Indian incarnation, is now the most popular of Chinese cooking styles in India. I doubt you will find tamarind or potatoes being used in a Chinese restaurant anywhere else in the world, but this irresistible combination has become all the rage in India. Serve it with fried rice and Sweet Corn Soup, page 212.

- Preheat the oven to 400°F. In a mixing bowl, combine the potatoes, salt, pepper, vegetable oil, and sesame oil. Toss to coat well. Bake the potatoes in a single layer on a baking tray or cookie sheet for 30 minutes, shaking the tray occasionally for the potatoes to roast evenly. Turn off the heat and let the potatoes roast for another 10 minutes in the fading heat of the oven.

- In a microwave-safe bowl, microwave the tamarind and ½ cup of the water uncovered on high for 2 minutes. Mash well with a fork and set aside to cool for 10 minutes. (If you prefer, you can soak the tamarind in the water for 2 hours.) Pass the tamarind and its liquid through a sieve set over a bowl, discarding the fibrous residue. You should have about 5 tablespoons of tamarind extract. If not, make up the remainder with a little water. Dissolve the cornstarch in it and add the sesame oil, soy sauce, chili sauce or paste, sugar, and ketchup. Mix in the remaining ½ cup of water. Stir well and set aside.

- Warm the oil in a nonstick wok or skillet over high heat. Add the dried chilies, grated garlic, and ginger. Sauté for 30 seconds, until crisp, then add the chopped onions. Sauté for 4 minutes, until lightly browned, then add the roasted potatoes and stir-fry for 1 minute. Turn off the heat, then mix in the tamarind-cornstarch mixture. Stir well to coat the potatoes and let it thicken over the stove for a minute. Transfer to a serving bowl. This dish can be made up to 3 days ahead of time.

  - SERVES 3 TO 4 AS A SIDE DISH

Breakfast Mushroom Spread

Sautéed mushrooms and onions, cooked with tomatoes and cheese

 The English in India had no difficulty in finding good domestic help. Isabella Fane, whose father was the commander-in-chief of the British army in India, wrote home in 1836, describing their household staff:

The number of servants my father keeps, who wait upon him and me, is sixty-eight, and this is reckoned a *small* number for the Commander-in-Chief. . . . At dinner I have three

2 tablespoons butter

1 cup finely chopped onions

½ cup canned crushed tomatoes

½ pound white mushrooms, washed, dried, and finely chopped

Salt to taste

¼ to ½ teaspoon ground black pepper

1 tablespoon all-purpose flour
½ cup milk
1 cup grated cheddar cheese

khitmagurs or waiting servants behind my chair. My father has six to his portion, everyone else one or two. Then there is the khansamar or butler, the plate butler, the wine cooler and his mate, the jelly maker, and many whose avocations I know nothing about; but I should think at our meals we are when *quite alone* surrounded by nearer thirty much, than twenty.

This magnificence was not reserved for senior officers alone. A young army captain, campaigning in Mysore in 1780, was accompanied by a cook, steward, valet, groom, groom's assistant, barber, washerman, and fifteen porters to carry his baggage, wine cellar, live poultry, and goats. This was the minimum complement required by the captain when roughing it in the field; the rest of his servants were at his house.

Even at breakfast, a dozen servants stood in attendance. English breakfasts were huge spreads that included chops, steaks, fish, eggs, rice, and curries. Mushrooms, which Indians rarely ate, were a favorite of the English. A popular Victorian recipe for mushroom ketchup was one in which mushrooms were marinated in salt and spices and cooked until very thick. This mushroom spread, my father's version, includes sautéed onions, tomatoes, and cheddar cheese.

- Warm the butter in a nonstick skillet over medium-high heat. Add the onions and sauté for about 3 minutes, until they lose their raw aroma and become limp.
- Reduce the heat to medium and add the crushed tomatoes. Cook for about 5 minutes, until they thicken slightly. Add the mushrooms and cook for 4 to 5 minutes, until they soften and release their liquid. Add the salt, pepper, and all-purpose flour. Stir for 1 minute, then slowly add the milk, stirring all the while. Mix in the cheese and cook for 4 to 5 minutes, stirring constantly until the mixture has thickened. Let cool to room temperature before refrigerating, where it will thicken. It will keep for a week. Warm slightly and serve over toast.

- SERVES 3 TO 4 WITH OTHER DISHES

Dak Bungalow Omelet

Omelet made with chopped onions, tomatoes, chili,
and fresh coriander

 The safest means of passage for British travelers in
early nineteenth-century India was to accompany
the postal delivery service (known as *dak* in
Hindi). Gradually, a network of rest houses called dak bungalows was established along these routes, many of which are in
use to this day.

Dak bungalow caretakers also doubled as cooks, and the
quality of the food they served was notoriously poor. On one
rare occasion when the cook seems to have made an effort, a
Mr. Brown was moved to leave this testimonial:

> So I will praise Peter wherever I go,
> And always speak well of his Dak bungalow;
> If I always gets food just as good as he gives
> In time I shall get jolly fat—if I lives!

My own memories of staying in dak bungalows as a child,
when I accompanied my father on trips, are happier ones. I
particularly remember the omelets served for breakfast; this
was the only place I knew where omelets were cooked with
fresh coriander and green chilies, which I adored. I have tried
to recreate those well-remembered flavors in this recipe. You
can eat the omelet with toast, or if you want to be totally
Indian, eat it with parathas (shallow-fried wheat bread).

3 large eggs

1 cup finely chopped onions

1 plum tomato, finely chopped

*1 hot green chili, deseeded if desired,
    finely chopped*

*3 tablespoons chopped fresh
    coriander leaves*

3 tablespoons milk

Salt to taste

¼ teaspoon ground black pepper

2 tablespoons vegetable oil or butter

- Break the eggs into a large bowl and beat well with a fork.
  Add the onions, tomato, chili, fresh coriander, milk, salt, and
  pepper. Mix well again.
- Warm the oil or butter in a large nonstick frying pan over
  medium-high heat. Pour the eggs into the pan, tipping the

pan in a circular motion to spread them. Lift the edges of the omelet and tip the excess liquid from the eggs into the edges to cook it evenly. Cook for about 2 minutes, then reduce heat to medium and carefully flip the omelet to cook it on the other side. Cook for about 2 minutes, then divide the omelet into half and transfer to two plates.

• SERVES 2

Bhindi Hariyali

Okra sautéed with onions, tomatoes, and fresh coriander

1 pound fresh okra

1½ cups finely chopped onions

1 garlic clove, chopped

¼-inch piece of ginger, chopped

1 cup packed fresh coriander leaves
    and tender stems, washed and
    drained

1 hot green chili, stemmed

2 tablespoons vegetable oil

½ teaspoon cumin seeds

2 plum tomatoes, chopped

½ teaspoon ground coriander
    seeds

½ teaspoon ground cumin seeds

½ teaspoon turmeric

¼ teaspoon cayenne pepper

½ teaspoon garam masala

Salt to taste

1 tablespoon lemon juice

 Sindh became part of the British Empire in 1842, after it was invaded by a force led by Sir Charles Napier, who is famous for issuing the shortest military communiqué in history. His message announcing the conquest of the province was the single Latin word "*Peccavi*" (I have sinned). Fortunately, he could safely assume that his superiors, all having received a sound classical education, would get the pun. I needed to have it translated.

I don't know if Sir Charles got a chance to sample any Sindhi cooking, but had he done so, it would have made the campaign worthwhile. Sindhi food uses relatively few ingredients and is simple to prepare. Yet when the dish finally appears on the table, the result is impressive. Fresh coriander and crushed cardamom seeds are used generously in almost every dish and lend the exquisite aroma that characterizes Sindhi food.

This recipe is a classic from Sindhi cuisine; chicken, fish, rice, and even raita (yogurt relish) are cooked in this sautéed onion-tomato herb sauce. Choose small okra for this dish so you can leave them whole. You can serve Bhindi Hariyali with Seyal Gosht (lamb marinated and cooked in onions, yogurt, and fresh coriander, folded with sautéed onions, tomatoes, cardamom, and tamarind, page 249) and rice.

- Wash the okra and trim off the ends. Leave whole if not too large; otherwise, halve. Put the onions, garlic, ginger, fresh coriander, and green chili in the jar of a blender or food processor and mince well.
- Warm the oil in a nonstick skillet over medium-high heat. Add the cumin seeds and, after a few seconds, the minced onion mixture. Sauté, stirring occasionally for 10 minutes, until the onions are lightly browned.
- Stir in the tomatoes and cook for about 5 minutes, blending them in with the back of your spoon. Add all the spices and salt and cook for 1 minute. Add in the okra. Gently mix. Cover and cook on medium-low heat for 30 minutes, stirring occasionally, or until the okra is tender. (If the okra seems to be getting too mushy at the end of cooking time, uncover and turn up the heat slightly. Stir-fry for a few minutes to dry up excess liquid.) Mix in the lemon juice and serve.

- SERVES 3 TO 4 WITH OTHER DISHES

Grilled Hot Pepper Chicken

Chicken marinated in a paste of roasted spices, chilies, herbs, and vinegar

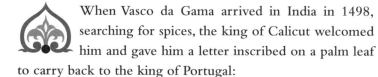

When Vasco da Gama arrived in India in 1498, searching for spices, the king of Calicut welcomed him and gave him a letter inscribed on a palm leaf to carry back to the king of Portugal:

Vasco da Gama, a gentleman of your household, came to my country, whereat I was much pleased. My country is rich in cinnamon, cloves, ginger, pepper, and precious stones. That which I ask of you in exchange is gold, silver, corals, and scarlet cloth.

1 pound skinless, boneless chicken breast, washed and dried
½ teaspoon whole black pepper
1 dried hot red chili (optional)
2 whole cloves
2 whole cardamom
½-inch cinnamon stick
½ teaspoon cumin seeds
½ teaspoon whole coriander seeds
1 bay leaf

½ teaspoon black mustard seeds

2 garlic cloves, chopped

½-inch piece of ginger, chopped

1 cup fresh coriander leaves and
    tender stems, washed and drained

1 hot green chili, stemmed

4 tablespoons white vinegar

Salt to taste

1 medium sweet red or green pepper,
    seeded and cubed into 1-inch pieces

Before leaving, Vasco da Gama asked the king of Calicut for a pepper plant that he could carry back to grow in Portugal. The king was untroubled by this request, replying, "You can take our pepper, but you will never be able to take our rains." The heavy monsoon rains of Kerala are essential for the pepper vines to flourish. The red and green chili plants that the Portuguese brought to India from the West Indies were much less particular about where they grew. Chili plants flourished all over the country, and chilies became an indispensable item in Indian kitchens.

This recipe from Goa celebrates the exchange of peppers between the New and Old Worlds. If you find it too hot, you can cut the amount of hot peppers or deseed the chilies to temper their heat. The chicken is interspersed with sweet peppers to mellow some of the fire. When I make Grilled Hot Pepper Chicken, I serve a soothing yogurt dip on the side.

- Cut the chicken into thin strips across the grain, about 1 inch in length (this is easier to do if the chicken is partially frozen). Set aside.
- Warm a small nonstick frying pan over medium heat and add the black pepper, red chili, cloves, cardamom, cinnamon, cumin seeds, coriander seeds, bay leaf, and mustard seeds. Toast for 4 to 5 minutes, stirring occasionally, until they darken and smell roasted. Cool and powder in a clean coffee or spice grinder.
- In a food processor, process the garlic, ginger, fresh coriander, green chili, vinegar, and salt until smooth. Transfer to a large mixing bowl and add the toasted spice powder. Mix well, then add the chicken strips. Toss well to coat, cover, and refrigerate for 1 hour.
- When you are ready to grill, lift the chicken strips out of the marinade and thread onto skewers, alternating with pieces of the sweet peppers. Grill covered in a medium-hot barbecue for about 8 minutes per side, turning the skewers occa-

sionally. Heap the skewers on a platter and serve, or slide the chicken and sweet peppers off the skewers and serve on a platter.

- SERVES 3 TO 4 WITH OTHER DISHES

Grilled Chicken Curry

Grilled marinated chicken thighs in a spicy coconut milk–tamarind sauce

Domenico Selvo, doge of Venice in the eleventh century, had married a Byzantine princess whose shocking behavior appalled the city. At the wedding celebrations, the bride refused to eat with her fingers like all the others present. Instead, she had her servant cut up the food, which she then daintily ate with a newfangled implement—a golden fork. "Decadence!" thundered the Cardinal Bishop of Ostia. In the face of such opposition, the use of forks in Europe disappeared, not to return for several centuries. The Portuguese who lived in sixteenth-century Goa had no difficulty eating with their fingers, as was the Indian custom.

Many of the Portuguese men living in Goa married Indian women who blended Indian and Portuguese cooking styles to suit their husbands' tastes. Goans use local ingredients such as coconut milk, tamarind, and curry leaves, but combine them with vinegar, reflecting the Portuguese influence on their cooking.

This Goan dish combines spicy marinated grilled chicken thighs with a mild coconut milk–based sauce. I like to fold in fresh tomatoes, scallions, and coriander to give the dish more flavor. Try using naan to scoop with instead of a fork.

- In a small microwave-safe bowl, microwave the tamarind and ½ cup of water uncovered on high for 2 minutes. Mash

Walnut-size piece of seedless tamarind (2 ounces)
½ cup water

FOR THE MARINADE
½-inch piece of ginger, grated
¼ cup white vinegar
½ teaspoon cumin seeds
½ teaspoon black mustard seeds
¼ teaspoon black pepper
½-inch cinnamon stick
4 whole cloves
2 small green cardamom
Salt to taste
1 tablespoon vegetable oil
1 pound boneless, skinless chicken thighs (about 8), washed and dried

FOR THE SAUCE
2 tablespoons vegetable oil
¼ teaspoon black mustard seeds
¼ teaspoon fenugreek seeds
10 to 15 curry leaves, preferably fresh

1 large garlic clove, finely chopped

1¼ cups finely chopped onions

1 cup canned unsweetened
coconut milk

½ teaspoon sugar

Salt to taste

1 tablespoon chopped fresh
coriander leaves

1 ripe tomato, finely chopped

1 green onion (scallion), finely
chopped with all its green parts

well with a fork and set aside to cool. (If you prefer, you can soak the tamarind in the water for 2 hours.)

- In a bowl, combine the ginger and vinegar. Powder the cumin seeds, mustard seeds, black pepper, cinnamon, cloves, and cardamom in a clean coffee or spice grinder. Mix this powder into the ginger vinegar, then add the salt and vegetable oil. Rub this marinade all over the chicken and refrigerate, covered, for at least 4 hours or overnight.

- When ready to grill, place the chicken thighs in a covered barbecue over medium-low heat and cook for 25 minutes or until tender, turning occasionally for even grilling. The grilling can be done up to 3 days ahead of time.

- To make the sauce, first strain the tamarind in a sieve set over a bowl. Squeeze out all the liquid, discarding the fibrous residue. Reserve this tamarind extract.

- Warm the vegetable oil in a nonstick skillet over medium-high heat. Add the mustard seeds and fenugreek seeds, then, after a second, the curry leaves and garlic. Sauté for a few seconds, then add the onions. Sauté, stirring occasionally for about 5 minutes, until the onions are lightly browned. Reduce the heat to low and add the coconut milk, tamarind extract, sugar, and salt. Cook for 5 minutes, then fold in the chopped fresh coriander leaves, tomato, green onion, and grilled chicken thighs. Remove from the heat and serve.

- SERVES 3 TO 4 WITH OTHER DISHES

Hara Masala Murgh

Chicken cooked in a sauce of onions, tomatoes, coconut, cashews, and fennel seeds with fresh herbs

 The city of Bombay started its life in rather unpromising fashion—as a wedding present that the groom wasn't very pleased with. Originally a Portuguese possession, Bombay was part of the dowry of Catherine of Braganza, sister of the Portuguese king, when she married King Charles II of England. The king's ministers were at first uncertain about the exact location of their newest colony: the Lord Chancellor, Clarendon, proclaimed it a valuable island "within a very little distance of Brazil." The king consulted a map and, disappointed to discover that it was a fairly worthless piece of land on the other side of the world, leased it to the East India Company in 1668. Bombay, blessed with a great natural harbor, became the center of British trade.

The British invited traders and craftsmen to settle in Bombay. Many of those who came were Parsis, people of Persian origin who had been living in India since the eighth century. They were quick to learn English and prospered in Bombay, becoming indispensable middlemen in British dealings with Indians.

Parsis, who practice the Zoroastrian religion, don't keep the dietary restrictions of Muslims and Hindus; their cuisine includes many chicken, lamb, fish, and, unusually for India, egg dishes. A popular Parsi dish is akoori, an exotic version of scrambled eggs. Ingredients can include chopped green peppers, hot green chilies, onions, tomatoes, herbs, spices, potatoes, almonds, and cream. Dhansak, the most famous of Parsi dishes, combines lamb with eight or nine varieties of lentils, vegetables, and spices. Patra ni Machali is fish coated with spices, coconut, and herbs, wrapped tightly in banana leaves and steamed.

1 teaspoon white poppy seeds (optional)

20 raw cashews

1 tablespoon plus 1 teaspoon whole fennel seeds

1½ cups finely chopped onions

3 garlic cloves, chopped

½-inch piece of ginger, chopped

2 tablespoons grated coconut, fresh or desiccated unsweetened

1 cup diced tomatoes, fresh or canned

2 tablespoons vegetable oil

¼ teaspoon cumin seeds

¼ teaspoon black mustard seeds

20 curry leaves, preferably fresh

Salt to taste

½ teaspoon turmeric

1 teaspoon ground coriander seeds

½ teaspoon ground cumin seeds

½ teaspoon garam masala

¼ to ½ teaspoon cayenne pepper

1 tablespoon sugar

½ cup water

3 pounds skinned chicken thighs and/or drumsticks, washed and drained

1 cup packed fresh coriander leaves and tender stems, washed and drained

½ cup packed fresh mint leaves, washed and drained

1 hot green chili (optional)

3 tablespoons lemon juice

In this Parsi recipe the chicken is cooked in a sautéed sauce of onions, tomatoes, herbs, and nuts. It goes well with rice or naan.

- Powder the poppy seeds, cashews, and fennel seeds in a clean coffee or spice grinder. In a blender, process the onions, garlic, ginger, coconut, and tomatoes to a smooth paste.
- Warm the oil in a nonstick skillet over medium-high heat. Add the cumin seeds, mustard seeds, and half of the curry leaves. After a few seconds, when they sputter, add the minced onion paste. Sauté, stirring for 10 to 15 minutes, until the moisture evaporates and the onions are lightly browned.

Gateway of India, Bombay

- Reduce the heat to medium and add the powdered cashew mixture, then stir in the salt, turmeric, ground coriander, ground cumin, garam masala, cayenne, and sugar. Sauté for 1 minute, then add ½ cup of water. Mix in the chicken, coating well. Now cover and bring to a boil. Immediately reduce the heat to medium-low and cook for 30 minutes, stirring occasionally.
- While the chicken is cooking, prepare the herbs. In a blender, combine the coriander, mint, remaining curry leaves, green chili, and lemon juice and blend to a smooth paste, adding 2 tablespoons of water if needed. After the chicken has been cooking for 30 minutes, pour in the herb paste and mix well. Cover and cook for another 20 minutes, or until the chicken is tender. This dish can be cooked up to 3 days ahead of time.

● SERVES 4 TO 6

Murgh Masale Mein

Chicken marinated with sautéed onions, spices, and thickened yogurt, sautéed with tomatoes and cardamom

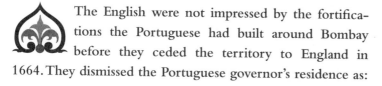 The English were not impressed by the fortifications the Portuguese had built around Bombay before they ceded the territory to England in 1664. They dismissed the Portuguese governor's residence as:

a pretty well Seated, but ill Fortified House, four Brass Guns being the whole Defence of the Island. . . . About the House was a delicate Garden, voiced to be the pleasantest in *India*, intended rather for wanton Dalliance, Love's Artillery, than to make resistance against an invading Foe.

Keen to show that they were made of sterner stuff, the English drafted the mystified Indians. After much protest,

FOR THE MARINADE

½ cup plain yogurt, not low-fat

2 tablespoons vegetable oil

½ teaspoon cumin seeds

1½ cups finely chopped onions

2 garlic cloves, chopped

½-inch piece of ginger, chopped

Salt to taste

½ teaspoon turmeric

1 teaspoon ground coriander seeds

1 teaspoon ground cumin seeds

½ teaspoon garam masala

¼ to ½ teaspoon cayenne pepper

3 pounds chicken drumsticks and/or
thighs, bone in, washed and
drained

FOR THE SAUCE
½ cup canned diced plum tomatoes,
drained
1 tablespoon vegetable oil (optional)
15 cardamom, powdered with skins
in a spice or coffee grinder
½ cup chopped fresh coriander leaves
1 tablespoon lemon juice
¼ teaspoon garam masala

Bombay merchants were exempted from serving in the army, instead contributing money that was used to hire a regiment of Germans. Though more martial, these soldiers had an unfortunate tendency to get drunk, and often proved more dangerous to public safety than any invader. Not only did they augment their salaries by periodically engaging in armed robbery, but on one occasion a bored corporal tied a "fired bandoleer" to the tail of a dog, which then ran into a store containing thirty-five barrels of gun powder, resulting in a considerable loss of life.

In spite of the hazards of life in Bombay, merchants from all parts of India continued to settle there. Many came from the province of Sindh; today's Sindhi community is an important part of the city. The cuisine is rarely found in restaurants, so to taste some you either have to know a Sindhi cook or make it yourself. I was fortunate enough to sample it in the home of my mother's Sindhi friend and neighbor, the late Roma Ramchandani, who was a wonderful cook. To make this curry, she marinated the chicken in yogurt and spices, then cooked it with tomatoes until the sauce thickened and smelled wonderful. She usually served Murgh Masale Mein with a simple rice pulao.

- Line a fine mesh sieve with 2 layers of cheesecloth or a coffee filter and set over a bowl. Pour in the yogurt and let it drain for an hour.
- Warm the oil in a nonstick skillet over medium-high heat. Add the cumin seeds and, after a few seconds, the chopped onions, garlic, and ginger. Sauté, stirring for about 8 minutes, until the onions are golden. Cool slightly and lift them out, reserving the oil. In a food processor, mince the onions with the thickened yogurt, then scrape down the sides and add the salt, turmeric, ground coriander, ground cumin, garam masala, and cayenne pepper. Process until everything is well blended, then transfer to a large mixing bowl. Toss in the chicken, coating well. Cover and refrigerate for an hour.

In the same food processor, puree the drained tomatoes and transfer to a small bowl.

- When you are ready to cook, warm the leftover oil in the skillet over medium heat, adding 1 tablespoon more if needed. Pour in the chicken and all its marinade and cook uncovered for 10 minutes, stirring occasionally. Add the pureed tomatoes and cook uncovered for about 8 minutes, until the oil floats on top. Add 1 cup of water, cover, and bring to a boil, then reduce heat to medium-low and cook for 30 minutes or until the chicken is tender. Mix in the powdered cardamom, fresh coriander leaves, lemon juice, and garam masala. There is a fair amount of sauce in this dish and it is usually not very thick. You can make this dish up to 3 days in advance.

- SERVES 6

Jardaloo Murgh

Chicken and dried apricots cooked in a sweet-and-sour sauce of sautéed onions, tomatoes, spices, and vinegar

Parsis are an Indian community of Iranian origin, most of whom now live in Bombay. Their ancestors sailed to India in the eighth century, after their ancient Zoroastrian religion was wiped out by the advent of Islam in Iran. Folklore has it that when the first Parsis arrived on Indian shores, they sent a delegation to the king of the region requesting permission to live there. The king replied with a brimming bowl of milk, indicating that his land, though prosperous, was already full. The Parsis added some sugar to the milk and returned it to demonstrate that they would enrich his kingdom. They were then welcomed into India and allowed to practice their religion. In the seventeenth century, most of the Parsi community migrated to the

2 tablespoons vegetable oil

¼ teaspoon cumin seeds

¼ teaspoon black mustard seeds

1 whole clove

1 whole cardamom

½-inch cinnamon stick

2 garlic cloves, grated

½-inch piece of ginger, grated

1 cup finely chopped onions

1 cup diced tomatoes, canned or fresh

Salt to taste

½ teaspoon turmeric

¼ to ½ teaspoon cayenne pepper

1 teaspoon ground coriander seeds

½ teaspoon ground cumin seeds

½ teaspoon garam masala

2 pounds skinned chicken thighs
   and/or drumsticks, washed
   and drained

20 dried, pitted apricots

1 tablespoon white vinegar

1 tablespoon sugar

1 tablespoon Worcestershire sauce

2 tablespoons chopped fresh
   coriander leaves

British settlement of Bombay, where they prospered as traders, merchants, and shipbuilders.

Parsi food reflects both its Iranian origin and later Indian and British influences. Jardaloo Murgh is a wonderful Parsi dish in which the chicken is cooked with dried apricots in a sweet-and-sour sauce. The use of dried apricots is characteristic of Iran, but spices such as garam masala, cumin, and coriander are typically Indian; the Worcestershire sauce must be thanks to the British. If you want to serve this dish the authentic Parsi way, top with deep-fried potato sticks and have rice on the side.

- Warm the oil in a large heavy nonstick skillet over medium-high heat. Add the cumin and mustard seeds and the whole clove, cardamom, and cinnamon. After a few seconds, when they begin to sputter, add the grated garlic and ginger. Sauté for about 30 seconds, then stir in the chopped onions and sauté, stirring occasionally for about 5 minutes, until lightly browned. Reduce heat to medium and add the tomatoes. Cook for 5 minutes, blending occasionally with the back of your spoon. Add the salt, turmeric, cayenne, ground coriander seeds, ground cumin seeds, and the garam masala. Sauté for 1 minute, then add the chicken and apricots. Coat well with the sauce, cover, and bring to a boil. Reduce the heat to medium-low and cook for about 30 minutes or until the chicken is tender.

- Add the vinegar, sugar, and Worcestershire sauce and cook covered for 5 minutes. The sauce should be quite thick. Fold in the chopped fresh coriander leaves and serve. This dish can be made up to 3 days ahead of time.

- SERVES 3 TO 4 WITH OTHER DISHES

Chicken Curry

Chicken cooked with onions, tomatoes, yogurt, and spices

Dinner for travelers stopping at the rest houses known as dak bungalows invariably consisted of chicken curry. This dish was popularly known as "sudden death," which newcomers to India were relieved to discover referred to the demise of the fowl. Within minutes of a guest arriving, one of the chickens that ranged free in the dak bungalow yard would be summarily executed and simmering in a pot. Diners did not always appreciate this menu: William Tayler wrote in 1881 that the cook "when asked, unblushingly professes to provide every delicacy of the season; but when he appears and uncovers his dishes, there is fowl, and nothing but fowl, of every age, size and degree of toughness." The stringy flesh of the chickens brought many complaints: "we rest satisfied with the assurance that we are tackling the identical cock that came out of the Ark," said another dissatisfied customer, George Atkinson.

Despite these criticisms, well-made chicken curry is easily prepared and a delight to eat. The classic recipe for chicken curry uses yogurt in the sauce, but I have substituted sour cream for half the yogurt, making the sauce richer and creamier. Serve with plain cooked rice and Saag Matar (spinach cooked with green peas, onions, tomatoes, and spices, page 21).

1¼ cups finely chopped onions

2 garlic cloves, chopped

½-inch piece of ginger, chopped

1 hot green chili (optional)

2 tablespoons vegetable oil

½ teaspoon cumin seeds

1 cup diced tomatoes, canned or fresh

2 tablespoons sour cream

2 tablespoons plain yogurt,
    not low-fat

1 teaspoon ground coriander seeds

½ teaspoon ground cumin seeds

½ teaspoon turmeric

¼ teaspoon cayenne pepper

¼ teaspoon ground black pepper

½ teaspoon garam masala

1 teaspoon kasoori methi
    (dried fenugreek leaves)

Salt to taste

2 pounds skinned chicken thighs,
    bone-in, washed and drained,
    or 8 boneless thighs

1 tablespoon lemon juice

2 tablespoons chopped fresh
    coriander leaves

- Mince the onions, garlic, ginger, and chili in a food processor. Warm the oil in a nonstick skillet over medium-high heat. Add the cumin seeds. After a few seconds, when they begin to sputter, add the minced onion mixture. Sauté, stirring occasionally for 5 to 10 minutes, until the onions are browned.

- Process the tomatoes in the food processor until smooth. Reduce the heat to medium under the skillet and add the tomatoes. Cook for 5 to 8 minutes, until all the liquid has evaporated and the oil appears around the edges.

- Add the sour cream and yogurt and stir continuously for about 5 minutes, until the oil appears again. Add all the spices and salt and cook for 1 minute. Now add the chicken thighs, coating well with sauce. Cover and bring to a boil. Immediately reduce the heat to medium-low and cook, stirring occasionally, for 30 minutes, or until the chicken is tender. Uncover and mix in the lemon juice and the fresh coriander leaves. Transfer to a serving dish. This dish can be made several days ahead of time.

- SERVES 3 TO 4 WITH OTHER DISHES

Chili Chicken

Chili chicken stir-fried with mushrooms and eggplant

FOR THE CHICKEN

4 boneless, skinless chicken
  thighs or breasts,
  about 10 ounces
¼-inch piece of ginger, chopped
1 garlic clove, chopped
1 hot green chili, stemmed
2 tablespoons chopped fresh
  coriander leaves
1 tablespoon soy sauce
1 teaspoon sesame oil
¼ teaspoon ground black pepper
2 tablespoons cornstarch
1 tablespoon all-purpose flour
2 tablespoons vegetable oil
2 medium long purple Chinese
  eggplant

"Soon the waters of my beloved Walden will blend with the sacred waters of the Ganges," wrote Henry David Thoreau. His poetic imagery was inspired by the ship *Tuscany,* which sailed from Boston to Calcutta in 1833 carrying a cargo of ice packed in felt and sawdust. It arrived with 180 tons of ice intact, two-thirds of its original freight. The ship's load was quickly snapped up by grateful residents of Calcutta, many of whom had never seen ice before. The successful voyage of the *Tuscany* encouraged other American entrepreneurs, and soon regular shipments of ice were arriving in Calcutta, where special warehouses were built to store it. This trade flourished until 1874, when it was abruptly killed by the announcement of the International Ice Company that it was about to commence manufacturing ice in Madras by the "steam process." Refrigeration had arrived in India, and summers would never be the same.

The constant flow of foreign traders through the port of Calcutta made it a bustling hub of commerce where different cultures often rubbed shoulders. The city's cuisine is a delightful mix of influences from around the world. This recipe—typical of Calcutta's Chinese cooking—creatively blends chicken and eggplants with Indian and Chinese spices. The chicken is first tossed with a fragrant marinade of ginger, garlic, chilies, and fresh coriander, then stir-fried until crisp. It is served with mushrooms and eggplant in a sautéed sauce of onions, tomatoes, black bean paste, and soy.

- Partially freeze the chicken to make slicing it easier. Slice it thinly across the grain in long strips. If using thighs, cut them into 1-inch pieces after trimming off all fat.
- Mince the ginger, garlic, green chili, and fresh coriander in a food processor. Transfer to a mixing bowl and add the chicken. Mix in the soy sauce, sesame oil, black pepper, cornstarch, and flour, coating the chicken well. Cover and refrigerate for 1 hour.
- Warm 2 tablespoons of oil in a nonstick wok or skillet over medium-high heat. Add the chicken and marinade and stir-fry until cooked through, crisp, and lightly browned. This should take about 3 minutes for chicken breasts and about 5 minutes for chicken thighs. Reserve oil, drain chicken on paper towels, and set aside.
- Cut the eggplant into 2-inch-long fingers (quarters). Warm the remaining oil, adding another tablespoon of oil if necessary. Stir-fry the eggplant over medium-high heat until cooked through and lightly browned. Drain on paper towels.
- Dissolve the cornstarch in the water and add the soy sauce, sesame oil, vinegar, black and red peppers, honey, black bean paste, and ketchup. Mix well and set aside.
- Warm 2 tablespoons of oil in a nonstick wok or skillet over medium-high heat. Add the chilies. As soon as they puff up and darken—this will take only a few seconds—stir in the chopped onions, garlic, and sweet pepper. Sauté them for 4

FOR THE SAUCE

1 teaspoon cornstarch
½ cup water
1 tablespoon soy sauce
1 teaspoon sesame oil
1 tablespoon rice vinegar
¼ teaspoon ground black pepper
¼ teaspoon red pepper flakes
1 teaspoon honey
1 teaspoon thick black bean paste
1 tablespoon tomato ketchup
2 tablespoons vegetable oil
2 dried red chilies, broken into bits (optional)
1¼ cups finely chopped onions
1 garlic clove, finely chopped
½ small sweet green pepper, cut into ½-inch cubes
6 small shiitaki mushrooms, washed, dried, and stemmed
4 tablespoons canned diced tomatoes, drained
2 green onions (scallions), chopped, white and green parts
2 tablespoons chopped fresh coriander leaves
1 hot green chili, sliced thin

to 5 minutes, then add the mushrooms. Sauté for 2 to 3 minutes, then mix in the diced tomatoes and cook for 2 to 3 minutes, until some of their liquid has evaporated. Give the cornstarch mixture a quick stir and pour it over the tomatoes. Cook for 1 minute, stirring gently, till the sauce has thickened. Gently mix in the chicken and eggplant. Remove from heat and fold in the chopped scallions, fresh coriander, and sliced green chili. Serve immediately.

• SERVES 4 WITH OTHER DISHES

Chicken Manchurian

Crisp morsels of chicken served in a garlic-flavored sauce
with fresh coriander and scallions

FOR THE CHICKEN

4 boneless, skinless chicken thighs
2 tablespoons cornstarch
1 tablespoon all-purpose flour
1 tablespoon water
1 tablespoon soy sauce
1 tablespoon sesame oil
½ teaspoon ground black pepper
Vegetable oil for deep frying

FOR THE SAUCE

1 teaspoon cornstarch
½ cup water
1 tablespoon thin black bean sauce
1 teaspoon sugar
¼ teaspoon ground black pepper
½ teaspoon red chili flakes
1 tablespoon soy sauce

The emperor of China wanted to just say no to drugs. The British East India Company was growing opium in Bengal and selling it in China. The Chinese government, alarmed by the increasing number of addicts, banned import of opium. Commissioner Lin Tse-Hsu, sent in 1839 to negotiate with the British, pleaded, "Your heartlessness in continuing to sell opium has made you the object of widely spread popular indignation. . . . What reason have you to cling to something which you are not allowed to sell and which no one is allowed to buy?" The British, affronted by this restriction on free trade, promptly invaded China in what became infamous as the Opium War. The war ended three years later with the Chinese defeated, Hong Kong a British possession, and the opium trade legalized. British ships sailed from Calcutta to Canton laden with opium and returned with tea.

Chinese merchants frequently traveled to Calcutta, and many settled there in what eventually grew into a large community that developed its own distinct cuisine. Many Chinese restaurants opened in Calcutta and, over time, developed a repertoire of dishes that appealed to their Indian customers. Chicken Manchurian is the most popular dish served in Indian Chinese restaurants—most people would think their meal incomplete without it. In my version of the recipe, the marinated chicken is fried until crisp, then served in a hot, gingery, soy-based sauce.

1 tablespoon sesame oil

1 tablespoon rice vinegar

2 garlic cloves, finely chopped

1-inch piece of ginger, chopped

1 green chili, stemmed

1 tablespoon vegetable oil

2 dried red chilies, broken in half

1 tablespoon chopped fresh
    coriander leaves

2 green onions (scallions), chopped,
    white and green parts

- Wash the chicken and cut into bite-size pieces (about ½ inch). Combine in a large mixing bowl with the cornstarch, flour, water, soy, sesame oil, and black pepper. Mix well to coat the chicken and refrigerate, covered, for half an hour.
- To make the sauce, dissolve the cornstarch with the water in a small bowl and mix in the black bean sauce, sugar, pepper, chili flakes, soy sauce, sesame oil, and vinegar. Set aside.
- Mince the garlic, ginger, and green chili in a food processor. Warm 1 tablespoon oil in a wok or nonstick skillet over medium heat. Add the dried red chilies and sauté for a few seconds. Stir in the minced garlic, ginger, and green chili and sauté, stirring for about 30 seconds, then turn off the heat and pour the dissolved cornstarch mixture into the wok. Stir well and let the sauce thicken over the fading heat of the stove for a minute or two. Mix in the chopped coriander and scallions.
- Cook the chicken just before you are ready to serve to retain crispness. Warm the oil in a wok over high heat. Make walnut-size balls out of the chicken mixture (they don't have to be perfectly smooth and round) and drop them gently into the hot oil. Fry gently until crisp, cooked through, and browned lightly. This should take about 5 minutes. Drain on paper towels, then fold gently into the sauce. Serve immediately.

- SERVES 3 TO 4 WITH OTHER DISHES

Goan Shrimp Curry

Shrimp cooked in a sautéed onion, tomato, and coconut-milk sauce with almonds

2 tablespoons vegetable oil

¼ teaspoon black mustard seeds

¼ teaspoon fenugreek seeds

1 garlic clove, grated

¼-inch piece of ginger, grated

10 to 15 curry leaves, preferably fresh

1 cup finely chopped onions

10 raw almonds, powdered fine in coffee or spice grinder

½ cup crushed tomatoes, fresh or canned

½ teaspoon ground coriander seeds

½ teaspoon ground cumin seeds

½ teaspoon turmeric

¼ teaspoon ground black pepper

¼ teaspoon cayenne pepper

Salt to taste

½ teaspoon sugar

½ cup canned unsweetened coconut milk

½ cup water

1 pound raw jumbo shrimp, peeled and deveined, washed and drained

4 tablespoons chopped fresh coriander leaves

1 tablespoon lemon juice

¼ teaspoon garam masala

 May 20, 1498. After a ten-month voyage from Lisbon, the Portuguese ships could clearly see the Indian coastline. The dream of generations of European seafarers—a direct sea route to India—was almost in their grasp. What lay ahead, wondered Vasco da Gama, as his men disembarked and approached the first native they saw. "The devil take you!" cursed the man in fluent Spanish. "What are you doing here?" The sailors had encountered an Arab trader from Tunis who was quite familiar with Europeans and was infuriated by their encroaching upon his turf.

Fortunately for them, the king of Calicut was quite willing to trade spices. But the Portuguese were chagrined to discover that the shipload of glass beads and brass bells that they had brought to barter with the simple natives wasn't going to get them much pepper. The Indians—shrewd bargainers that they were—demanded hard cash, preferably gold.

The Portuguese paid up and made good use of the spices, as is displayed in this recipe. This is a simply cooked, delicious dish from Goa where the shrimp are simmered in a sautéed onion, tomato, powdered almond, and coconut-milk sauce. This dish goes well with plain cooked rice.

- Warm the oil in a nonstick skillet over medium-high heat. Add the mustard and fenugreek seeds. As soon as they sputter—this will take only a few seconds—add the grated garlic and ginger and the curry leaves. Sauté for 30 seconds, then add the chopped onions. Sauté for 6 to 8 minutes until lightly browned. Reduce heat to medium, then add the powdered almonds and cook for 1 minute. Now stir in the crushed tomatoes and cook for about 5 minutes, until the moisture has evaporated. Add all the spices, salt, and sugar except for the garam masala and cook for 1 minute, then add the coconut milk. Cook for 2 minutes, then add the water and the shrimp.

- Cover and bring to a boil. Immediately reduce the heat to low and cook for 12 to 15 minutes, until the sauce is well cooked and the shrimp are cooked through. Mix in the fresh coriander leaves, lemon juice, and garam masala.

- SERVES 3 TO 4 WITH OTHER DISHES

Hot Garlic Shrimp

Crisp marinated shrimp served in a hot garlic sauce

 Foreign travelers to India have always been puzzled by the lack of eating implements at the table. The Chinese monk Xuan Zang visiting India in A.D. 629 commented:

They have many vessels made of dried clay; they seldom use red copper vessels: they eat from one vessel, mixing all sorts of condiments together, which they take up with their fingers. They have no spoons or cups, and in short no sort of chopsticks.

Indians still like to eat with their fingers, though nowadays you can find chopsticks in Chinese restaurants. Not everyone has mastered the art of eating with them, but eating Chinese food such as noodles with your fingers is too awkward; a fork seems a sensible compromise.

In this recipe from the Hakka Chinese community of Calcutta, the marinated shrimp are stir-fried until crisp, then folded in a thick, delicious sauce of onions, tomatoes, and red peppers. The shredded lettuce on which the shrimp are laid

FOR THE MARINADE

1 tablespoon cornstarch

1 teaspoon all-purpose flour

1 tablespoon water

½ of a beaten egg

1 teaspoon soy sauce

1 teaspoon sesame oil

¼ teaspoon ground black pepper

1 pound raw jumbo shrimp
  (about 20), peeled and deveined,
  washed and drained

1 tablespoon chopped fresh
  coriander leaves

3 tablespoons vegetable oil

FOR THE SAUCE

1 teaspoon cornstarch

½ cup water

1 tablespoon soy sauce

1 tablespoon rice vinegar

1 teaspoon sesame oil

1 teaspoon sugar

1 teaspoon red chili paste
  or chili sauce

¼ teaspoon ground black pepper

¼ teaspoon red pepper flakes

3 garlic cloves, grated

2 whole dried red chilies,
  broken in half

1¼ cups finely chopped onions

½ cup diced tomatoes, canned or
  fresh

1 small sweet red pepper, diced into
  1-inch cubes

2 scallions (green onions), chopped,
  white and green parts

1 cup finely shredded iceberg lettuce

out is the best part of this dish—it softens slightly with the heat of the shrimp and mixes with the sauce. I usually serve Hot Garlic Shrimp with fried rice.

- Combine the cornstarch, flour, and 1 tablespoon of water. Add the egg, soy sauce, sesame oil, and ground black pepper, stirring until smooth. Mix in the shrimp and the chopped fresh coriander leaves. Cover and refrigerate for at least half an hour.

- To make the sauce, mix together the cornstarch, ½ cup water, soy sauce, vinegar, sesame oil, sugar, chili paste, ground black pepper, and the red pepper flakes. Set aside.

- Cook the shrimp just before you are ready to serve. Warm the oil in a nonstick skillet or wok over high heat. Add the shrimp and all the marinade. Stir-fry for 2 to 3 minutes, until they are cooked through and slightly crisp. Drain on paper towels.

- Warm the remaining oil over medium-high heat and add the grated garlic and broken red chilies. Fry for 30 seconds, until the garlic turns golden, then add the onions. Sauté for 5 minutes, then reduce the heat to medium and stir in the tomatoes. Cook for another 5 minutes, mashing the tomatoes with your spoon to soften them. Give the cornstarch mixture a quick stir and pour it over the tomatoes. Stir to mix, then add the shrimp, coating well with sauce, and cook for 1 minute, until the sauce has thickened. Remove from heat. Fold in the sweet red pepper and the scallions. Spread the shredded lettuce evenly over a platter and transfer the shrimp onto it. Serve at once.

- SERVES 3 TO 4 WITH OTHER DISHES

Goan Fish Curry

Grilled salmon chunks served in a sauce of sautéed onions, tomatoes, coconut, and fresh coriander

 Have you ever complained about fish not being fresh? Sympathize with the plight of sixteenth-century cooks in Europe, trying their best to make dried salt cod palatable. In 1497 John Cabot, sent by Henry VII of England on a voyage to find a western sea route to India, landed in Newfoundland instead, where he found the waters teeming with fish. Soon European fishermen were sailing to Newfoundland every summer. While camping on the island, they lived on a diet of fish stew, named chowder after the pot it was cooked in—a *chaudière*. The fishermen caught cod, which was salted and dried on wooden racks (called stocks) for the long journey home, where it could be stored for years. It was a daunting task to make ten-year-old stockfish edible: "It behoves to beat it with a wooden hammer for a full hour and then set it to soak in warm water for a full two hours or more, then cook it and scour it very well." The resurrected fish was drowned in spicy sauces: ginger and saffron in *sauce jaune;* ginger, cloves, and cardamom and herbs in *sauce verte;* or ginger, cinnamon, cloves, cardamom, pepper, and mace in *sauce cameline.* Business had never been better for the Portuguese spice merchants.

The Portuguese in Goa had no shortage of fresh fish, which were plentiful all along the coastline. Goan fish curry, which combines fresh coconut, tamarind, red chilies, sautéed onions, tomatoes, and spices, is a very popular dish. There are many variations of the basic recipe, and in Goa it is usually cooked with a lot of fiery red chilies that give it a bright red color and a scorching hot taste. In this recipe I have substituted green chilies, which are somewhat milder. If you want to get the authentic shade of red, use a combination of paprika

1 pound thick-cut salmon fillet or other firm-fleshed fish

FOR THE MARINADE
½ teaspoon salt
¼ teaspoon turmeric
1 tablespoon lemon juice

FOR THE SAUCE
Walnut-size lump of seedless tamarind (2 ounces)
1½ cups water
2 tablespoons grated coconut, preferably fresh unsweetened
1 cup loosely packed fresh coriander leaves and tender upper stems, washed and drained
2 hot green chilies, stemmed, deseeded if desired
¾ teaspoon ground coriander seeds
¾ teaspoon ground cumin seeds
2 tablespoons vegetable oil
½ teaspoon black mustard seeds
2 garlic cloves, grated
½-inch piece of ginger, grated
1¼ cups finely chopped onions
½ cup diced tomatoes, canned or fresh
½ teaspoon turmeric
Salt to taste

and cayenne pepper. Serve plain cooked rice and lots of cold water on the side.

- Wash the fish well and dry with paper towels. Lay the fillets skin side down in a single layer in a large flat dish. Make a paste of the salt, turmeric, and lemon juice and rub it all over the flesh of the fish. Cover and refrigerate for 1 hour.
- In a small microwave-safe bowl, microwave the tamarind and ½ cup of the water uncovered on high for 2 minutes. Mash with a fork to soften and set aside to cool for 10 minutes. (If you prefer, you can soak the tamarind in the water for 2 hours.) Strain the liquid through a fine mesh sieve set over a bowl, discarding the fibrous residue. Combine this tamarind extract, coconut, fresh coriander, green chilies, ground coriander, and cumin in a blender and blend to a smooth paste. Transfer to a bowl and set aside.
- Warm the oil in a nonstick skillet over medium-high heat. Add the mustard seeds and, after a few seconds, the grated garlic and ginger. Sauté for 30 seconds, then mix in the chopped onions. Sauté, stirring occasionally for 5 minutes, until the onions are lightly browned. Add the tomatoes and cook for 5 minutes, blending with the back of your spoon. Add the turmeric and salt and cook for 1 minute. Now add the coconut-coriander paste and cook for 2 minutes. Add the remaining 1 cup of water, cover, and bring to a boil. Reduce heat to medium-low and cook for 10 minutes. This sauce can be prepared and refrigerated up to 2 days ahead of time.
- When you are ready to grill, lift the fish out of its marinade. You can either grill it in a medium-hot barbecue or under the preheated broiler in your oven. Grill it skin side down for about 8 minutes, then flip gently and grill for another 8 minutes, or until done to your liking. Remove the skin, divide the fish into 2-inch pieces, and stir into the prepared sauce (reheating first if refrigerated). Gently toss the fish to coat well and serve hot.
  - SERVES 3 TO 4 WITH OTHER DISHES

Machali Patia

Fish cooked in a sweet-and-sour sautéed onion and tamarind sauce

 Lord Marcus Sandys, formerly governor of Bengal, returned home to Britain in 1835. He went to the store of John Lea and William Perrins in Worcester and asked them to make a sauce according to a recipe he had brought back from India. The mixture proved so fiery that Messrs. Lea and Perrins abandoned further attempts and relegated the barrel to their cellar. Months later, as they were about to throw the cask away, they decided to taste some of its contents and discovered that the sauce had mellowed deliciously. Within two years Lea and Perrins were bottling Worcestershire sauce commercially, and it quickly became the most popular sauce in Britain.

Exported all over the world, Worcestershire sauce soon found its way back to India, where a Parsi cook must have discovered how good it tasted in patia. Patia is a Parsi dish usually made with seafood and served with rice at festive occasions. It combines the tart flavors of tamarind and lemon juice with the bite of cayenne pepper and the sweetness of brown sugar, all topped off with a dash of Worcestershire sauce. This eclectic mix of flavors will leave your palate tingling!

- Wash the fish and pat dry with paper towels. Lay the fillets skin side down in a single layer in a large flat dish. Combine the marinade ingredients and rub all over the flesh of the fish. Marinate in the refrigerator for 15 minutes.
- Line an ovenproof dish with foil and place a grilling rack over the dish. Lift the fillets out of their marinade and place them on the rack. Place the oven rack on the second rung from the top and preheat the broiler. Broil the fillets for 5 minutes. The purpose of this is not to cook the fish but to

1¼ pounds thick-cut firm
  fish fillet

FOR THE MARINADE

Salt to taste
½ teaspoon turmeric
¼ teaspoon ground black pepper
2 tablespoons lemon juice

FOR THE SAUCE

Walnut-size piece of seedless
  tamarind (2 ounces)
1½ cups water
2 tablespoons vegetable oil
¼ teaspoon cumin seeds
¼ teaspoon black mustard seeds
10 curry leaves, preferably fresh
1 garlic clove, grated
¼-inch piece of ginger, grated
1¼ cups finely chopped onions
½ cup diced tomatoes, canned
  or fresh
Salt to taste
¼ to ½ teaspoon cayenne pepper
¼ teaspoon turmeric
½ teaspoon ground coriander
  seeds
¼ teaspoon ground cumin seeds
½ teaspoon garam masala
1 tablespoon dark brown sugar
1 tablespoon Worcestershire sauce

1 tablespoon lemon juice
½ cup chopped fresh coriander leaves
 and tender stems

loosen its skin. When the fillets are cool enough to handle, remove their skin, dividing the flesh into 2-inch chunks as you do so. Set aside in a bowl.

- In a small microwave-safe bowl, microwave the tamarind and ½ cup of the water on high for 2 minutes, mash with a fork, and set aside to cool for 10 minutes. (If you prefer, you can soak the tamarind in the water for 2 hours.) Set a fine mesh sieve over a bowl and pour the tamarind and its liquid through. Squeeze the pulp and discard the fibrous residue. Reserve this extract.

- To make the sauce, warm the oil in a large nonstick skillet over medium-high heat. Add the cumin, mustard seeds, and curry leaves and, after a few seconds, the grated garlic and ginger. Sauté for about 30 seconds, then stir in the chopped onions. Sauté, stirring for about 5 minutes, until lightly browned. Reduce heat to medium, add the tomatoes, and cook for 5 minutes, blending them in with the back of your spoon. Add the salt, cayenne, turmeric, ground coriander seeds, ground cumin seeds, garam masala, sugar, and Worcestershire sauce and cook for 1 minute, then mix in the tamarind extract and cook for another minute. Add the remaining 1 cup of water, cover, and bring to a boil. Reduce heat to medium-low and gently slide in the fish. Cook for 20 minutes, stirring occasionally. Mix in the lemon juice and chopped fresh coriander. This dish can be made up to 3 days ahead of time and reheated before serving.

- SERVES 3 TO 4 WITH OTHER DISHES

Macher Jhol

Fillet of fish cooked with tomatoes and ground mustard seeds

 François Bernier was a French doctor who spent seven years traveling around India in the late seventeenth century. He was deeply impressed by the beauty of Bengal, which he described vividly in his writings:

> The rich exuberance of the country, together with the beauty and amiable disposition of the native women, has given rise to a proverb in common use among the Portuguese, English and Dutch, that the Kingdom of Bengale has a hundred gates open for entrance, but not one for departure.

Bernier also described the good food, including the profusion of "fish of every species, whether fresh or salt." All Bengalis love fish. They may dispute where the best fish comes from—in the east they insist that the tastiest fish is caught in rivers, while in the west they prefer fish from lakes—but all agree that a meal without fish is incomplete. For breakfast, minced fish is mixed with mashed potatoes and spices, shaped into cutlets and deep-fried. Doi Maach, an unusual pairing of fish and yogurt, is served at lunch with dal and rice. Even the dal may be flavored with fish heads. Macher Jhol is another classic fish preparation from Bengal: the fish is first marinated in a pungent mustard seed paste, then lightly grilled, and finally simmered in a sauce of sautéed onions and tomatoes spiced with powdered mustard and poppy seeds. Serve plain cooked rice on the side to sop up all the delicious sauce.

- Wash the fillets well and dry them with paper towels. Put them in a single layer, skin side down, in a large flat dish. Powder the mustard seeds in a clean coffee or spice grinder, then transfer half of this powder to a small bowl (leave the

1¼ pounds firm fish fillet, such as rainbow trout, thick-cut

FOR THE MARINADE
2 tablespoons black mustard seeds
2 tablespoons lemon juice
Salt to taste
¼ teaspoon turmeric
½ teaspoon ground black pepper

FOR THE SAUCE
1 tablespoon white poppy seeds
¼ teaspoon fennel seeds
¼ teaspoon fenugreek seeds
¼ teaspoon black mustard seeds
¼ teaspoon cumin seeds
¼ teaspoon kalonji (onion seeds)
3 whole cardamom
3 whole cloves
½-inch cinnamon stick
1 bay leaf
2 tablespoons vegetable oil
1 cup finely chopped onions
½-inch piece of ginger, grated
1 hot green chili, chopped fine
Salt to taste
½ teaspoon turmeric
½ teaspoon ground coriander seeds
½ teaspoon ground cumin seeds
1 cup diced tomatoes, canned or fresh

1 cup water

2 tablespoons chopped fresh
coriander leaves

remaining half in the spice grinder) and add the lemon juice, salt, turmeric, and ground black pepper. Make a smooth paste and rub this all over the flesh side of the fish. Cover and refrigerate for an hour.

- Preheat your oven broiler. Line a large flat baking dish with foil and put a grilling rack on top. Place the fillets in a single layer on the rack. Move your oven rack to its second rung and broil the fillets for 5 minutes. Remove and cool slightly. Skin and debone the fillets, dividing them into 2-inch pieces as you do so. Set aside in a bowl.

- Put the poppy seeds in the spice grinder with the remaining mustard seed powder and powder again. Transfer to a small bowl. Combine the fennel, fenugreek, mustard, cumin, and onion seeds in another small bowl, then add the cardamom, cloves, cinnamon, and bay leaf.

- Warm the oil in a nonstick skillet over medium-high heat. Add the whole-spice mixture and sauté for about 30 seconds. Mix in the onions and sauté for 5 minutes, stirring occasionally. Reduce the heat to medium and add the grated ginger and green chili along with the poppy seed and mustard powder, salt, turmeric, ground coriander, and ground cumin seeds. Sauté for 1 minute, then add the tomatoes and cook for about 8 minutes, until the tomatoes are blended into the sauce and the oil appears around the edges. Add the water and bring to a boil. Gently slide in the fish, cover, and reduce heat to medium-low. Cook for 15 minutes, stirring gently once in a while. Mix in the fresh coriander leaves and serve. You can make this dish up to 3 days ahead of time and reheat gently.

  - SERVES 3 TO 4 WITH OTHER DISHES

Mangsho Jhol

**Lamb cooked with tomatoes, yogurt, mustard seeds,
baby potatoes, and shallots**

The Calcutta satirist who wrote under the name of Quiz was shocked at "the indelicate method both ladies and gentlemen eat." He reported seeing "one of the *prettiest girls* in Calcutta eat about two pounds of mutton-chops at one sitting!" Calcutta table manners were not improved by the ladies at a dinner party in 1775, who, after imbibing copious amounts of cherry brandy, began throwing bread pellets at each other. This practice became all the rage, and the acknowledged bread pellet

1¼ cups finely chopped onions

½ cup diced tomatoes

½ cup plain yogurt, not low-fat

2 hot green chilies, stemmed

2 garlic cloves, chopped

½-inch piece of ginger, chopped

*1 tablespoon grated unsweetened
   coconut (optional)*

Salt to taste

Writers' Building, Calcutta, 1915

1 teaspoon ground coriander seeds

½ teaspoon ground cumin seeds

½ teaspoon garam masala

2 tablespoons black mustard seeds,
    powdered fine in coffee or
    spice grinder

½ teaspoon turmeric

1 pound cubed lamb, bone-in,
    washed and drained

¼ teaspoon cumin seeds

¼ teaspoon fennel seeds

¼ teaspoon black mustard seeds

¼ teaspoon fenugreek seeds

¼ teaspoon kalonji (onion seeds)

2 tablespoons vegetable oil

6 shallots (small onions), peeled

6 baby potatoes, peeled

1 cup water, or more if needed

1 tablespoon lemon juice

½ cup chopped fresh coriander leaves

champion was Mr. Daniel Barwell, who could extinguish a candle four yards away. Fortunately, the fashion did not last long. Captain Morrison, after being hit by a pellet, retaliated by hurling a leg of mutton. This exchange was followed by a duel in which the bread pellet thrower was almost killed, somewhat dampening the exuberance of Calcutta diners.

This popular Calcutta dish is so good that your guests will not be tempted to hurl pieces of it at each other. It is cooked in typical Bengali fashion, using a lot of powdered mustard seeds, which give it a pleasant pungency. Mustard seeds are used in three different ways in Bengali cooking: their oil is used for cooking; the seeds are crackled in hot oil to give the food a delicious nutty taste; or the seeds are ground into a paste and added to the food as it simmers. A unique spice mixture called panchphoran (literally meaning "five spices") is used in almost every Bengali dish. It is a blend of cumin, mustard seeds, fenugreek seeds, fennel seeds, and onion seeds, which is added to the hot oil before the food. Mangsho Jhol is usually served with rice, which Bengalis eat at almost every meal.

- Mince the onions, tomatoes, yogurt, green chilies, garlic, ginger, and coconut in a food processor or blender. Add the salt, ground coriander seeds, ground cumin seeds, garam masala, powdered mustard seeds, and turmeric and blend again. Transfer to a large bowl and toss in the lamb, coating well with marinade. At this point you can either marinate the meat in the refrigerator for a few hours or overnight, or proceed with the recipe.

- Combine the cumin seeds, fennel seeds, mustard seeds, fenugreek seeds, and onion seeds together in a small bowl near the stove. Warm the oil in a nonstick skillet over medium-high heat, then add the mixed whole spices. After about 30 seconds, when they begin to crackle, add the lamb and all its marinade. Stir-fry continuously for 10 minutes, browning lightly. Add the shallots, potatoes, and 1 cup of water and mix well. Cover and bring to a boil. Immediately reduce heat to medium-low and cook for 1 hour or until the lamb is tender and the sauce fairly thick.

- Stir occasionally, and if the meat seems to be sticking to the bottom of the skillet, add ¼ cup water. When done, add the lemon juice and fresh coriander and mix again. This dish can be cooked up to 3 days ahead of time.

- SERVES 3 TO 4 WITH OTHER DISHES

Goan Lamb Curry

Lamb cooked in a sauce of sautéed onions, tomatoes, and coconut milk with vinegar and spices

 In medieval Europe, spices were wealth, often hoarded like treasure. The Venerable Bede, an English scholar, carefully distributed among his friends his most precious possession—a handful of pepper—as he lay on his deathbed in 735.

The wealthy stocked huge amounts of spices and used them liberally in cooking. A 1328 inventory of spices in the kitchen of Jeanne d'Evreux, widow of the king of France, listed: 3 bales of almonds, 6 pounds of pepper, 13½ pounds of cinnamon, 23½ pounds of ginger, 5 pounds of cardamom, 3½ pounds of cloves, 1½ pounds of saffron, ⅜ pound of mace, 5 pounds of cumin, and 20 pounds of sugar. I use spices freely and keep a well-stocked pantry, but I stand in awe of Jeanne's stash!

Many of the spices sold in Europe were shipped from Goa, where local cooks used them too. This lamb curry from Goa contains all the spices cherished by medieval chefs, though used with more restraint. The lamb is first soaked in a spicy sautéed marinade until it absorbs the flavors, then cooked until tender in a coconut milk sauce which mellows the spices

1 pound boneless or bone-in lamb

FOR THE MARINADE

2 tablespoons vegetable oil

¼ teaspoon black mustard seeds

¼ teaspoon fenugreek seeds

10 curry leaves, preferably fresh

1¼ cups finely chopped onions

2 garlic cloves, chopped

½-inch piece of ginger, chopped

½ cup diced tomatoes, canned or fresh

¼ teaspoon ground black pepper

½ teaspoon turmeric

½ teaspoon ground coriander seeds

½ teaspoon ground cumin seeds

½ teaspoon garam masala

Salt to taste

½ teaspoon cayenne pepper

4 tablespoons rice vinegar

1 tablespoon vegetable oil

½ teaspoon cumin seeds

1 cup finely chopped onions

½ cup canned unsweetened
   coconut milk

½ cup water

Salt to taste

4 tablespoons chopped fresh coriander
   leaves

deliciously. You can serve this lamb curry with Vendakai Thengai Mundri Poriyal (okra cooked with cashews and coconut, page 52) and plain cooked rice.

- If you are using bone-in lamb, have the butcher cut it into cubes. If you are using boneless lamb, cut it into 2-inch cubes. Wash and set aside in a colander to drain.
- Warm the oil in a nonstick skillet over medium-high heat. Add the mustard and fenugreek seeds and, after a few seconds, the curry leaves, chopped onions, garlic, and ginger. Sauté for about 5 minutes, until lightly browned. Let cool for a few minutes, then lift out of the oil with a slotted spoon, leaving behind as much oil as possible. Reserve the skillet and its oil for later use.
- Put the onions, garlic, ginger, and spices in a food processor or blender, combine all the remaining ingredients for the marinade, and blend till smooth. Transfer to a large mixing bowl. Toss in the lamb and coat well. Cover and refrigerate overnight if possible, or for at least 2 hours.
- To make the sauce, warm the leftover oil in the skillet over medium-high heat, adding 1 more tablespoon of oil if necessary. Add the cumin seeds, then, after a few seconds, the chopped onions. Sauté for 5 minutes, then stir in the lamb and all its marinade. Stir-fry for 5 minutes, then add the coconut milk, water, and salt to taste. Cover and bring to a boil, then reduce heat and cook for 1 hour, or until the lamb is very tender and the sauce is thick. Stir occasionally. If the meat seems to be sticking to the bottom of the pan, add an additional ½ cup of water. For faster results, you can transfer the lamb from the skillet to a pressure cooker and cook it for 15 minutes. The sauce should be very thick when the meat is done. Mix in the chopped fresh coriander leaves and serve.

- SERVES 3 TO 4 WITH OTHER DISHES

Seyal Gosht

Lamb marinated and cooked in onions, yogurt, and fresh coriander, folded with sautéed onions, tomatoes, cardamom, and tamarind

 Although the British had conquered most of India in the nineteenth century, social life wasn't always scintillating. Maria Graham wrote about her experiences in Bombay in 1809:

> The parties in Bombay are the most dull and uncomfortable meetings one can imagine. Forty or fifty persons assemble at seven o'clock, and stare at one another till dinner is announced. . . . The repast itself is as costly as possible, and in such profusion that no part of the table-cloth remains uncovered. But the dinner is hardly touched, as every person eats a hearty meal called tiffin, at two o'clock, at home.

Almost thirty years later, Emily Eden was still complaining:

> After dinner all the ladies sit in a complete circle around the room, and the gentlemen stand at the farther end of it. I do not suppose they would have anything to say if they met, but it would look better. Luckily it does not last long.

This lamb curry from Bombay will certainly please your dinner guests, but you're on your own for sparkling conversation.

"Seyal" means cooking with sautéed onions, herbs, and spices, with no water added. Seyal Gosht is cooked in classic Sindhi style, with plenty of fresh coriander and crushed cardamom seeds; the sautéed onion, tomato, and spicy tamarind sauce makes the dish distinctive. Serve with plain cooked rice or Indian bread.

FOR THE MARINADE

1 cup finely chopped onions

2 garlic cloves, chopped

½-inch piece of ginger, chopped

1 hot green chili, stemmed

1 cup packed fresh coriander leaves
   and tender stems, washed and
   drained

1 cup plain yogurt, not low-fat

Salt to taste

½ teaspoon turmeric

½ teaspoon ground coriander seeds

½ teaspoon ground cumin seeds

½ teaspoon garam masala

2 pounds cubed lamb, bone-in,
   washed and drained

1 tablespoon vegetable oil

FOR THE SAUCE

Walnut-size piece of seedless
   tamarind (2 ounces)

½ cup water

20 whole cardamom

1 teaspoon whole fennel seeds

2 tablespoons vegetable oil

½ teaspoon cumin seeds

1¼ cups finely chopped onions

1 cup diced tomatoes, canned or fresh

½ teaspoon ground black pepper

- Combine all the marinade ingredients except the vegetable oil in a food processor and mince well. Transfer to a large mixing bowl and add the cubed lamb. Toss well to coat, cover, and refrigerate overnight or for at least 4 hours.

- Warm the oil in a nonstick skillet over high heat. Stir in the lamb and all its marinade. Cover and bring to a boil, then reduce heat to medium-low and cook for 1½ hours, stirring occasionally. Toward the end, stir more often to prevent the sauce from sticking. It should be very thick and clinging to the meat when the dish is done.

- While the lamb is cooking, prepare the sauce. In a small microwave-safe bowl, microwave the tamarind and ½ cup of water on high for 2 minutes, then mash well with a fork. Set aside to cool for 10 minutes. (If you prefer, you can soak the tamarind in the water for 2 hours.) Place a fine mesh sieve over a bowl and pour the tamarind and all its liquid through. Squeeze out the thick pulp, discarding the fibrous residue. Reserve this extract in a small bowl.

- Powder the whole cardamom and the fennel seeds in a clean coffee or spice grinder. Mix into the reserved tamarind.

- Warm the oil in a skillet or frying pan over medium-high heat and add the cumin seeds, then, after a few seconds, the chopped onions. Sauté, stirring for about 5 minutes, until lightly browned. Reduce the heat to medium and mix in the diced tomatoes. Cook for about 8 minutes, until the tomatoes are well blended and the oil appears around the edges. Add the spiced tamarind extract and ground black pepper and cook for 1 minute.

- When the lamb is done, gently fold in the sautéed onion-tomato-tamarind sauce and cook on medium heat for 2 minutes. You can make this dish up to 3 days in advance.

  • SERVES 4 TO 6 WITH OTHER DISHES

Fusion Cuisine:
East Meets West

"There's McDonald's!" As we walked down a street in Delhi, the familiar golden arches elicited shrieks of joy from my children. Others may grumble about the ubiquitous presence of American fast food around the globe, but my North American born-and-bred boys had no such complaint. After a month in India filled with overwhelming new experiences, sights, and flavors, the restaurant seemed like a little piece of home. But its menu left them bewildered: in lieu of the usual roster of hamburgers, we found the Maharaja Burger, a ground lamb patty in a bun; in the land of the sacred cow, even McDonald's has had to improvise. Searching for something familiar, we ordered french fries, but when my three-year-old son tasted them, he burst into tears. They were spiced with lots of ground black pepper, the better to appeal to Indian palates.

India has always welcomed new foods, but on its own terms, confident that a judiciously chosen sprinkling of spices can transform even the blandest dish into something quite savory. In the hands of Indian cooks, Persian, Arab, Chinese, and Portuguese recipes have all become part of the national cuisine. This process of assimilation continues—only the sources of inspiration have changed. In recent years, Indian restaurants have played an important part in adapting foreign dishes to suit Indian tastes. Restaurant chefs are acutely sensitive to the preferences of their clientele and are also keen to substitute local ingredients, which are cheaper and more easily available. The end product is a fine example of fusion cuisine, though that isn't usually the cooks' intention.

It is only in the last few decades that restaurants have played a significant role. Fifty years ago, Indian cities had few restaurants, and those that existed catered largely to the British; Indians reasoned that they could get better food at home. The restaurant boom in India was spurred by the upheaval that followed when the British left India in 1947, finally bowing to the country's demand for independence. Their departure marked the birth of two nations: India was partitioned to create the new, largely Muslim, country of Pakistan. The many autonomous kingdoms such as Hyderabad, Jaipur, Udaipur, and Kashmir that had existed as British protectorates were all absorbed into either India or Pakistan.

Indian independence was followed by a huge displacement of people, as Hindus moved to India and Muslims to Pakistan. Punjab was the province most affected, for the new international boundary ran right through its middle. Punjabi Hindus who found themselves in Pakistan migrated en masse to India; most of them settled in Delhi, where they struggled to find work and rebuild their lives. Many of them opened small restaurants whose inexpensive, hearty food proved popular, but what really made them successful was the introduction of the *tandoor*. The clay oven sunk into the ground and lined with glowing charcoal had been used for centuries in Punjabi villages to grill food, but it was a novelty in Delhi. At that time the repertoire of dishes cooked in tandoors was quite restricted, consisting of a few varieties of kababs (skewers of spiced ground or cubed meat), naan (leavened flatbread), and, most popular of all, tandoori chicken—marinated, delicately spiced, whole chickens cooked on skewers. In spite of their limited menus, tandoori restaurants proved an instant hit in Delhi and finally gave people a reason to eat out, for tandoors are difficult to build and maintain at home.

Indian independence also signaled the demise of the princely states, in whose palaces some of the finest chefs in the country had worked. The elaborate recipes of the royal kitchens, whose origins could be traced back to the days of the Moghuls, had been kept a closely guarded secret, handed down by each generation of master chefs to their apprentices. With the end of the princely era, these cooks found themselves without aristocratic patrons and had to offer their services to less exalted customers. Their misfortune had the happy consequence of allowing a large number of people to taste the food previously reserved for nobility.

By the 1960s, restaurants in India had hit upon a successful menu: tandoori food combined with some Moghlai dishes such as biryanis and kormas. Restaurants all over the country served much the same fare, apparently assuming that there would be little demand for the fresh, exquisitely spiced dishes that Indians ate every day at home. Dining out meant rich curries, tandoori chicken, and naan. Cookbooks written at that time were filled with warnings that the best samples of Indian food were not to be found in restaurants, and they were quite right.

Indian restaurants had opened in Europe long before they did in India: London coffeehouses were serving Indian curries as early as 1770. Pierre Jouhard, a French lawyer, claimed in 1809 that Parisian restaurants conveyed each customer to "the land that saw his birth, and seated him at the table of his forefathers," and if "you were born in those burning lands watered by the Indus . . . you were offered a *carrick à l'indienne*." But these dishes demanded ingredients the Europeans often did not have, with results that were only rough approximations of the original. People who sought authenticity had to wait until Indians opened restaurants in the West.

Where there was a demand for Indian food, Indian entrepreneurs were quite happy to satisfy it. But the people who first opened Indian restaurants in Western cities followed what they considered a tried-and-true formula, serving the hybrid Punjabi-Moghlai cuisine popular in India. This standardization of restaurant menus led the rest of the world to believe that was all there was to Indian cuisine.

The lack of variety in Indian restaurants did not prove an impediment; in recent times Indian cuisine has experienced an explosive worldwide growth in popularity. The British, who carefully avoided eating any Indian food during their three centuries in India, have rediscovered it with a passion. There were ten Indian restaurants in London in 1955; now there are thousands, with more opening every day. Every major city in the world has at least a few Indian eating places. Fortunately, Indian restaurants have grown not just in numbers but also in sophistication. At one time Indian food meant quick, cheap curry. Now you can find excellent restaurants in London and New York where skilled chefs offer a variety of Indian dishes to an increasingly discriminating and knowledgeable clientele.

The job of these chefs has been simplified, and their dishes made more authentic, by the widespread availability of Indian spices and vegetables in Western cities. Western cooks have also discovered these Indian ingredients. I am no longer surprised to find garam masala paired with oregano, or to taste tamarind in a French sauce.

Indians, too, are exploring the rich variety of cooking styles available in their own country. You can now find restaurants devoted to specialized regional cuisines that serve food with painstaking attention to detail. The quest for authenticity may sometimes prove a little excessive—some restaurants recreate the entire experience of dining in an Indian village, down to seating their diners on extremely uncomfortable, though unquestionably rural, furniture. Indian restaurant-goers are also increasingly demanding in their search for authentic dishes. Connoisseurs in Bombay ordering Bengali *macher jhol* not only request the correct seasoning, but also specify that it be made from the traditional *hilsa* fish, freshly caught in a Bengali river.

In recent years, large numbers of Indians have discovered foods from other countries and taken to the spicier cuisines of the world with gusto. Chinese eating places had long existed in Calcutta, but are now found everywhere in India. Mexican and Thai restaurants are becoming familiar sights in the big cities. Indian restaurant owners, noting the success of these establishments, were quite willing to diversify, and it is not unusual to see an eatery with a sign outside proclaiming that Tandoori, Moghlai, Chinese, and Continental (this last term encompassing all cuisines west of the Suez Canal) dishes are available. Some of the more imaginative cooks have abandoned any pretense of keeping these cuisines separate and offer intriguing hybrids such as *uthappam pizza*s (fermented rice batter made into pancakes topped with cheese, tomato sauce, onions, and peppers), *dosa Manchurian* (fermented rice crepes stuffed with Chinese chicken), *tandoori croissants* (croissants stuffed with tandoori chicken), *keema pizza*s (pizzas topped with spicy ground lamb and cheese), and *chole burgers* (spicy mashed chickpea patties in a bun).

The mingling of cuisines is not confined to restaurants. The growth of a worldwide Indian diaspora means that many Indians have a cousin in Sydney or aunt in Vancouver urging them to visit. The food they taste on these trips provides inspiration for their own kitchens. This cross-pollination of cultures is producing exciting new dishes with combinations of ingredients and flavors unheard of even a few years ago.

Indian cuisine has developed over thousands of years, influenced by the many new ingredients and cooking styles that reached Indian shores. This process continues at an ever-increasing speed; recipes that were once handed down from mother to daughter now whiz over the Internet, and each person trying them adds a new twist. In spite of this incessant evolution, the flavors and spices that characterize Indian food have remained much the same over the centuries.

In this chapter you will find a few examples of how nontraditional ingredients blend harmoniously with traditional Indian cooking styles. If they inspire you to experiment in your own kitchen, then so much the better!

Samose • Puff pastry turnovers stuffed with spicy ground lamb, mixed vegetables, or spicy crumbled cottage cheese

Pao Bhaji Roll-ups • Rolled-up pizza dough stuffed with spicy mixed vegetables

Masala Macaroni • Macaroni and cheese baked with tomatoes, Parmesan, bread crumbs, and spices

Bhutta Malaidaar • Corn baked with cottage and cheddar cheeses

Yogurt Dill Dip with Sun-dried Tomatoes

Yavani Kabab • Ground lamb kababs marinated with onions, sun-dried tomatoes, spices, and herbs

Grilled Soy-Coconut Fish • Fish marinated in soy sauce and vinegar, served in a sautéed onion, tomato, and coconut-milk sauce with scallions and fresh coriander

Samose

Puff pastry turnovers stuffed with spicy ground lamb, mixed vegetables, or spicy crumbled cottage cheese

A nasty international incident seemed imminent in 1942. Mrs. Soli Bilimoria, a former Seattle schoolteacher then working in India as a reporter for the American Office of War Information, was writing anti-British columns. It was bad enough that she opposed British rule over India; even more seriously, she objected to their custom of dining at nine, complaining that the British "think all Americans barbarians because we don't like their damn eating hours." British Military Intelligence was so alarmed ("I say, old chap, dining at six! Not quite *pukka,* what?") that it asked for her removal, a request that the Americans refused.

Though the British left India long ago, Indians continue to dine late. At some Delhi dinner parties I have attended, the main meal was served around midnight; we kept starvation at bay by nibbling on the many hors d'oeuvres. Samosas are a favorite appetizer at parties, with fillings varying from spicy potatoes to ground meat. Traditionally samosas are deep-fried, but here I have encased the spicy filling in puff pastry and baked them. You can use leftover keema (spicy ground lamb) from any recipe in this book or other leftovers of your choice.

1 package frozen puff pastry (2 blocks), thawed

2 to 3 cups Hariyali Keema (ground lamb cooked with spinach and sour cream and a fresh herb chutney, page 180), Keema Guchchi (portobello mushrooms stuffed with spicy ground lamb and peas, page 130), or Paneer ki Bhurji (crumbled cottage cheese stir-fried with sautéed onions, tomatoes, and spices, page 157)

1 egg, beaten

- Preheat the oven to 350°F. Roll each block of puff pastry into a sheet about ¼ inch thick. Cut each sheet lengthwise into 3 strips, then each strip into 3 squares. Put about 2 teaspoonfuls of the filling in the center of a square and fold to form a triangular pouch, pressing the edges lightly to seal them. Put all the pouches in a single layer on a lightly greased baking tray and brush them lightly with the beaten egg. Bake for 25 minutes, until the tops are golden and the puff pastry is cooked through. Transfer to a platter and serve.

- SERVES 4 TO 6

Pao Bhaji Roll-ups

Rolled-up pizza dough stuffed with spicy mixed vegetables

2 tablespoons vegetable oil

1 teaspoon cumin seeds

2 garlic cloves, finely chopped

1 large bulb onion (large scallion),
 finely chopped, with green parts, or
 4 scallions (green onions),
 finely chopped

1 small sweet green pepper,
 finely chopped

1 small sweet red pepper,
 finely chopped

1 cup shredded cabbage

1 cup finely chopped cauliflower
 florets

1 small zucchini, diced into
 small pieces

1 carrot, peeled and diced into
 small pieces

1 medium cooked potato, peeled
 and diced

2 medium tomatoes, finely chopped

Salt to taste

½ teaspoon turmeric

1 teaspoon ground coriander seeds

1 teaspoon ground cumin seeds

¼ teaspoon ground black pepper

¼ teaspoon cayenne pepper

1 teaspoon garam masala

1 tablespoon kasoori methi
 (dried fenugreek leaves)

1 teaspoon ground fennel seeds

Indians have created a huge variety of breads that are usually made from unleavened flour and cooked on a griddle. However, the technique of baking bread in ovens from leavened dough was something they learned from Europeans. The Portuguese introduced *pao*, a square bun whose top is divided into four sections, making it easy to break apart. Cooks in Bombay discovered that pao tastes really good topped with bhaji (spicy mixed vegetables) and made pao-bhaji one of the most popular street foods in the city. You will find a vendor on almost every street with a pushcart equipped with a small stove on top of which sits a huge griddle. The bhaji stays warm on the periphery of the griddle, and every time a customer stops by, the vendor will melt some butter in the center of the griddle and toast some pao.

Here, I have stuffed the bhaji into pizza dough, rolled it up, and baked it. When sliced, it makes an appetizing dish that can be served as a snack or accompaniment. You can also toast some rolls in lieu of the traditional pao and serve the bhaji on the side instead of stuffing it in the pizza dough. I recommend chopping all the vegetables before cooking, because you will need them in quick succession once you start stir-frying. You can make the filling ahead of time and freeze unused portions.

- In a nonstick skillet, warm the oil over high heat. Add the cumin seeds, then, after a few seconds, the chopped garlic and bulb onion or scallions. Sauté for 1 minute, then stir in the green and red peppers. Sauté for 1 minute, then add the cabbage and stir-fry for 1 minute. Add the cauliflower, zucchini, and carrot, sautéing for a minute after the addition of each vegetable. Add the potato and tomatoes and cook for 2 minutes. Now add salt and all the spices and cook for 1 minute. Remove from heat and mix in the lemon juice. Cool to room temperature.

- Preheat the oven to 400°F. Sprinkle the pizza dough with some flour and roll it out into a rectangular shape, about ¼ inch thick and 12 by 15 inches in size. Spread half the filling evenly over the dough in a thin layer, leaving a ¼-inch border on all sides. Now lift one edge and roll it tightly over the filling, jelly roll–fashion. Pinch the edges together to seal. Place it seam side down on a lightly greased baking sheet and let it sit at room temperature for 15 minutes. Just before putting the pizza roll in the oven, brush it all over with the cream or the beaten egg. Sprinkle over the chopped onion, green chili, and fresh coriander, then the sesame seeds on top. Make 4 deep diagonal slashes across the surface of the top of the pizza roll and bake for 30 minutes. Transfer to a chopping board, cool slightly, and cut into ½-inch-thick slices. Proceed similarly with the remaining filling. You can make 2 loaves this way.

• SERVES 8

¼ teaspoon dry ground ginger
  (optional)
2 tablespoons lemon juice
1 package store-bought pizza dough
  (about 1 pound)
2 tablespoons white all-purpose flour
1 tablespoon heavy cream or
  1 beaten egg
1 small onion, finely chopped
1 hot green chili
2 tablespoons chopped fresh
  coriander leaves
1 teaspoon white sesame seeds

Street vendor's food stand

Indian cook carrying a tureen, nineteenth century

Masala Macaroni

Macaroni and cheese baked with tomatoes, Parmesan, bread crumbs, and spices

The British discovered that one of the greatest rewards of building an empire in India was the number of servants they could employ. Unfortunately, since few British residents of India learned any local language, communication with these retainers could prove difficult, as recounted by an English official in 1878:

Our khansamar, or head table-servant, was supposed to know English, or at any rate the English names of the table necessaries; and on the morning after we had entered on possession of our house, he came to inform me that it was advisable to lay in a small stock of certain kitchen requisites. "Would I be pleased to make a list, and get them from the European shops?"

Accordingly I took my pen, while he, standing with his hands clasped in the native attitude of deferential respect, commenced: "Makrakurma." "What?" said I. "Makrakurma," he repeated.

I had never heard of any English eatable of this name; but he assured me it was very common and absolutely necessary. "Well," said I, wishing to temporize, "pass on to the next thing." "Burrumchellee," he said.

The author finally had to pay a translator to find out that the two items requested were macaroni and vermicelli.

The British introduced macaroni to India, but Indian cooks were not content to follow bland English recipes. Soon they were tossing in a pinch of this and a dash of that, and macaroni and cheese was transformed into a dish that no

2 cups dry elbow macaroni
2 tablespoons vegetable oil
¼ teaspoon cumin seeds
2 garlic cloves, chopped
1¼ cups finely chopped onions
1 cup diced tomatoes, canned or fresh
½ teaspoon ground black pepper
¼ teaspoon turmeric
¼ teaspoon ground cumin seeds
¼ teaspoon ground coriander seeds
Salt to taste
1 tablespoon all-purpose flour
1 cup milk
½ cup grated cheddar cheese
½ cup grated mozzarella cheese
½ cup plain bread crumbs
2 tablespoons grated Parmesan cheese

Englishman would recognize but which tastes wonderful. Even though this dish has traveled far from home, it is still good with garlic bread.

- Bring a large pot of water to boil and add the macaroni. Cook it over medium heat until al dente, about 10 minutes. Drain and set aside. Preheat oven to 400°F.
- Warm the oil in a nonstick skillet over medium–high heat and add the cumin seeds, then after a few seconds, the chopped garlic and onions. Sauté for about 5 minutes, until lightly browned. Reduce heat to medium, add the tomatoes, and cook for about 5 minutes, blending them in with the back of your spoon. Stir in all the spices and salt and cook for 1 minute. Mix in the flour and turn off the heat. Add the milk in a slow stream to avoid curdling, stirring gently all the while. Mix in the cheddar and mozzarella cheeses, then gently stir in the cooked macaroni. Transfer to a large flat baking dish. Mix the bread crumbs with the Parmesan cheese and spread evenly over the macaroni. Bake uncovered for 30 minutes.
- SERVES 3 TO 4

Bhutta Malaidaar

Corn baked with cottage and cheddar cheeses

6 ears of peaches-and-cream corn, shucked

3 medium cooked potatoes, peeled and grated (about 1½ cups)

½ cup crumbled paneer (cottage cheese)

½ cup grated cheddar cheese

Salt to taste

Corn has never been very important in Indian cuisine. Originally an American crop, it was brought to India by Europeans, and Indians never quite figured out how to cook it. Corn on the cob has long been a popular snack, sold by street vendors who roast it over an open fire and serve it with a sprinkling of salt and lemon juice. In Punjab *makke di roti*, flatbread made from corn flour, is eaten with freshly harvested, cooked greens. Apart from these two examples, I cannot think of any traditional recipes for corn. One reason may be that, unlike Western varieties, the corn commonly available in India was not very sweet or tender. However, good-quality corn goes very well with Indian ingredients, and imaginative cooks in India are finding new ways to use it.

This recipe for baked corn is contributed by my mother. Here, fresh corn is combined with potatoes and cottage and cheddar cheeses, then mixed with spices and sautéed onions, chilies, and garlic. The whole thing is topped with a delicious crust of cheese and cream, which in my opinion is the best part of this dish. If it is not hot enough for you, you can serve with Tabasco or chili sauce. You can also shape the corn mixture into croquettes, roll them lightly in bread crumbs, and shallow-fry them. They make great appetizers with a fresh herb chutney on the side.

- Wash the corn, cover each cob tightly with plastic wrap, and microwave on high for 3 minutes each. (You can also cook the corn with water in a saucepan.) Cover with water, bring to a boil, and simmer for 4 to 5 minutes. Remove and unwrap the cobs. When they are cool enough to handle, remove the kernels and collect in a large mixing bowl—you should have about 3 cups. Whirl them lightly in a food processor to mash slightly. Transfer back to the large mixing bowl and set aside.

- Mix the potatoes with the corn and add the ½ cup crumbled cottage cheese, ½ cup cheddar cheese, salt, pepper, roasted ground cumin seeds, and lemon juice.

- Warm the oil in a nonstick skillet set over medium-high heat. Add the cumin seeds and, after a few seconds, the green chili, chopped garlic, and ginger. Sauté for 30 seconds, then stir in the chopped onions. Sauté for 2 to 3 minutes, until the onions are translucent and slightly tender. Remove from the heat and add to the corn mixture. Mix well with a fork or with your hands and transfer to a lightly greased flat baking dish. Preheat the oven to 400°F.

½ teaspoon ground black pepper
¼ teaspoon roasted ground
    cumin seeds
2 tablespoons lemon juice
2 tablespoons vegetable oil
¼ teaspoon cumin seeds
1 hot green chili, finely chopped
1 garlic clove, finely chopped
¼-inch piece of ginger, finely chopped
½ cup finely chopped onions

FOR THE TOPPING
½ cup crumbled or grated paneer
    (cottage cheese)
¾ cup grated cheddar cheese
Salt to taste
¼ teaspoon ground black pepper
4 tablespoons heavy cream
Butter to dot the corn

- To make the topping, combine the ½ cup crumbled cottage cheese and ½ cup of the grated cheddar cheese in a small mixing bowl. Add the salt, pepper, and heavy cream and mix well. Spread this mixture evenly over the corn and sprinkle over the remaining ¼ cup grated cheddar cheese. Dot with butter and bake uncovered for 30 minutes or until the top is golden. Serve with a dash of Tabasco. You can make this dish up to two days ahead of time.

- SERVES 4

Yogurt Dill Dip with Sun-dried Tomatoes

1 cup plain yogurt, not low-fat

6 sun-dried tomato halves, either
   frozen or oil-packed,
   finely chopped

1 tablespoon finely chopped fresh dill

½ of a medium cucumber, peeled
   and grated

1 garlic clove, grated

1 teaspoon lemon juice

Salt to taste

¼ teaspoon ground black pepper

½ teaspoon roasted ground
   cumin seeds

Mahatma Gandhi bent down and picked up a few grains of sea salt from the beach at Dandi, a village on the western coast of India, on the morning of April 5, 1930. He was immediately arrested, because manufacturing salt was a jealously guarded government monopoly in British India. The leader of India's freedom struggle had deliberately broken the law to protest the injustice of India's colonial administration. His act of civil disobedience so captured the public imagination that soon people all over the country were making their own salt and courting arrest by selling it. India's first prime minister, Jawaharlal Nehru, reminisced years later: "We knew precious little about it, and so we read it up where we could, and issued leaflets giving directions, and collected pots and pans and ultimately succeeded in producing some unwholesome stuff, which we waved about in triumph, and often auctioned for fancy prices."

Salt is a necessity of life to Indians, because it enhances the taste of spices in the food. I emphasize this point when teaching Indian cooking to Western students, who often don't use salt in their cooking at all. Even though this dish sounds very Western, it has been Indianized with the use of spices, and salt is necessary to draw out the flavors. You can serve this dip with kababs or use it as a topping on kababs wrapped in pita bread.

- Line a fine mesh sieve with 2 layers of cheesecloth or with a coffee filter and set it over a bowl. Pour the yogurt into this, cover, and refrigerate overnight.
- Scrape the thickened yogurt into a serving bowl. Add the tomatoes and dill. Squeeze all the excess liquid from the cucumber and add, along with the garlic, lemon juice, salt, black pepper, and roasted cumin. Mix well and serve chilled.

- SERVES 4 TO 6

Yavani Kabab

Ground lamb kababs marinated with onions, sun-dried tomatoes, spices, and herbs

 The last time Greek and Indian cultures collided was in 327 B.C., when Alexander the Great invaded India. Alexander's brief foray left little lasting impact on Indian culture. The Greek settlements were soon absorbed by the surrounding Indian kingdoms and disappeared without a trace. So fleeting was the Greek sojourn in India that it is doubtful they had any significant influence on Indian food. However, I am so fond of Greek food that I wanted to make up for this omission with this recipe, which nicely blends Greek ingredients with Indian spices.

Inspired by the Greek gyros, these kababs are skewered and grilled on the barbecue. The addition of sun-dried tomatoes and bread makes these kababs very soft and delicious. Greek

1 pound lean ground lamb

1¼ cups chopped onions

3 garlic cloves, chopped

½-inch piece of ginger, quartered

1 hot green chili, stemmed (optional)

1 cup fresh coriander leaves, washed and well drained

12 sun-dried tomato halves, oil-packed or frozen, well drained and dried with paper towels

½ teaspoon dried oregano

¼ teaspoon ground black pepper

Salt to taste

¼ teaspoon cayenne pepper

½ teaspoon roasted ground cumin
   seeds

¼ teaspoon paprika

¼ teaspoon powdered cinnamon

2 bay leaves, well crushed

1 egg

2 slices white bread, broken into
   pieces

Lemon juice

spices such as oregano, bay leaves, and cinnamon blend well with Indian ingredients such as roasted ground cumin seeds and fresh coriander. You can also shape the kababs into patties and shallow-fry them. Serve with Yogurt Dill Dip with Sun-dried Tomatoes, page 264. You can also lightly cook leftover kababs in any sauce from this book.

- Wrap the ground lamb in 3 layers of paper towels to absorb the juices and set aside. Combine the onions, garlic, ginger, green chili, fresh coriander leaves, and sun-dried tomatoes in a food processor and mince well. Scrape down the sides and add all remaining ingredients except the lemon juice and ground lamb. Mince well again, then add the lamb and process until everything is well blended and the meat is ground fine. Transfer to a bowl, cover, and refrigerate for an hour or longer.

- When you are ready to grill, mold lemon-size balls of the ground meat mixture onto skewers in 4- to 6-inch sausage shapes, wetting your hands whenever necessary. Grill the skewers in a covered medium-hot barbecue until cooked through and lightly browned all over. Slide the kababs off the skewers onto a platter and sprinkle liberally with lemon juice. You can also make balls out of the meat mixture and broil in the oven, or shape into patties and shallow-fry.

- SERVES 4 TO 6

Grilled Soy-Coconut Fish

Fish marinated in soy sauce and vinegar, served in a sautéed onion, tomato, and coconut-milk sauce with scallions and fresh coriander

Fusion cuisine in India is not being shaped by Western influences alone: Thai, Indonesian, Malaysian, and Chinese restaurants are becoming familiar sights in big Indian cities, and their seasonings and cooking styles are finding their way into Indian dishes. In this recipe I have blurred the boundaries between different Asian cooking styles. Ingredients such as onions, garlic, tomatoes, and fresh coriander are common to all these cuisines. Soy sauce is typically Chinese, while coconut milk is essential in Southeast Asian and southern Indian cooking. In this dish all these ingredients blend together deliciously.

The fish in this recipe is first marinated in a mixture of cornstarch, soy, and vinegar. When grilled, the fish coating thickens and becomes slightly crisp. The grilled fish is then lightly cooked in a sauce of sautéed onions, tomatoes, coconut milk, soy, and vinegar. Chopped green onions and fresh coriander folded in at the very end complete this dish. Serve with plain cooked rice.

- Wash the fish and pat dry with paper towels. Lay the fillets skin side down in a single layer in a large flat dish. Mix together the marinade ingredients and pour over the fish. Cover and refrigerate for at least 2 hours. Place your oven rack on the second rung and preheat the broiler. Line an ovenproof dish with foil and place a grilling rack on it. Lift the fish out of its marinade and place it on the grilling rack. Spoon some of the marinade on top of the fish. Place the fish under the broiler for 10 to 12 minutes, until it is done from the thickest part of its center. Remove, cool slightly, and remove the skin from the fish, dividing the meat into

1 pound thick-cut firm fish fillet

FOR THE MARINADE

1 teaspoon cornstarch

¼ teaspoon ground black pepper

2 tablespoons soy sauce

2 tablespoons rice vinegar

1 tablespoon sesame oil

FOR THE SAUCE

2 tablespoons vegetable oil

1 cup finely chopped onions

1 garlic clove, finely chopped

¼ cup canned diced plum tomatoes

1 hot green chili, thinly sliced

¼ cup canned unsweetened coconut milk

1 cup water

1 teaspoon cornstarch

Salt to taste

¼ teaspoon ground black pepper

1 teaspoon sugar

1 tablespoon soy sauce

2 tablespoons rice vinegar

2 scallions (green onions), finely chopped, white and green parts

1 tablespoon chopped fresh coriander leaves

2-inch chunks as you do so. Set aside. (You can also grill the fish on an outdoor barbecue on medium heat, for 12 to 15 minutes until cooked through.)

- To make the sauce, warm the oil in a nonstick skillet over medium-high heat. Add the onions and garlic. Sauté for about 5 minutes, until lightly browned. Reduce the heat to medium and add the tomatoes. Cook for 3 to 4 minutes, mashing lightly with the back of your spoon. Add the sliced green chili, coconut milk, and ½ cup of the water. Cook for 2 minutes, then add the fish and cook for another 2 minutes. Mix the cornstarch, salt, pepper, and sugar with the remaining ½ cup of water, then add the soy sauce and vinegar. Pour this mixture into the skillet and cook for 1 minute, until the sauce thickens. Gently fold in the chopped scallions and fresh coriander and serve.

  - SERVES 3 TO 4 WITH OTHER DISHES

Bibliography

Achaya, K.T. *Indian Food: A Historical Companion*. Delhi: Oxford University Press, 1994.

Auboyer, Jeannine. *Daily Life in Ancient India*. New York: Macmillan, 1965.

Barr, Pat. *The Memsahibs: The Women of Victorian India*. London: Martin Secker & Warburg, 1976.

Bhisham Pal, H. *Historic Rajasthan*. New Delhi: Sagar Publications, 1974.

Blake, Stephen P. *Shahjahanabad: The Sovereign City in Mughal India 1639–1739*. Cambridge: Cambridge University Press, 1991.

Brennan, Jennifer. *Curries and Bugles: A Cookbook of the British Raj*. New Delhi: Penguin Books, 1992.

Constable, Archibald and Vincent A. Smith. *Travels in the Mogul Empire*. London: Oxford University Press, 1916.

Coryat, Thomas. *Greeting from the Court of the Great Mogul*. Amsterdam: Da Capo Press, 1968.

Beveridge, Annette. *The History of Humayun: Humayun-nama*. Delhi: Idarah-I Adabiyat-I Delli, 1972.

Brown, Hilton. *The Sahibs*. London: William Hodge, 1948.

Burton, David. *The Raj at the Table*. London: Faber and Faber, 1993.

Dunbar, Janet. *Golden Interlude: The Edens in India 1836–1842*. Gloucester, UK: Alan Sutton, 1985.

———. *Tigers, Durbars and Kings: Fanny Eden's Indian Journals 1837–1838*. London: John Murray, 1988.

Eden, Emily. *Up the Country*. London: Curzon Press, 1978.

Editors of Time-Life Books. *What Life Was Like in the Jewel in the Crown: British India A.D. 1600–1905*. Alexandria, VA: Time-Life Books, 1999.

Edwardes, Michael. *The Orchid House*. London: Cassell, 1960.

Elliot, H. M. and John Dowson. *The History of India by Its Own Historians*. New York: AMS Press, 1966.

Fane, Henry Edward. *Five Years in India*. Patiala, India: Director Languages Department Punjab, 1970.

Fay, Eliza. *Original Letters from India*. London: Hogarth Press, 1986.

Findly, Ellison Banks. *Nur Jahan: Empress of Mughal India*. New York: Oxford University Press, 1993.

Foster, William. *The Embassy of Sir Thomas Roe to the Court of the Great Mogul*. Liechtenstein: Kraus Reprint Limited, 1967.

Foster, William. *Early Travels in India, 1583–1619*. New Delhi: Oriental Books Reprint Corporation, 1985.

Fryer, John. *A New Account of East India and Persia*. Liechtenstein: Kraus Reprint Limited, 1967.

Gascoigne, Bamber. *The Great Moghuls*. London: Jonathan Cape, 1971.

Grew, Raymond. *Food in Global History*. Boulder, CO: Westview Press, 1999.

Grey, Edward. *The Travels of Pietro Della Valle*. New York: Burt Franklin, 1973.

Gupta, Shakti M. *Festivals, Fairs and Fasts of India*. New Delhi: Clarion Books, 1990.

Hamilton, Alexander. *A New Account of the East Indies*. London: Argonaut Press, 1930.

Hanchett, Suzanne. *Coloured Rice: Symbolic Structure in Hindu Family Festivals*. Delhi: Hindustan Publishing, 1988.

Hart, Henry H. *Sea Road to the Indies*. Westport, CT: Greenwood Press, 1971.

Hasan, Amir. *Vanishing Culture of Lucknow*. Delhi: B. R. Publishing, 1990.

Henisch, Bridget Ann. *Fast and Feast: Food in Medieval Society*. University Park, PA: Pennsylvania State University Press, 1976.

Hickey, William. *Memoirs of William Hickey*. London: Hurst and Blackett, 1913.

Hyman, Mavis. *Jews of the Raj*. London: Hyman, 1995.

Irvine, William. *Niccolao Manucci, A Pepys of Mogul India*. London: John Murray, 1913.

Jaffrey, Madhur. *A Taste of India*. London: Pan Books, 1985.

James, Lawrence. *Raj: The Making and Unmaking of British India*. London: Little, Brown, 1997.

Jayne, K. G. *Vasco da Gama and His Successors 1460–1580*. London: Methuen, 1910.

Katz, Nathan and Ellen S. Goldberg. *The Last Jews of Cochin-Jewish Identity in Hindu India*. Columbia, SC: University of South Carolina Press, 1993.

Khare, R. S. and M. S. A. Rao. *Food, Society and Culture*. Durham, NC: Carolina Academic Press, 1986.

Kincaid, Dennis. *The Grand Rebel*. London: Collins, 1937.

———. *British Social Life in India*. New York: Kennikat Press, 1971.

Knighton, William. *Elihu Jan's Story or The Private Life of an Eastern Queen*. London: Oxford University Press, 1921.

———. *The Private Life of an Eastern King*. London: Oxford University Press, 1921.

Lee, Samuel. *The Travels of Ibn Batuta*. New York: Burt Franklin, 1971.

Lynton, Harriet R. and Mohini Rajan. *The Days of the Beloved*. Berkeley: University of California Press, 1974.

Mackenzie, Donald A. *Indian Myth and Legend*. London: Gresham, 1913.

MacMillan, Margaret. *Women of the Raj*. London: Thames and Hudson, 1988.

Mahindru, S. N. *Spices in Indian Life*. New Delhi: Sultan Chand, 1982.

Mathur, N. L. *Red Fort and Mughal Life*. New Delhi: N. L. Mathur, 1964.

McCrindle, J. W. *Ancient India as Described by Megasthenes and Arrian*. Calcutta: Chuckervertty, Chatterjee, 1926.

Miller, J. Innes. *The Spice Trade of the Roman Empire*. London: Oxford University Press, 1969.

Moreland, W. H. and P. Geyl. *Jahangir's India: The* Remonstrantie *of Francisco Pelsaert*. Delhi: Idarah-I Adabiyat-I Delli, 1972.

Nayeem, M. A. *The Splendour of Hyderabad—Last Phase of an Oriental Culture*. Bombay: Jaico, 1987.

Ovington, John. *A Voyage to Surat in the Year 1689*. London: Oxford University Press, 1929.

Oxfeld, Ellen. *Blood, Sweat and Mahjong: Family and Enterprise in an Overseas Chinese Community*. Ithaca, NY: Cornell University Press, 1993.

Parks, Fanny. *Wanderings of a Pilgrim in Search of the Picturesque*. Karachi: Oxford University Press, 1975.

Parry, John W. *Spices*. New York: Chemical Publishing, 1969.

Pemble, John. *Miss Fane in India*. Gloucester, UK: Alan Sutton, 1985.

Polo, Marco. *The Travels of Marco Polo*. London: Routledge & Kegan Paul, 1931.

Prakash, Om. *Economy and Food in Ancient India*. Delhi: Bharatiya Vidya Prakashan, 1987.

Rama Rau, Santha. *The Cooking of India.* Time–Life International, 1969.

Ritchie, Carson I. A. *Food in Civilization: How History Has Been Affected by Human Tastes.* New York: Beaufort Books, 1981.

Shalleck, Jamie. *Tea.* New York: Viking Press, 1971.

Sharar, Abdul Halim. *Lucknow: The Last Phase of an Oriental Culture.* London: Paul Elek, 1975.

Sheppard, Samuel T. *Bombay.* Bombay: Times of India Press, 1932.

Singh, Khushwant. *A History of the Sikhs.* Princeton, NJ: Princeton University Press, 1963.

Smith, V. A. *Akbar the Great Mogul.* Oxford: Clarendon Press, 1917.

Spear, Percival. *India: A Modern History.* Ann Arbor, MI: University of Michigan Press, 1961.

———. *The Nabobs.* London: Oxford University Press, 1963.

———. *A History of India, Volume II.* New Delhi: Penguin Books India, 1965.

Tannahill, Reay. *Food in History.* New York: Stein and Day, 1973.

Thackston, Wheeler M. *The Baburnama: Memoirs of Babur, Prince and Emperor.* New York: Oxford University Press, 1996.

———. *The Jahangirnama: Memoirs of Jahangir, Emperor of India.* New York: Oxford University Press, 1999.

Thapar, Romila. *A History of India, Volume I.* New Delhi: Penguin Books India, 1966.

Wheeler, J. Talboys. *Early Travels in India.* Delhi: Deep Publications, 1975.

Woodcock, George. *Kerala: A Portrait of the Malabar Coast.* London: Faber and Faber, 1967.

Index

methi gosht, 192–94
milk:
    ice cream made with mangoes,
      pistachios and, 135–36
    rice dessert with sugar, saffron,
      almonds and, 39–40
mint, xxvi
    chicken and portobello
      mushrooms with walnuts,
      yogurt, spices and, served in
      tortillas, 106–8
    chicken with onions, tomatoes,
      yogurt, nuts, spices, raisins
      and, 169–71
    tamarind chutney, sweet and
      sour, with bananas, 29–30
molagu koli thakkali biryani,
    73–75
mookal, 126–27
moong ki dal palakwali, 25–26
mughlai kadhai paneer, 98–100
mung bean(s), xxvii
    dumplings in tomato-herb
      sauce, 92–93
    yellow, with spinach, 25–26
murgh dumdaar, 165–66
murgh kabab, 103–4
murgh korma biryani, 194–95
murgh masale mein, 227–29
murgh nizami, 169–71
murgh paneer anardaana, 173–74
murgh tamatari, 175–76
mushrooms:
    and chickpeas, in onion, tomato,
      and fenugreek sauce, 20–21
    chili chicken stir-fried with
      eggplant and, 232–34
    cottage cheese, and cashews in
      tomato sauce, 95–98
    cottage cheese, and peas in
      onion, tomato, and yogurt
      sauce, 17–18
    cottage cheese, and sweet
      peppers, stir-fried with spices
      and tomatoes, 18–19
    dry lamb curry folded with
      spinach, onions and,
      189–90
    and onions, sautéed, with
      tomatoes and cheese,
      217–18

and spinach with onions,
    tomatoes, and yogurt, 15–16
spring rolls, 214–15
see also portobello mushrooms
mustard seeds:
    black, xxvii
    fish with tomatoes and, 243–44
    lamb with tomatoes, yogurt,
      baby potatoes, shallots and,
      245–47

nigella, xxvii
nut(s):
    chicken with onions, tomatoes,
      yogurt, spices, mint, raisins
      and, 169–71
    fish with yogurt, spices and,
      120–21
    mixed vegetables with onions,
      coconut, spices and, 54–55
    onion, and yogurt sauce, lamb
      in, 182–84
    rice with spicy chicken, cream
      and, 194–95
    spicy cauliflower with cottage
      cheese, bread crumbs and,
      155–56
    tomato, and cream sauce,
      chicken in, 110–12
    tomato, raisin, and cream sauce,
      cottage cheese and sweet
      peppers in, 98–100

okra:
    with cashews and coconut,
      52–54
    with onions, tomatoes, and
      coriander, 220–21
    shrimp stir-fried with spices
      and, 118–19
    spicy, chicken with onions,
      spices, tamarind and, 58–60
    stir-fried with onions, garlic,
      and spices, 158–59
omelet with onions, tomatoes,
    chili, and coriander, 219–20
onion(s), xxvii
    and mushrooms, sautéed, with
      tomatoes and cheese, 217–18
    rings marinated in vinegar, 32
    see also scallion

onion seeds, xxvii

palak ka raita, 27–28
paneer khumb aur mirch ki
    sabzi, 18–19
paneer ki bhurji, 157–58
paneer makhani masala, 95–98
paneerwale kulche, 199–202
pao bhaji roll-ups, 258–61
Parmesan, macaroni and cheese
    with tomatoes, bread crumbs,
    spices and, 261–62
patty pan squash korma, 10–11
peas:
    beaten rice with tomatoes,
      spices and, 9–10
    chicken with cashews, yogurt,
      spices and, 115–16
    cottage cheese, and mushrooms
      in onion, tomato, and yogurt
      sauce, 17–18
    and grated cauliflower stir-
      fried with onions and spices,
      23
    portobello mushrooms stuffed
      with spicy lamb and, 130–31
    spinach with onions, tomatoes,
      spices and, 21–22
peas, yellow split, xxix
    deep-fried dumplings with dill
      and, 50–51
    with zucchini, tomatoes, and
      spices, 94–95
pepper:
    black, xviii–xix
    cayenne, xx
    chicken with tomato rice,
      73–75
    hot, grilled chicken, 221–23
peppers, sweet:
    cottage cheese, and mushrooms,
      stir-fried with spices
      and tomatoes, 18–19
    and cottage cheese, in tomato,
      nut, raisin, and cream sauce,
      98–100
    red, rice pilaf with shrimp,
      asparagus, dill and, 196–97
pilaf, rice, with shrimp, sweet red
    pepper, asparagus, and dill,
    196–97

Photo by Rohan Chandra

About the Authors

Smita Chandra is the author of two previous cookbooks, *From Bengal to Punjab: The Cuisines of India* and *Indian Grill: The Art of Tandoori Cooking at Home*. She teaches cooking and writes on the subject of Indian food.

Sanjeev Chandra teaches engineering at the University of Toronto. He loves good food and delving into history.

Sanjeev and Smita live in Toronto with their two sons, Rohan and Varun, and their cat, KitKat.